The Future Wallet

The Future Wallet

Managing Money in a Borderless World

Darius Kelmori

Mindful Pages

Published in 2026

ISBN: 9789374597019 (PB)
ISBN: 9789374592663 (eBook)

Published by

Mindful Pages
Imprint of Alpha Editions LLC
312 W. 2nd St #1834
Casper, WY 82601, USA

This book was developed using advanced writing tools to support the drafting and ideation process. All content has been thoughtfully curated, refined, and reviewed to ensure quality and relevance.

Content

Introduction viii

Chapter 1 When Money Became Software 1

Chapter 2 Digital Wallets 101 32

Chapter 3 Stablecoins Without the Hype 62

Chapter 4 Cross-border in Practice 89

Chapter 5 Privacy, Identity, and You 115

Chapter 6 Earning and Getting Paid 137

Chapter 7 Spending, Subscriptions, and Commerce 159

Chapter 8 Saving and Safeguarding 181

Chapter 9 Risk Maps, Not Predictions 203

Chapter 10 Families, Teams, and Communities 224

Chapter 11 Regulation and Freedom in Tension 247

Chapter 12 A Personal Operating System for Borderless Money 269

About the Author 294

Introduction

The nurse leans against the corrugated wall outside a clinic in Nairobi, her scrubs still creased from the morning rush. With a few taps she sends part of her wages to her mother, who lives two counties away. The transfer takes less time than it takes her tea to cool. In Lisbon, a designer submits her invoice and receives payment not in euros but in digital dollars, a quiet advantage in a country where her rent climbs faster than her traditional bank moves funds. Meanwhile, a student in Mumbai pauses between classes to tip a gamer livestreaming from Seoul—two strangers whose paths would never have crossed were it not for a thin thread of code carrying value across continents. Money is now a message: immediate, fluid, borderless. And yet, for many, it has never felt so fragile.

This is the paradox of our age. Money travels at extraordinary speed, but our sense of control slips through our fingers. We wake to headlines about frozen accounts, fluctuating tokens, platform outages, and policy changes written in a vocabulary few civilians fully grasp. Traditional finance offers predictability without flexibility. Newer systems promise freedom but often leave people navigating a labyrinth of interfaces, jargon, and risk. The nurse, the designer, and the student are not outliers; they are early representatives of a new economic citizenry—people who earn, spend, and save in ways previous generations could scarcely imagine.

For years, experts have dramatised the shift with either apocalyptic warnings or utopian visions. Yet the lived reality is more ordinary, more human, and far more complex. The way we handle money today is not only shaped by technology; it is shaped by family obligations, personal ethics, local laws, historical memory, and the silent expectations of everyday life. This book is written for the kinds of people who are increasingly caught between worlds: those who need the speed of digital tools but crave the reliability of traditional assurances; those who want autonomy yet must meet documentary demands; those who sense that money has changed but do not yet have a stable framework with which to make sense of that change.

At its core, *The Future Wallet* is a study of stewardship—how ordinary people can manage their resources wisely when cash becomes code and borders grow porous. It asks how one can preserve dignity, clarity, and foresight when the financial ground beneath them is constantly shifting. The chapters ahead do not teach speculation, nor evangelise for any particular technology or ideology. Rather, they offer a practical, principled way to navigate a world where our transactions carry both unprecedented convenience and unfamiliar exposure.

Money has always been a story of systems and their consequences. Long before wallets lived in our pockets or our browsers, value moved through communities by means of trust networks: kinship arrangements, temple authorities, guild notaries. The form mattered less than the promise behind it. When banknotes emerged, they became tangible representations of institutional commitments. When card networks arrived, they added global reach at the expense of opacity. Now we enter a period where money behaves like software: programmable, fast, and maddeningly complex beneath the interface.

This shift did not happen overnight. Each chapter of financial history is a response to the constraints of the last. Slow settlement demanded batch processing; batch processing demanded intermediaries; intermediaries created bottlenecks that modern networks now bypass. Yet the human concerns remain astonishingly consistent. People want to send money without delay. They want to store value without constant fear of loss. They want to transact without surrendering more information than necessary. They want to pay the right people, at the right time, in the right form. They want backup plans for when things go wrong, and they want those plans to be simple enough to use under pressure.

Still, something genuinely new has emerged. For the first time, individuals can choose the rails their money travels on. A payment may begin in one currency, traverse a second network, settle in a third, and record itself across systems that operate outside the boundaries of any single nation-state. To many, this feels like standing on the shoreline during low tide, watching the sea pull back further than expected. The danger is not the water; it is the unfamiliar landscape it reveals.

This book attempts to chart that landscape without melodrama. It recognises the ingenuity of the new tools and the enduring wisdom of the old. It approaches the digital wallet not as a fad but as a frontier, one that blends technical architecture with social custom. The wallet becomes more than a container for balances; it is a control panel for permissions, identities, and responsibilities. It determines not only what we can spend but how we authenticate ourselves, what we expose, whom we trust, and what safety nets we design for tomorrow.

At the heart of the book is a simple motif: the map. Not the kind etched in cartographers' ink, but the kind sketched by navigators. A map does not tell you where to go; it tells you what exists. It reveals paths and boundaries, shows the hidden currents, and gives you the confidence to choose your own route. In a borderless financial world, such a map is indispensable. Far too many people leap into new systems without understanding the terrain. Others avoid new possibilities because they fear losing their footing. This book meets both groups where they stand, offering a balanced, intelligible guide for moving through interconnected digital economies with intention rather than impulse.

To understand what is at stake, consider how identity now threads through every transaction we make. A century ago, paying someone rarely required sharing anything beyond physical proximity. Today, each payment leaves a trail, whether through a bank ledger, a private server, or a public blockchain. This trail can be a shield or a vulnerability, depending on who controls it and how it is accessed. Privacy, once a natural by-product of physical cash, has become a strategic decision. Identity, once local and self-evident, now spans multiple systems, each with their own standards and assumptions. The future wallet must therefore help us negotiate what we reveal, when, and why.

But privacy is only one piece of the puzzle. The rise of digital earning—freelancing, remote work, gig markets, creative economies—means that many people now deal with foreign clients, fluctuating currencies, and unpredictable payment rails by default. The Lisbon designer receiving dollar-denominated tokens is not participating in a speculative subculture; she is preserving her purchasing power in a city where inflation outpaces wage growth. The student sending value from Mumbai to Seoul is not performing a radical act; he is demonstrating how culture, identity, and commerce blend seamlessly across continents.

With this globalisation of daily financial life comes new exposure to volatility. Contrary to popular belief, volatility is not solely the province of decentralised tokens. A family in Argentina must plan around currency instability; a small business in Turkey faces sudden rate adjustments; a migrant worker sending remittances across borders contends with fees that behave like unpredictable tides. In environments like these, stability is not a luxury but a lifeline. The book therefore introduces frameworks that allow readers to evaluate stablecoins without hype, use them without blind faith, and integrate them into diversified financial routines with clarity and caution.

Another essential theme is responsibility. Not the punitive kind, but the thoughtful kind—the kind that recognises that financial tools shape our behaviour. The moment someone moves from a bank account to a digital wallet, even a custodial one, they take on new forms of stewardship. Keys, recovery phrases, backup methods, identity checks, transaction previews: these become part of the discipline of modern finance. Far from being a burden, they can foster resilience. The diligent saver who performs regular wallet hygiene or keeps accurate transaction notes is not playing at being an accountant; they are cultivating a habit of attention that pays dividends in autonomy.

This book asks its readers to treat money not as a passive utility but as an operating system. A personal operating system is not judged by the number of features it possesses but by how well it supports daily life. It must be intuitive enough to use under stress, flexible enough to adapt to new circumstances, and strong enough to protect against foreseeable threats. The chapters ahead gradually build this system layer by layer: how to choose a wallet model that matches your capability; how to move funds across jurisdictions with confidence; how to construct privacy boundaries that protect without isolating; how to earn, spend, and save with routines that withstand shocks; how to understand regulation without being paralysed by it; and ultimately, how to design a financial life that reflects your values, not just the demands of institutions.

As the introduction closes, several questions begin to surface—questions that will accompany the reader throughout the book, shaping their understanding and sharpening their sense of agency. What does sovereignty mean in a world where money flows through private networks rather than national ones? How does one preserve privacy without undermining legitimate obligations? What does stability look like when your income arrives through rails your grandparents would not recognise, and your savings sit partly outside the banking sector? How can families build shared financial structures that remain robust when one member falls ill or travels abroad? How should we think about risk when prediction has become an unreliable compass?

Most crucial of all: how do we build a future wallet that serves human dignity rather than eroding it?

These questions are not rhetorical flourishes; they are the living concerns of anyone navigating cross-border financial life today. They will recur throughout the chapters, each time with greater precision and more useful guidance. The aim is not to offer easy answers, but to equip readers with a mental model strong enough to handle complexity and flexible enough to adapt as the landscape evolves.

In the end, this book invites readers to reclaim something quietly revolutionary: confidence. Confidence to understand the tools they use. Confidence to design their own routines. Confidence to question platforms and institutions without retreating into cynicism. Confidence to build financial habits that are both modern and humane. If the past century taught us to let institutions handle our money, the coming decades will require a different posture: alert, informed, and willing to take responsibility for choices both small and significant.

The nurse in Nairobi, the designer in Lisbon, the student in Mumbai—all three represent the world that now surrounds us. Their wallets may be digital, but their needs are deeply human. They want safety, speed, clarity, and fairness. They want to support their families, express their identities, and plan their futures with peace of mind. The pages that follow aim to meet these needs with honesty and practical wisdom, offering a grounded guide for anyone who wishes to manage their money in a world where borders blur, systems multiply, and the flow of value becomes as fluid as thought.

The future wallet is already here. This book will help you learn to hold it well.

Chapter 1
When Money Became Software

The first hint that money was about to change came quietly, without grand announcements or global campaigns. It emerged in small, pragmatic gestures: a shopkeeper in rural Kenya topping up phone credit instead of counting shillings; a student in London tapping her card without a second thought; a programmer in Buenos Aires refreshing an online balance that lived nowhere she could physically visit. These moments seemed trivial, even mundane, but together they marked a turning point. Money, once defined by the tangibility of coins and banknotes, began dissolving into networks, interfaces, and code. What mattered was no longer the object, but the system behind it.

Consider the scene that unfolded in Nairobi in the late 2000s. A young man living in the city would receive his wages in cash, walk to a kiosk, hand over a portion of it, and watch as the attendant typed a few digits into a battered handset. Moments later, his mother—many miles away—would see a balance appear on her phone. The value moved without the money itself moving. It was a domestic convenience at first, then a national infrastructure, and eventually a global reference point. What M-Pesa revealed, long before cryptocurrency advocates made similar claims, was that money's power lies less in its physical form than in the certainty of its message. When the message travels reliably, the medium becomes negotiable.

And yet, even as money dematerialised, its risks became more visible. The digital ledger was swift but unforgiving. A mistyped digit could redirect funds to a stranger. A lost device could break the link between a person and their financial identity. Speed brought reach; reach brought new vulnerabilities. The shift from paper to software was not merely a story of convenience—it was a story of custody, control, and the human desire for finality. Who truly holds the money when money is a record, not a thing?

This chapter steps into that question. It begins with the historical drift from paper promises to programmable value, not as a linear march of progress but as a series of contested transitions. It then turns to the wallet—the object we think we understand but rarely examine. Finally, it explores how networks and nations now coexist in uneasy tension, and why trust, once anchored in the weight of metal or the watermark of paper, now stretches across time and code.

The leap from banknotes to networks is often described as an evolution, but it was more like a quiet revolution. For centuries, money depended on physicality. You held it, weighed it, verified its texture. Even early banknotes, despite their fragility, represented something tangible elsewhere—a promise tied to reserves, vaults, or the authority of a central institution. When card networks emerged, they redefined the relationship between people and their money, but they did not abolish the underlying metaphor of possession. They simply masked it behind a plastic card and a signature strip.

What truly changed was the idea of settlement. With paper money, settlement was instantaneous: handover equalled transfer. With cards, settlement became a multi-stage negotiation involving banks, processors, clearing houses, and risk systems. The transaction you thought happened at the point of sale was, in reality, an IOU passing through layers of trust. We acclimatised to this complexity because the interface was simple. But underneath it, money had already become a message that needed routing, confirmation, and eventual reconciliation.

Mobile money made this shift visible to ordinary people. In Nairobi, the queue at the M-Pesa kiosk was not just a line of customers; it was a living demonstration of network effects. Each new participant made the system more useful. The rails were no longer ATMs or branches—they were SIM cards and cell towers. When value moved, it travelled through infrastructure built for communication, not finance. That inversion changed expectations everywhere. People began to believe that sending money should be as easy as sending a text, and that belief reshaped global attitudes faster than any policy paper or market prediction.

Today's crypto rails—public blockchains, stablecoin issuers, decentralised networks—extend this logic. They promise a kind of finality that earlier systems struggled to guarantee. A transfer is not a request awaiting approval; it is an executed change on a shared ledger. But that finality brings its own discomfort. When there is no reversal mechanism, the user must become more careful. When no one can undo a mistake, the burden of accuracy becomes personal. This is the paradox of programmable value: the system is stronger, but the individual carries more responsibility.

To navigate this new terrain, we must rethink the humble wallet. Most people still imagine a wallet as an account—an object that holds money. But accounts belong to institutions. Wallets, in the digital sense, belong to people. They are not containers; they are interfaces. They manage keys, permissions, identities, and signatures. When you approve a transaction, you are not "moving funds" in the old-fashioned sense; you are authorising the release of a cryptographic command. The money moves because the system recognises your instruction as legitimate.

The distinction between custodial and self-custodial models is not theoretical. It shapes the very nature of responsibility. A neobank app provides convenience because it holds the keys on your behalf. You log in, see a balance, and transact. Everything behind the scenes—security, recovery, authentication—is delegated. A browser wallet, by contrast, places the keys in your hands. You own the authority, which is empowering until the moment it becomes daunting. A forgotten seed phrase can lock you out of your own assets; a compromised device can expose them to theft.

Between these extremes sit hybrid models: social recovery schemes, multi-party arrangements, hardware devices paired with software interfaces. Each approach offers a different balance between autonomy and assistance. Understanding these trade-offs is not optional. It is foundational to the future of financial self-management. Without it, one risks treating software wallets as if they were merely modern bank accounts, expecting safeguards that may not exist and missing opportunities for control that traditional institutions rarely grant.

If wallets redefine custody, networks redefine geography. Payment networks and blockchain systems route around borders as if they are little more than historical curiosities. Yet laws remain bound to jurisdiction. A freelancer in Manila who receives stablecoins for work performed for a client in Berlin may bypass traditional remittance channels, but she does not bypass the tax authorities, reporting obligations, or exchange rules that apply in her home country. The tension is not abstract: it is lived in the gap between what the network allows and what the law expects.

Messaging layers complicate matters further. A payment may appear to be "on-chain" but may actually rely on off-chain communication for pricing, routing, or confirmation. Different systems overlap, each with its own assumptions about identity, time zones, and risk. When these layers misalign, friction emerges. The freelancer may receive funds instantly, but converting them into local currency, proving their origin, or integrating them into existing records can become an administrative maze. The border has not vanished; it has moved. It now sits at the point where digital freedom meets territorial rules.

Place still matters—for protection, for recourse, for governance. No network, however elegant, can erase the significance of legal jurisdiction. What networks do is challenge the monopoly of borders, forcing nations to adapt their frameworks to flows they can no longer fully control. This creates uncertainty for individuals who must operate within both worlds. The chapter will show how to navigate this uncertainty with clarity rather than anxiety.

Underlying all these shifts is a deeper theme: the relationship between value, trust, and time. Money is not merely a medium of exchange; it is a claim about the future. When you hold a balance—whether in a bank account, a mobile wallet, or a blockchain address—you are trusting that it will remain redeemable, stable, and accessible when needed. But different systems anchor that trust differently. A stablecoin may rely on collateral reserves and attestation reports. A volatile asset may rely on market perception and scarcity. A bank balance may rely on regulation, deposit insurance, and institutional authority.

Each model carries its own timeline of trust. A volatile token may swing within minutes. A stablecoin may hold steady until the issuer falters. A bank deposit may remain safe for decades unless the institution collapses or the state intervenes. Time exposes assumptions. To navigate digital finance intelligently, one must understand not only how assets behave but why they behave as they do, and at what cadence their risks unfold.

This chapter introduces that lens. It sets the vocabulary for everything that follows: settlement, finality, custody, keys, permissioning, jurisdiction, counterparty risk, collateral, volatility. These terms are not technical ornamentation; they are the grammar of borderless money. Without them, the rest of the book would be a set of anecdotes. With them, it becomes a coherent framework.

As we step into the full chapter, several questions linger. What does it mean to "own" money when ownership is expressed through cryptographic authority rather than possession? How do we evaluate networks that promise freedom but depend on assumptions we cannot see? How should we balance convenience against control, speed against safety, autonomy against the comfort of delegation? And how do we prepare for a world where the financial tools we rely on may outpace the laws that govern them?

These questions are not obstacles. They are invitations. They invite us to understand money not as a static object but as a living system shaped by technology, society, and time. They invite us to step beyond the surface of glowing interfaces and confront the structures beneath. And they invite us to consider what kind of financial future we want to inhabit—and what kind of responsibility we are willing to assume.

The chapter ahead does not offer simple answers. It offers something more valuable: a clear-eyed examination of the moment money became software, and the tools to navigate that transformation with knowledge, confidence, and purpose.

From banknotes to networks

In March 2007, in Kisumu, a port city on the shores of Lake Victoria, a market trader named Salome Oketch stood in a Safaricom queue with an unusual request. She wanted to send her sister 500 Kenyan shillings immediately, but she had no bank account, no card, and no time for paperwork. The Safaricom agent tapped her details into the terminal, her cash was accepted, and within seconds her sister's basic Nokia handset chimed with confirmation. The transfer cost less than a bus fare. That small exchange, repeated across Kenya in the months following M-Pesa's launch by Safaricom in February 2007, did more than speed up payments. It revealed a shift already under way: money, once confined to paper and metal, had begun living inside networks. A few taps, a short message, and value moved without a handover. It felt simple. It was anything but.

The paradox was stark. How could something so intangible command so much trust from people who had spent lifetimes treating cash as the anchor of certainty? The answer lay not in the novelty of mobile phones but in the behaviour the system made visible. A kiosk agent accepted cash, a server recorded the instruction, a handset displayed the new balance. Settlement—a word few outside banking once used—was suddenly part of daily life. And beneath the smooth surface of the transaction, custody was quietly changing hands.

By the time Salome's sister checked her phone, the idea that value must be passed physically from one person to another had already begun to unravel. That moment, grounded in one place, one date, and one named organisation, stands as a hinge between eras. It shows how financial systems evolve long before language catches up. What moved that day was not merely money; it was the very notion of what money could be. It was.

The movement from banknotes to networks is often summarised as a story of speed, but speed is only the most visible layer. What truly changed was the meaning of finality. With a banknote, finality is immediate: once exchanged, the transaction is complete and irreversible. With cards—first standardised widely by BankAmericard in the United States in 1958 and later embedded into Visa and Mastercard networks—finality became conditional. A transaction might be authorised in Paris at 14:03 but not settle until days later through clearing houses in London or Frankfurt. Beneath every swipe lay a chain of institutions agreeing, in stages, that the payment would stand. The customer experienced convenience; the system bore complexity.

Consider an example from 1999, when Brazil's central bank launched the Sistema de Transferência de Reservas (STR), a real-time gross settlement system meant to prevent cascading delays in payment finality. It reduced settlement times dramatically, but its design also exposed a truth: when money lives as a ledger entry rather than a physical token, the timing of recognition matters as much as the amount. A transfer recorded at 10:01 is not the same—legally, operationally, or psychologically—as one recorded at 10:01 but settled later. The system may carry billions, but each entry rests on a shared assumption about when a promise becomes real. That assumption is fragile.

A counter-example, however, reminds us that not all digital innovations rewrite the rules. Japan's Konbini payment system, which became widespread by the mid-1990s, allows online shoppers to pay with cash at convenience stores. The custodian is digital; the settlement is physical. The model proved remarkably resilient, especially among consumers wary of card debt. This hybrid system shows that networks do not automatically displace paper; they coexist with it, shaped by cultural habits and institutional trust. The limitation is instructive: technology only transforms finance when it aligns with behaviour people already practise or secretly desire.

These examples reveal a simple motif running through the story: the ledger. Whether carved on clay, printed on paper, or encoded into servers, the ledger reflects a collective decision about what counts. Once the ledger becomes programmable, its influence expands. It determines not only who owes what, but when, how, and under whose authority. The ledger is silent, but decisive.

Mobile money demonstrated how quickly a new ledger model could take hold when it met real needs. By 2010, M-Pesa processed more transactions annually in Kenya than Western Union handled globally. Researchers at MIT (Jack and Suri, 2011) later documented that access to mobile money increased household resilience to income shocks. People behaved differently when value could move at the speed of a message rather than at the speed of transport.

The power of the system was not technological sophistication—early M-Pesa ran on SMS—but the network effect. Every new user expanded the viable set of recipients. Every agent increased the density of cash-in and cash-out points. Network effects rarely appear in physical currency because its utility does not increase with the number of holders. But networked money thrives on participation. When communities begin to rely on instantaneous transfers, the paper system that once held them together starts to feel slow, precarious, even archaic.

Card networks had matured through decades of institutional agreements. Mobile money leapt ahead by appealing to basic behavioural aims: immediacy, convenience, safety in public spaces, and the reassurance of seeing a balance on a screen. It reframed trust from the object (the banknote) to the system (the network). This shift created a baseline expectation: money should arrive when promised.

Crypto rails extended that baseline into a new domain. Bitcoin's first block in January 2009 introduced a ledger verified by distributed consensus rather than central authority. Ethereum's public launch in July 2015 added programmability, allowing money to carry instructions. Stablecoins—particularly those issued on audited reserves such as USDC by Circle, launched October 2018—further altered the equation by preserving a reference value while enabling global settlement layers outside traditional banking hours. Transfers that took days on card or bank systems now take minutes or seconds, settled by validators rather than correspondent banks.

But programmable finality has a sharp edge. When a blockchain transfer is confirmed, it is not a request; it is a decision executed. The user must commit in full knowledge that no dispute mechanism stands behind an error. The speed is seductive. The responsibility is heavy.

The shift from banknotes to networks also redefined custody. A decade ago, most people assumed custody meant possession of the physical asset or reliance on a bank whose obligations were insured. Networked money changes that posture. Custody becomes the act of controlling credentials—passwords, PINs, keys. Losing a banknote means losing the value; losing a cryptographic key means losing the authority to instruct the network.

A named example sharpens this point. In June 2016, The DAO—a decentralised investment vehicle built on Ethereum—was compromised due to a flaw in its smart contract logic. Approximately 3.6 million ETH were diverted. The incident led to a contentious hard fork on 20 July 2016, splitting Ethereum into two chains: Ethereum and Ethereum Classic. The episode did not merely expose a technical weakness; it illustrated the fragility of custody in a programmable environment. The ledger recorded what the code permitted, not what participants intended. The community had to choose between rewriting history and accepting the consequences. The ledger motif returned, but this time with an ethical sting.

A limitation must be acknowledged. Not every part of the world experiences custody risks equally. In Sweden, where cash usage declined sharply between 2010 and 2020 according to Sveriges Riksbank, digital payments rely heavily on institutional trust in banks, regulators, and identification systems. For many Swedes, the notion of self-custody is unnecessary, even undesirable. Their behaviour shows that technological shifts do not impose a uniform financial culture; they reveal alternatives. The reconciliation lies in recognising that networked money reshapes possibility, not necessity. Individuals and societies gravitate to the model that fits their tolerance for risk, autonomy, and administrative burden.

As networks expanded, the meaning of reach changed with them. A card network operates within a consortium of banks and regulators; a mobile network operates where agents and signal towers exist; a blockchain operates wherever there is an internet connection and a node. These layers overlap, collide, and sometimes eclipse one another.

In 2021, a Ghanaian freelance designer receiving USDC payments for work commissioned by a company in London found her earnings travelling across rails that no single authority fully controlled. The stablecoins settled on a public network, priced on global exchanges, and were converted to local cedi through a licensed platform in Accra. Each step carried a different settlement model, legal assumption, and exposure point. Her behaviour—waiting for two confirmations on-chain before acknowledging receipt, checking local FX spreads before converting—was shaped by these mechanics, not by any ideological stance. The network's reach gave her speed; the fragmentation gave her operational risk.

The visible implication is simple: the geography of money has stretched, but not disappeared. A transaction may move across three jurisdictions in seconds, yet the user must still reckon with the laws, taxes, and reporting rules of the place they inhabit. The border now sits at the interface between systems, not the crossing between countries.

Through these developments, the motif of the ledger threads again. Paper money carries value embedded in its physicality. Card networks carry value embedded in institutional agreements. Mobile money carries value embedded in telecom infrastructure. Crypto rails carry value embedded in code and consensus. At each transition, the ledger expands its territory. What matters is no longer what you hold, but what the system you rely on can guarantee—and when.

As money becomes programmable, the difference between an instruction and a transaction narrows. To press "send" is to commit. To approve is to authorise. To control a key is to hold the authority once represented by possession of a physical object. That shift brings efficiency and exposure in equal measure.

The unresolved question follows naturally: when value moves across networks as fluidly as a message, where should we ground our sense of certainty? The answer is not obvious. It requires choosing which ledger to trust, which authority to accept, and which form of finality we are willing to live with.

Wallets as interfaces, not accounts

In October 2014, in a supermarket car park in San Francisco, an early Apple Pay user held an iPhone to a terminal and watched the screen flash green. The bank card on file sat in a vault at a data centre hundreds of kilometres away. The plastic card itself remained inside a wallet that never left his pocket. Yet the terminal printed a receipt, the bank authorised the charge, and the customer left with his groceries. The key moment was not the contactless beep, but the quiet realisation that the object in his hand had become a control panel rather than a purse. The "wallet" was now an interface. The same month, a software engineer in Berlin opened a very different sort of wallet: MetaMask, first released publicly as a browser extension in 2016 by ConsenSys, but already prototyped and whispered about in developer circles. Instead of a card token, he saw a twelve-word recovery phrase—the seed that generated cryptographic keys. There was no bank logo, no customer service line, no assurance that a mistaken transfer could be reversed. Yet the balance, when it arrived, felt more like "his" than any number printed on a bank statement. Two apps, two screens, very similar layouts. Completely different responsibilities. That contrast is the hinge for this chapter. When money becomes software, the wallet stops being merely a storage object and starts acting as a cockpit. Buttons, sliders, approval screens: these are how we steer value. What looks like a balance screen is, in truth, a permission console—one that shapes what you can do, who can act on your behalf, and what happens if something goes wrong. Once you see the wallet as an interface rather than an account, the stakes of design and habit come sharply into focus.

The first shift is almost invisible: the move from "where is my money?" to "who can speak for my money?". Traditional accounts answer the first question. They tell you which institution holds your deposits, what jurisdiction governs them, and what number you can quote on a form. A modern wallet, whether a neobank app like Monzo (launched in the United Kingdom in 2015) or a self-custodial browser extension, answers the second. It governs which keys can sign instructions to a ledger. That distinction sounds technical; it shows up in everyday behaviour. Losing a debit card means cancelling it and waiting for a replacement. Losing a seed phrase means something else entirely. Neobank apps demonstrate how far interfaces can distance us from the underlying machinery while offering slick, controlled experiences. Open a Revolut account in London in 2018 and you are walked through identity checks, card selection, and optional budgeting tools. The app organises accounts by currency, offers analytics, and lets you freeze or unfreeze cards with a tap. It invites you to behave as if the screen *is* the money. Yet every action you take is, technically, a request relayed to Revolut's systems, which in turn hold balances at partner banks and payment institutions. The interface hides the plumbing and centralises control with the provider. The implication is clear: the user experiences granular control, but the legal and technical authority sits elsewhere.

A self-custodial browser wallet presents the opposite pattern. Open MetaMask in Amsterdam in 2021 and the very first thing you see after installation is a seed phrase—typically twelve or twenty-four words in a specific sequence. The software urges you to store it somewhere safe and warns that no one can restore it for you. This phrase is not a password in the usual sense; it is a compressed representation of a cryptographic root from which all your keys derive. Show: you write the words on paper, perhaps twice. Name: this is your seed phrase. Explain: anyone who sees it can re-create your wallet on another device and make any transaction the network allows. Lose it, and the network has no way to distinguish you from anyone else. Implication: the interface has handed you real power, but also irreversible risk.

If the neobank app is a hotel keycard, the browser wallet is a set of house keys cut uniquely for you. In one case, losing the card is an inconvenience; the staff can issue a new one and invalidate the old. In the other, losing the keys may lock you out of a home full of possessions unless you have made prior arrangements. That quiet metaphor of the key runs through every modern wallet. It is the motif that reveals who truly controls what.

Custodial wallets—those managed by exchanges, fintech firms, and payment apps—rely on institutional key management. A company like Coinbase, founded in San Francisco in 2012, holds underlying keys in complex security setups and presents users with a login screen. You reset your password with an e-mail, contact support if locked out, and trust that the combination of internal controls and external regulation will keep your balances intact. Your visible behaviour is familiar: you choose strong passwords, enable two-factor authentication, and check your balance on a dashboard. The keys stay out of sight. Self-custodial wallets command a different discipline. You may purchase a hardware device from a firm such as Ledger (founded in Paris in 2014), connect it to a computer, and approve each transaction with a physical button press. The visible behaviour here is almost ritualistic: check the address, check the amount, press the button. The device never exposes the private key to the computer. The implication is stark:

security becomes a routine you perform with your hands and eyes, not a service you outsource. Custodial arrangements optimise for convenience and customer support; self-custody optimises for direct control and independence from institutional failure.

A credible limitation challenges this dichotomy. In Estonia, where the national eID system underpins banking and public services, many residents comfortably manage digital access with centrally issued credentials. A single smart card or mobile ID unlocks tax filing, banking, and signing legally binding documents. From the citizen's perspective, this is not "custody versus self-custody"; it is a unified digital identity experience. The state and its partner institutions handle keys; individuals handle PINs and usage. The model works because institutional trust and service reliability are high, and because the interface feels coherent. This does not invalidate the key metaphor; it refines it. Sometimes, the most practical key is one shared with a trusted steward, rather than clasped tightly in one's own hand.

Recovery is where the notion of wallet-as-interface becomes most vivid. With a conventional bank account, recovery routines revolve around identity verification: show a passport, answer security questions, wait while someone in a call centre reconfigures access. The institution assumes the role of guardian. The interface simply displays the outcome—a reset password, a new card, a confirmation message. Responsibility is diffuse, and failure is social: you might complain, escalate, or switch banks.

In a self-custodial wallet, recovery is no longer a customer-service function. It is a design problem, handled at the level of keys and permissions. Social recovery models, for example, allow a user to designate several trusted contacts whose combined approval can reconstruct access. Vitalik Buterin proposed such schemes publicly in 2021 as part of discussions around smart contract wallets. The behaviour changes subtly:

instead of hoping a distant institution will help if things go wrong, you must choose living, named individuals or devices that can, together, unlock your funds. The implication is intimate. Your financial continuity becomes tied to a small social graph: family members, colleagues, or hardware you maintain. The wallet's interface—showing "guardians", thresholds, recovery workflows—becomes a visual representation of your personal safety net.

Seed phrases, too, embody this shift. When a wallet generates a recovery phrase, it is not being dramatic; it is unmasking the bare minimum required to control a suite of addresses. Writing those words in a notebook, splitting them between locations, committing them to a safety deposit box: these visible acts give form to an otherwise abstract claim. The motif of the key reappears, now turned into language. A phrase you can read becomes a key you can carry across borders without metal or plastic. The consequence is double-edged. It becomes harder for governments or companies to seize assets without physical access to you and your secrets. It also becomes easier to lose everything through misplacement, fire, or forgetfulness.

The interface differences between a neobank app and a browser wallet crystallise at the moment of approval. In a Monzo-style interface, a user in Manchester might tap "Pay", see a merchant name, a pound amount, and a confirmation tick. The app may display a reassuring message: "Protected by the Financial Services Compensation Scheme" or its local equivalent. The behaviour is almost casual. People send money while commuting, queuing, or glancing between messages. The implication is that the system, not the individual, handles the heavy lifting of correctness and recourse.

In a browser wallet like MetaMask, approving a transaction often means inspecting an address, a network fee, and sometimes opaque contract data. In 2022, users interacting with decentralised finance protocols in Singapore found themselves reading small hexadecimal strings before clicking "Confirm". Many skimmed; some took screenshots; a cautious minority pasted addresses into explorers to confirm legitimacy. These behaviours are not quirks; they are attempts to cope with the fact that the interface is no longer a mere viewing window but a signing device. The moment you consent, the ledger changes. There is no further referee. This sharpens every click into a decision rather than a routine tap.

A counter-example comes from highly abstracted mobile wallets in regions where regulators require "strong customer authentication". In parts of the European Union after PSD2 implementation in 2018, many consumers use banking apps that mix biometrics, device fingerprints, and time-limited codes. The experience remains smooth: face recognition, a tap, a green check mark. Under the surface, though, cryptographic keys, secure enclaves, and challenge–response flows are at work. The interface does not teach users about keys or addresses; it teaches them to trust the result of a biometric scan. The risk here is subtle. The citizen learns that a face or fingerprint is the master key, and may carry that assumption into contexts where it no longer holds. The reconciliation lies in acknowledging that good interfaces protect users most of the time, but may leave them under-prepared for environments where recourse is scarce.

As wallets absorb more functions—identity proofs, loyalty points, tickets, signing rights—the metaphor of the control panel becomes more accurate. A wallet deciding which decentralised application may access what data is closer to a permissions dashboard than a bank passbook. Approving a connection between a wallet and a third-party service is not simply "logging in"; it is granting that service a bundle of capabilities: see your addresses, request signatures, sometimes move certain tokens. The visible behaviour is a simple tap on a pop-up. The underlying reality is a delegation of power.

This is where understanding the interface clarifies responsibility. A person who thinks of a wallet as "just another bank app" may feel blindsided when a misclick approves a malicious contract. A person who understands it as a signing device will approach those same pop-ups with cautious attention, much as they would treat a blank contract placed in front of them in an office. The interface cannot change the underlying ledger rules, but it can either highlight or obscure the seriousness of each action. Fonts, colours, wording—all of these influence whether a user treats an approval as a trivial step or a binding decision.

The motif of the key returns one last time. Keys, in the physical world, are small, boring objects. Their boredom is a feature. They live on keyrings, hang by the door, rest in the bowl on the hallway table. You rarely think about them until they are missing. Digital wallet keys, by contrast, are invisible until something goes wrong or until a thoughtful interface chooses to bring them into view through seed phrases, backup prompts, or recovery flows. The danger is not that people will forget the word "key". It is that they will forget the role it plays in every interaction: quietly deciding who may speak to the ledger in their name.

Seen in this light, the central question is not whether one should choose a neobank app or a browser wallet, a custodial account or a hardware device. The harder question is this: how much of your financial life are you prepared to pilot directly from a control panel you manage, and how much are you willing to route through institutions that hold the keys for you? That choice will not be the same for every person, every family, or every stage of life. But it will need to be a choice, not an accident of default settings and glossy screens.

Networks vs nations

In March 2012, in Brussels, the Society for Worldwide Interbank Financial Telecommunication (SWIFT) disconnected a group of Iranian banks from its messaging system after pressure from the European Union and the United States. Overnight, thousands of legitimate businesses in Tehran, Hamburg, Dubai and beyond discovered that invoices could still be issued, goods could still be shipped, but bank-to-bank payment messages could no longer traverse the network. The accounts existed. The contracts stood. Yet the wires fell silent because a private network, headquartered in Belgium, flipped a switch in response to national sanctions. The border was suddenly visible.

That episode captured a new geometry of power. Money now moves through private and public networks that cross frontiers with ease, yet those networks remain entangled with governments that claim jurisdiction over people, banks, and servers located on their soil. A message from Hamburg to Tehran feels like a simple instruction between two firms. In reality, it is a packet moving across data centres, under legal regimes, and through compliance filters operated by an institution that answers to particular laws in Brussels. The same transfer, if executed in cash, would depend on smugglers and suitcases; executed via SWIFT, it depends on cables and policy. The route changes. The border does not.

Payment networks make this tension concrete long before anyone touches a blockchain. Consider a simple card transaction in Nairobi in 2019, when a traveller from London taps a Visa-branded card at a hotel terminal. The card number, merchant ID, and amount travel from Kenya to a Kenyan acquiring bank, then to Visa's data centres—historically centred in the United States and Europe—and eventually to the issuing bank in the United Kingdom. Show: the tourist sees "Approved" on a screen in seconds. Name: VisaNet, the global processing network that Visa has operated since 1976. Explain: VisaNet treats messages from Kenya and the UK as data packets subject to network rules and bilateral agreements. Implication: the transaction behaves as though distance and border checks are negligible, even though each bank, and the card network itself, must comply with domestic regulation in multiple countries. Contrast that with a cash payment. A British traveller handing over Kenyan shillings at the same hotel must first obtain that cash at a bureau de change or ATM. The exchange rate is printed, the fee is explicit, and the entire process locks the transaction into a local monetary system. The card network, by comparison, floats above these constraints while quietly enforcing them in the background through currency conversion tables, fraud rules, and sanctions screening. The card behaves like a passport. The message moves because the network recognises it as valid.

Now add mobile and account-to-account schemes. In the Single Euro Payments Area (SEPA), formalised in 2008, a transfer from Lyon to Lisbon in euros looks domestic, with harmonised formats and charges. The European Central Bank's TARGET2 infrastructure settles high-value payments in central bank money, giving banks across the eurozone a shared backbone. This is a deliberate policy choice: the network is regional by design, built to make national borders feel less economically relevant. Yet the legal framework remains layered. Consumer protection, tax rules, and anti-money-laundering enforcement still operate at the level of member states. A French resident who fails to report income from Portugal cannot claim ignorance because the payment "felt" local. The map on the app does not match the map in the law.

Public blockchains appear, at first glance, to wipe the map altogether. A transaction broadcast from Lagos, nodes validating in Frankfurt and Singapore, miners or validators rewarded in Reykjavik or Toronto—the system operates as if geography were irrelevant. When someone sends bitcoin or a dollar-denominated stablecoin, the message passes through a mesh of nodes that care about protocol rules, not passports. Show: a Brazilian developer in São Paulo receives USDC on Ethereum from a client in Zurich in under a minute in late 2021. Name: USDC, the stablecoin issued by Circle, first launched in 2018, and Ethereum, publicly live since 2015. Explain: the transfer settles when the network reaches consensus. No correspondent banks, no SWIFT fields, no business hours. Implication: from a network perspective, the transaction is locationless.

The illusion shatters at the edges. The Brazilian developer still lives under Brazilian tax law. The Swiss client still operates under Swiss reporting rules. If either party uses a regulated exchange such as Coinbase (United States, founded 2012) or Bitstamp (Luxembourg, founded 2011) to turn tokens into bank deposits, they encounter know-your-customer checks, suspicious-activity reporting, and withdrawal limits. The message may ignore borders; the humans cannot. The border reappears at the points where digital value meets people, banks, and state power.

The motif here is the map. Networks draw one map—nodes, latency, routes. Nations draw another—jurisdictions, tax codes, enforcement reach. Cross-border payments happen in the overlapping shapes between these maps. When those shapes align, life feels smooth. When they clash, friction becomes personal.

Messaging layers add a further twist. When a migrant worker in Dubai sends money home to Dhaka via a fintech app in 2022, several networks interact at once. The worker uses WhatsApp to share a payment screenshot with a relative. The fintech app routes the instruction through an internal ledger, settles foreign exchange via a liquidity provider in Singapore, and pays out via a local partner connected to Bangladesh's domestic real-time gross settlement system. Show: the worker taps send, takes a screenshot, and watches for the "got it" reply. Name: WhatsApp (owned by Meta Platforms, Inc.), the fintech brand, the domestic RTGS like Bangladesh Bank's Real Time Gross Settlement system. Explain: each layer obeys different rules—telecom regulation for messaging, financial licensing for the app, central bank oversight for the settlement system. Implication: a cross-border payment is no longer a single act but a stack of acts, each under a different flag.

A credible counter-example reminds us that not every stack is precarious. In China, WeChat Pay and Alipay—both launched in the early 2010s—operate primarily within a single national jurisdiction, alongside the People's Bank of China's oversight and domestic payment regulations. For a user in Shanghai in 2019 paying at a corner shop, the messaging layer (WeChat), the wallet, the bank connections, and the legal framework mostly share one territorial base. There are cross-border scenarios, but for daily life the network map and national map almost coincide. This makes enforcement, consumer protection, and policy experiments such as the digital yuan easier to coordinate. The limitation of this model is obvious once a person steps outside those borders: the same wallet may become difficult or impossible to top up or use fully, not for technical reasons but for regulatory ones. The reconciliation is straightforward: where networks and nations share boundaries, users feel coherence; where they diverge, users must stitch their own map.

The freelancer paid in stablecoins sits precisely in that gap. Picture a graphic designer in Lagos in 2023, contracted by a start-up in Berlin. They agree a fee of 2,000 USDC for a project, partly to avoid the volatility of naira and partly to sidestep the delays and charges of correspondent banking. The work is done. The tokens arrive at her self-custodial wallet address within minutes. Show: she refreshes her phone, sees "2,000.00 USDC", and exhales. Name: Lagos, Berlin, USDC, a public blockchain such as Ethereum or Polygon. Explain: the network has fulfilled the technical promise—fast, border-agnostic settlement in a unit both parties understand. Implication: at the level of code, this is success.

Her next steps reveal the real story. To pay rent and buy food, she must either find a local counterparty willing to accept USDC or convert it to naira. She chooses a regulated Nigerian exchange. The platform asks for identification documents, bank details, and sometimes a written note explaining the source of funds. These are not arbitrary hurdles; they arise from Nigerian anti-money-laundering regulations and central bank directives. The visible behaviour is familiar: upload a passport scan, type a bank account number, wait for "verified" status. The friction is the price of connecting a borderless balance to a local banking system with territorial obligations. Taxes loom in the background. The Berlin start-up must record the payment, possibly report it under German rules governing payments to foreign contractors, and handle value-added tax depending on the nature of the service. The designer in Lagos must, if she wishes to remain compliant, treat the 2,000 USDC as income when filing her returns under Nigerian law. The network does not care; it has no field for "jurisdiction". The tax authorities do. They care intensely. The border exists in Excel, not in code.

Two high-profile regulatory episodes underline how forcefully nations respond when networks stray too far from their map. In September 2017, regulators in Beijing banned initial coin offerings and instructed domestic cryptocurrency exchanges to close or move operations abroad. Show: Chinese traders suddenly found that platforms they used daily announced wind-downs, halted new registrations, or shifted servers to Hong Kong and beyond. Name: the People's Bank of China, the China Securities Regulatory Commission, the 2017 announcements. Explain: while the Bitcoin and Ethereum networks continued processing blocks globally, access points inside mainland China were curtailed through licensing, banking relationships, and pressure on internet service providers. Implication: nations cannot turn off a public blockchain, but they can make using it locally costly, awkward, or criminal.

In June 2019, Facebook (now Meta) announced Libra, a proposed global digital currency backed by a basket of assets, in Menlo Park, California. Within months, lawmakers in

Washington, Brussels, and other capitals raised concerns about monetary sovereignty, consumer protection, and systemic risk. Several original members of the Libra Association, including Visa and Mastercard, withdrew by October 2019 after regulatory pushback. Show: a project that seemed inevitable in June looked stalled by autumn. Name: Libra, later rebranded Diem, and its eventual wind-down announced in January 2022. Explain: a company with billions of users tried to overlay a private monetary network onto existing national systems. Governments saw a foreign map laid atop their own and reacted quickly. Implication: scale does not trump sovereignty. When networks threaten core national powers—such as control over money creation and payment rails—states assert themselves in very direct ways.

These episodes do not prove that networks always lose. They demonstrate that networks and nations negotiate, sometimes violently, over who draws the definitive map.

For individuals, this clash rarely appears as high politics. It shows up as blocked transfers, delayed withdrawals, or requests for "additional documentation". A British charity seeking to send funds to a partner organisation in Lebanon in 2020 may discover that its bank asks for detailed due diligence, not because the payment network cannot carry the message but because UK and EU sanctions regimes make banks cautious about exposure. The visible behaviours—answering more questions, filling forms, choosing different corridors—are responses to this layered map. A developer in Argentina who keeps part of her savings in a stablecoin to hedge against local inflation may find that certain exchanges restrict trading pairs for residents, reflecting local capital controls. She adapts by using peer-to-peer platforms, timing conversions, or retaining balances in token form for longer than she would prefer. Every workaround traces a border.

A quiet motif returns here: the line. A line on a satellite map marks a frontier; a line in a terms-of-service document marks a jurisdiction clause; a line in a regulator's guidance marks what is permitted. Payment networks draw lines through country codes and currency codes. Blockchains, at the protocol level, do not. But at every on-ramp, off-ramp, and user interface, someone draws them back in.

The deeper question is not whether networks will "win" against nations or vice versa. History suggests that neither can fully displace the other. Instead, they co-create a world in which money moves like data but settles into legal structures that remain tied to territory. For the individual using digital wallets and borderless rails, the practical challenge is more grounded. When you accept payment through a network that ignores borders, which map are you using to decide what you may do, what you must disclose, and what risks you are prepared to carry? Are you operating on the network's map of nodes and addresses, or the nation's map of residence, reporting, and recourse? And when those maps diverge, which line will you treat as the one that truly binds?

Value, trust, and time

On a Friday morning in March 2013, queues began forming outside bank branches in Nicosia, Cyprus. Cash machines had gone quiet. Customers who believed they held ordinary euro deposits at the Bank of Cyprus and Laiki Bank, institutions supervised under European rules, discovered that withdrawals were frozen while politicians in Brussels and Nicosia negotiated a rescue package. Within days, a "bail-in" was agreed: uninsured depositors at Laiki would face heavy losses; some deposits would be converted into bank equity. The account balances had not moved. The numbers on screens stayed the same. Yet their meaning had changed. What had looked like cash on Monday revealed itself, by Friday, as a claim whose value over time depended on decisions far beyond the depositor's control. The promise was deceptively simple.

The scene in Nicosia distilled a broader truth: money is not only a medium of exchange or a store of value. It is a dated promise. Every balance you hold is an agreement stretched across time, anchored in someone else's capacity and willingness to honour it later. When that "someone else" falters—a bank, a government, a protocol, a company—the erosion of trust shows up first not in abstract theory but in concrete behaviour. People queue, rush to transfer funds, scan news feeds, or shift balances into whatever feels safer. As money becomes software, this time dimension becomes sharper. A blockchain transfer settles quickly, but the value of the asset hours or months later can diverge dramatically from expectations. A stablecoin may hold its peg for years, only to unravel in a single week. A government bond may be treated as risk-free for decades until one auction fails. To understand what sits in a digital wallet, one must see each holding as *timed trust*: trust in a counterparty, secured (or not) by collateral, exposed (or cushioned) by volatility across a specific horizon.

Start with the simplest frame: money as a claim. When a salary in pounds lands in a current account in Manchester, the employee changes nothing physical in their home. No gold arrives. No notes fall through the letterbox. Instead, a bank's ledger updates to say: *we owe you this much*. Name this for what it is: counterparty risk. The employee now depends on that bank—and, indirectly, on the legal and regulatory scaffolding around it—to make good on the claim when rent is due or food must be bought. The visible behaviour is unremarkable: check the balance, set up a direct debit, move on. The implication is profound: what feels like "having money" is largely "trusting a timetable of obligations". The Northern Rock crisis in the United Kingdom in September 2007 dramatised this point. When the mortgage lender announced emergency support from the Bank of England, queues formed outside branches as savers sought to withdraw deposits. Many stood in line despite deposit insurance schemes that, on paper, protected much of their funds. The line itself was a vote of no confidence in the timetable. People did not only fear loss; they feared *delay*. A protected deposit that arrives months later may be legally sound but practically useless if bills are due this week. Trust, here, is not abstract belief; it is a very specific expectation about *when* value will be available.

Digital balances preserve this logic while hiding it behind smoother interfaces. Stable account views, instant transfers between users of the same platform, notifications when incoming payments clear—these design choices cultivate an impression of perpetual liquidity. Yet the claims beneath them remain contingent. A neobank that holds customer funds with a partner institution is, structurally, a layer of promises built on other promises. The user rarely sees that ladder. The calendar does.

Collateral is the second pillar tying value to time. Whenever money is lent, someone asks: "What stands behind this promise if the borrower fails?" The answer is collateral: property, securities, or other assets pledged to absorb losses. In traditional finance, government bonds dominate high-quality collateral markets. During the 2008 financial crisis, the discovery that US mortgage-backed securities rated as safe were, in reality, exposed to widespread default shook this assumption. Repossession and liquidation took longer than models had suggested. The clock misfired. Institutions that relied on certain securities as reliable collateral found that what had looked like a solid foundation was, over time, much less so.

In digital finance, collateral often appears in more programmable form. MakerDAO, launched in 2017 and governed by a decentralised community, issues the DAI stablecoin against overcollateralised positions in crypto assets such as ether (ETH). Show: a user in Zurich in 2021 locks $15,000 worth of ETH into a smart contract and mints $5,000 worth of DAI. Name: this is overcollateralisation, enforced by code rather than bank officers. Explain: if the value of ETH falls below a certain threshold, the position is liquidated automatically, selling collateral to cover the DAI in circulation. Implication: the stability of DAI depends on the future price path of ETH and the reliability of the liquidation mechanisms. The promise is not simply "one DAI ≈ one dollar"; it is "one DAI can be redeemed because enough valuable collateral stands behind it *in time*".

A counter-example tempers enthusiasm for collateral as a cure-all. During the COVID-19 market panic in March 2020, even traditionally safe collateral such as US Treasury bonds experienced sudden illiquidity, prompting extraordinary interventions by the Federal Reserve. In digital markets, similar liquidity crunches have seen automated liquidations cascade through decentralised finance protocols when collateral values dropped sharply within hours. The code performed exactly as written. The calendar did not care. What these episodes show is that collateral buys time *until* it is tested under stress. In those moments, what matters is not only the ratio of collateral to debt, but the speed at which assets can be sold at prices close to assumed values. The motif of timed trust resurfaces. You are not only trusting the collateral; you are trusting the path it will take through time and markets when trouble hits.

Volatility ties these threads together. A balance is not simply "there" or "gone". Its purchasing power can expand or contract dramatically along the timeline you care about. Compare two holdings in a digital wallet in Buenos Aires in late 2021: 1,000 USDC (a fiat-backed stablecoin issued by Circle) and 0.02 bitcoin. Nominally, at that moment, both might be worth roughly the same in US dollar terms. Show: the wallet screen displays similar figures side by side. Name: USDC and bitcoin. Explain: the trust models differ. The USDC holder relies on Circle to maintain reserves in cash and short-term US Treasuries, as attested in public reports, and on regulators in the US and elsewhere to supervise that arrangement. The bitcoin holder relies on mathematical scarcity and the collective belief of market participants that others will value bitcoin in the future, without a central issuer. Implication: over a week, USDC may track very close to one dollar, while bitcoin may swing substantially; over a decade, USDC may suffer from dollar inflation, while bitcoin may have either multiplied in price or collapsed.

When people talk about *risk*, they are rarely explicit about the timeline they have in mind. Behaviour reveals it. A parent saving for school fees due next quarter tends to favour assets whose value in local currency is relatively stable over months, even if they yield little. A young professional speculating in crypto-assets late at night may watch minute-by-minute price charts, refreshing constantly, implicitly anchoring their trust horizon to hours or days. The same asset can be low risk on a three-decade horizon and high risk on a three-day horizon, or vice versa. Money does not just measure value; it maps value onto time in different ways.

The collapse of TerraUSD (UST) in May 2022 drove this home for anyone watching. TerraUSD was marketed as an algorithmic stablecoin, designed to maintain a one-dollar peg through arbitrage with a companion token, LUNA, and through programmed incentives. For months, the peg held within a tight band. Balances sat calmly on screens. Then a combination of market stress and design weaknesses triggered a rapid loss of confidence. Within days, UST traded far below one dollar and never recovered. Holders who had treated UST as timed trust—a claim that one unit would reliably redeem around a dollar over practical horizons—discovered that the implicit collateral (LUNA and market incentives) could not sustain that promise once confidence cracked. The clock moved faster than their models.

This failure contrasts starkly with fiat-backed stablecoins where reserves are held in audited accounts and instruments such as US Treasuries. Those, too, carry risk—issuer default, regulatory freezes, banking crises—but of a different character. Time behaves differently. There is a meaningful difference between the volatility of a token backed by short-term government paper and the volatility of a token backed by an algorithm and market incentives. One model centralises risk in a corporate and regulatory structure; the other centralises it in code and crowd psychology. Both are trust structures; they simply locate trust in different places and across different timelines.

Counterparty risk, collateral, and volatility rarely appear one by one. They interact. A euro deposit at a bank in Paris in 2021 carries counterparty risk (the bank and the French financial system), typically little collateral transparency to the depositor, and low short-term volatility in nominal euro terms. A token like ether in a self-custodial wallet carries no direct bank counterparty risk, explicit collateral only if you use it as such, and high price volatility. A tokenised government bond, if widely adopted, would blend qualities: explicit collateral (the bond itself), issuer and state counterparty risk, and moderate volatility, depending on rates. Each position is a different configuration of *who* you trust, *what* stands behind that trust, and *how* value is likely to move between now and the moment you need it.

A limitation is worth stating. Not every holder actively analyses these components. Many people act through habit, social proof, or practical constraints. A worker in Lagos may accept volatile tokens because they settle quickly and offer some protection against local inflation, even if nominal dollar volatility is high. A retiree in Tokyo may hold most assets in yen deposits and domestic bonds because that is what local institutions and norms present as default, even if those balances quietly erode with inflation. The absence of explicit analysis does not mean the structure of timed trust disappears; it simply means choices reflect institutional defaults instead of personal models. The calendar still runs.

The motif that clarifies this is a simple one: the date stamp. Every claim you hold effectively carries one, even if you never see it. Some are obvious—the bond maturing in 2030, the invoice due next month. Others are implicit—the expectation that your bank will honour withdrawals every day, that a stablecoin will maintain its peg at least until you next pay rent, that a volatile token's price swings will average out over several years. To think clearly about value in a borderless financial system is to ask, again and again: *by what date must this promise hold for my purposes?*

Money as timed trust becomes especially vivid during crises, yet it operates quietly during normal periods. When a remittance corridor suffers a sudden regulatory clampdown, flows may be rerouted through informal channels. When a currency depreciates rapidly, households may switch to pricing goods in dollars while still paying in local notes. When a major stablecoin briefly "wobbles" from its peg, traders may sell it aggressively or diversify into competitors. These visible acts—changing corridors, re-denominating prices, swapping tokens—are not mere reactions. They are attempts to realign time and trust under pressure. A promise that felt solid on last month's calendar no longer fits next month's bills.

Framing money this way does not make choices easier. It makes them clearer. Instead of asking, "Is this asset safe?", a more precise question emerges: "Safe against *what*, and until *when*?". Instead of debating whether stablecoins are "good" or volatile assets are "bad", one asks, "What are the terms of the promise here, who can change them, and what paths could value take between now and the moment I care about?". The answers vary by person, place, and purpose.

That leaves a useful tension on the table. When you next glance at a balance—whether in a bank app, a mobile wallet, or a browser extension—can you name the counterparty behind it, the collateral (if any) that supports it, and the timescale over which its value matters to you? And if you cannot, what, precisely, are you trusting as the days on the calendar turn?

Chapter 2
Digital Wallets 101

The first time she held a hardware wallet in her palm, Ana, a software contractor living between Buenos Aires and Madrid, felt faintly ridiculous. The device looked like a minimalist car key, all brushed metal and tiny screen. Yet when she pressed the button and watched her balance appear, a quiet recognition settled in: this object was not a container but a responsibility. Months earlier, she had kept everything on a slick exchange app that demanded almost nothing from her—no seed phrase to protect, no backups to arrange, no rituals of checking and confirming. Now she held something that could protect her work, her savings, and her choices, but only if she learned the small disciplines that separated convenience from control. It was the moment she realised that a digital wallet is not a place but a role.

Across the world, people are encountering similar moments in quieter ways. A father in Nairobi tells his daughter the passcode to his mobile money account before travelling for surgery. A student in Warsaw writes twelve seed words on paper and hides them under a mattress, though he isn't entirely sure why they matter. A designer in Manila taps "Approve" on a browser wallet without realising she has just granted a loan protocol long-term access to her tokens. None of these acts feel like financial strategy; they feel like everyday life. Yet each contains a deeper truth: the shift from banks and platforms managing our money to us managing our interfaces is already underway, and most of us are improvising our way through it.

This chapter steps into that improvisation—not to tidy it into something perfect, but to illuminate its stakes. You do not need to be an engineer to understand digital custody. You do not need to be a crypto enthusiast to recognise that more of your financial life is being mediated through devices and screens governed by keys, permissions, and recovery choices. The key question is no longer simply *where* your money sits, but *who* can act on it, *how*, and *under what conditions*. That shift—from geography and institutions to interfaces and control paths—is reshaping how ordinary people relate to claims over their own value.

The world of wallets is often described as a spectrum, but the word hardly does justice to the psychological leap involved. On one end sit custodial services: centralised exchange apps, mobile payment accounts, neobank wallets—polished, supervised, and liberatingly simple. They resemble the familiar: forgotten passwords restored through customer support, balances synced across devices, lost phones handled through account recovery. These tools excel at confidence through abstraction. Yet their strength is also their hidden bargain. They hold the keys, set the rules, and promise to step in when things go wrong—but only within the limits of their own obligations and jurisdiction.

Move a little further along the spectrum and hybrid forms appear. Social-recovery wallets, contract-based accounts, and smart-signature models redistribute control across trusted people or devices. They introduce resilience without demanding total self-reliance. Here, the wallet begins to resemble a shared safe: you can regain access if you are locked out, yet no single person—including you—can act unilaterally without meeting a threshold. These arrangements force deliberate choices. Whose judgement do you trust? Which relationships can bear the weight of recovery? Where will you store instructions that may one day be needed but must not fall into the wrong hands? Hybrid custody is neither the comfort of a bank nor the solitude of full self-sovereignty. It is something more human: a system woven from people, tools, and planning.

At the far end lie self-custodial devices and apps that place the entire burden—and power—on the individual. A hardware wallet tucked in a drawer in São Paulo does not promise forgiveness if you forget your PIN. A seed phrase scribbled and hidden in Bangalore will not reappear if a fire sweeps through your home. These tools offer unmatched autonomy, but autonomy without habit is fragility disguised as freedom. Many enter self-custody imagining independence; they discover, quickly, that independence must be practised. The wallet is merely honest about the terms.

If this chapter were only a classification exercise, it would undersell the lived stakes. The deeper concern is continuity—the quiet, essential question of recovery. Most people treat recovery as an afterthought, something to confront when trouble arrives. Yet recovery is the backbone of custody. The dead phone, the stolen laptop, the corrupted backup, the forgotten passcode, the sudden illness, the unexpected absence: these are not exotic failure modes but the everyday hazards of being human. A digital wallet, whether custodial or not, is only as strong as the plan that governs access when you are not at your best.

Some plans are endearingly simple. An envelope in a desk drawer containing seed words, instructions, and a brief note for heirs may sound unsophisticated, yet it has rescued countless families from chaos. Others embrace cryptographic elegance: splitting secrets across locations, distributing shares among trusted people, or binding recovery to devices rather than memories. What matters is not the sophistication but the suitability. The act of thinking through continuity—*Who should know? Where should this live? How will someone access it if I cannot speak?*—is often more valuable than the tools themselves. A wallet without a recovery plan is not a wallet. It is a gamble.

Yet even the most carefully chosen custody model and recovery scheme falters without hygiene. This is the least glamorous part of digital finance and, for that reason, the most neglected. Hygiene lives in the margins of behaviour: installing updates, verifying send addresses, previewing transactions before approving them, running a five-second mental check before connecting a wallet to a new app, sending a small test transfer when moving large sums. It resembles brushing your teeth—repetitive, easy to skip, never dramatic until the day it is. People who maintain hygiene do not look more sophisticated. They simply avoid the avoidable. Over months and years, that avoidance compounds like interest.

Hygiene also requires emotional posture: enough scepticism to question what the screen says, enough calm to avoid rushing through steps, enough humility to know that no one is immune to mistakes. Every scam borne of haste, every accidental approval of a malicious contract, every irreversible transfer to a mistyped address shares the same origin: a moment of inattentiveness amplified by tools that execute instructions faithfully, not wisely. In this sense, hygiene is not about paranoia; it is about respect—for yourself, for the value you hold, and for the irreversibility of many digital actions.

Yet digital wallets are no longer mere vessels of payment and storage. They are becoming general-purpose interfaces for identity, access, and participation. A wallet can authenticate you to a service, grant privileges to an application, or sign a message that carries legal or financial weight. Connecting a wallet to a decentralised lending protocol, for instance, is not simply "trying an app". It is extending a line of trust. It is granting permissions that may persist long after the experiment has ended. The blast radius—the range of damage a single mistake can cause—grows when the wallet becomes an access hub rather than a one-purpose tool.

This composability is powerful. It allows a wallet to function as the digital spine of a life lived across services. But it also means that revocation—removing permissions, unpairing integrations, pruning connections—matters just as much as permission. People tend to remember the things they turn on, not the things they forget to turn off. A wallet connected to ten services is not "ten times more convenient"; it is ten doors left unlocked unless monitored. The responsibility shifts from isolated transactions to ongoing relationship management with the services that your wallet touches.

The motif that threads through all of this is the key. Not the cryptographic key in its mathematical form, but the human understanding of a key: the small, stubborn object that unlocks, secures, and signals authority. A custodial wallet asks you to trust someone else with the key. A social-recovery wallet invites you to distribute copies in a way that preserves safety without sacrificing accessibility. A hardware wallet asks you to protect the key with rituals, backups, and discipline. In every case, the key represents the same underlying truth: control over value is always a function of control over access. Everything else is decoration.

What lies ahead in this chapter is not a technical manual, nor a sermon on risk, nor a parade of gadgets. It is an attempt to decode the practical meaning of digital self-determination. You will move through the architecture of custody, the quiet craft of recovery, the daily discipline of hygiene, and the expanding universe of wallet-based applications. Each domain demands not expertise but attentiveness: a willingness to look beneath the frictionless surfaces of modern finance and see the mechanisms that grant or deny agency.

The reward is clarity. Clarity about who holds your keys. Clarity about what happens if you drop your phone into a river. Clarity about which permissions you have granted and which you might wish you hadn't. And clarity about how a device in your pocket became not just a tool for paying and receiving, but an instrument for choosing the kind of financial life you intend to lead.

The question waiting at the threshold of this chapter is simple: when your wallet asks you to trust it, what, exactly, are you trusting—and how will you take responsibility for the parts that no institution, no app, and no engineer can manage on your behalf?

Custodial, hybrid, self-custody

In late January 2022, after a routine maintenance notice from Coinbase, a London-based illustrator named Daniel opened his exchange app and found that his account was temporarily inaccessible. Nothing dramatic had happened: no hack, no lost password, no exotic misstep. The platform was simply performing an update. Yet the moment stayed with him. For the twelve hours the freeze lasted, Daniel could view his balances but not move them. He could not convert the tokens he had planned to sell, nor transfer the stablecoins he intended to use for rent. His money had not vanished. But his agency had. A button in someone else's system had temporarily outranked his intentions.

A few months later, in June 2022, a software engineer in Accra experienced the opposite problem. She kept her savings on a hardware wallet and had confidently dismissed the need for backups, convinced that her technical fluency would compensate for any setback. One humid afternoon, she discovered the device unresponsive after a home power surge. She searched drawers for the seed phrase she was sure she had written down. She could not find it. Her autonomy had been intact, right up to the moment she needed help. Then it collapsed into silence.

Two scenes, opposite failures. One reflects dependence without disaster; the other shows sovereignty without safety. They bracket the central question of wallet design: *who* holds the keys, *how* is access restored when things break, and *what* trade-offs flow from those choices as time and circumstance shift? Between these poles lies a spectrum of custody models—custodial, hybrid, and self-custodial—that define not only ownership but responsibility. They shape daily behaviour: how we approve transactions, how we sleep at night, and how we handle moments when life becomes inconvenient or cruel.

Custodial wallets occupy the familiar end of the spectrum. Show: when a user logs into Binance in Paris in 2021, they enter an e-mail address and password, pass a two-factor check, and are greeted by a neat dashboard of balances. Name: this is custodial access. Explain: the platform, not the user, holds the private keys. Transfers and trades are executed within the exchange's internal systems before eventually settling on-chain. Implication: the user enjoys speed, simplicity, and customer support, but must accept that access depends on the platform's infrastructure, policies, liquidity, and regulatory standing.

Visible behaviours illustrate the difference. Users of custodial apps often forget passwords, switch phones casually, or depend on customer service to restore access. They treat digital money like a streaming subscription or an online shop account: one more credential among many. The convenience is real. For many, it is indispensable. Yet convenience is purchased by outsourcing key risk—the risk that someone must hold the private keys securely, detect suspicious behaviour, and prevent unauthorised transfers. This outsourcing can be prudent if the institution is competent, solvent, and well supervised. But it is not a neutral act. It is a choice to place one's ability to transact inside another entity's operational timeline.

The collapse of FTX in November 2022 made this painfully concrete. Customers found that their balances were, in practice, claims against an insolvent exchange. They had entrusted keys to an institution that failed to safeguard user funds. The numbers on screen still appeared familiar, but the function of those numbers had changed from "accessible assets" to "potential claims in bankruptcy". The motif of the key, small but decisive, resurfaces here: *who holds it determines whose timeline wins.*

A counter-example softens this critique. Many custodial institutions, particularly regulated ones, have strong internal controls, segregated client funds, and legal obligations designed to protect users. A customer of Kraken in the United States or Bitstamp in Luxembourg in 2021 encountered stable operations, audit reports, and transparent regulatory relationships. These firms show that not all custodians are fragile or opaque. They prove that custodial models can be safe when governance is sound. But the underlying truth remains: custodial convenience always comes with custodial dependence. The reconciliation lies not in dismissing custodial services but in recognising them as a choice within a landscape of options—not the default, not the villain, but one instrument among many.

Move further along the spectrum and hybrid custody appears. This is the middle ground where technical autonomy meets social design. Hybrid wallets distribute control across multiple parties—people, devices, or both—so that no single actor, including the user, can act alone without meeting a threshold. Show: the social-recovery model of Argent (launched in 2018) used "guardians"—trusted individuals or devices—to help a locked-out user regain access without revealing the seed phrase. Name: social recovery. Explain: instead of one point of failure, the system uses multiple keys held across a small network. Recovery becomes a co-ordinated act rather than a solitary gamble. Implication: users gain resilience while avoiding the anxiety of sole responsibility.

Hybrid custody forces decisions that custodial users rarely make. Who should be trusted as a guardian? A partner who might later become estranged? A sibling who lives abroad? A second device that could be stolen or damaged at the same time as the first? These are not merely technical questions; they are social ones. They demand a level of honest self-assessment—about one's relationships, stability, and habits—that custodial models conveniently hide.

A second example widens the picture. In 2022, Gnosis Safe (now Safe) allowed organisations to store assets using multi-signature wallets in which multiple parties had to approve transactions. A start-up in Berlin could require three out of five executives to sign any major transfer. The system minimised internal fraud risk, created clear decision trails, and aligned digital signatures with governance structures. Here, hybrid custody served institutional discipline rather than personal recovery. It demonstrated that distributing control can mirror human reality: many significant financial decisions are, and should be, collective.

The limitation of hybrid systems is subtle but real. They assume stable relationships, functional communication, and consistent access to guardians or co-signers. During the war in Ukraine in 2022, for example, displaced individuals sometimes lost contact with trusted people who would have served as recovery partners. Hybrid custody can falter when social networks fracture suddenly. The reconciliation is to acknowledge that hybrid models excel in predictable social environments but require careful thought when lives are mobile, uncertain, or under political stress. The key motif returns again: a key shared wisely protects; a key shared carelessly dissolves protection into vulnerability.

At the far end is self-custody—the model that attracts the loudest rhetoric and the deepest misunderstanding. Here, the user alone holds the private keys. No institution, no friend, no helpdesk stands between the user and the asset. Show: a person in Mumbai using a Ledger Nano hardware wallet in 2021 sees their balance only after entering a PIN and physically approving actions on the device. Name: self-custody. Explain: the keys never leave the secure element; transactions are signed locally and broadcast by a companion app. Implication: the user enjoys maximal autonomy and minimal platform risk, but must practise disciplined recovery and vigilance.

Self-custody looks deceptively simple. It promises freedom: no freezes, no intermediaries, no gatekeepers. But every freedom imposes a cost, usually paid in habits. Forget the seed phrase? Funds are irrecoverable. Enter the wrong address? Transfers are irreversible. Misplace the device and backup? No amount of pleading will return the assets. For people accustomed to banking norms—fraud reimbursement, hotline support, reversible transactions—the psychological adjustment is significant. Every gesture carries weight. Every approval is a commitment. Self-custody is not just a technical model; it is a behavioural regime.

Yet it is powerful. Activists under authoritarian regimes, citizens in hyperinflationary economies, and migrants navigating financial exclusion have long valued the ability to store and move value independently of institutions. A journalist in Minsk in 2020 receiving support through crypto-assets depended on self-custody precisely because custodial accounts were monitored or blocked. Here, the burden of responsibility is worth the protection it affords. The device becomes a quiet instrument of personal agency.

The counterpoint is predictable but necessary: self-custody is not universally suitable. People with unreliable living conditions, inconsistent device access, or limited capacity to manage backups may be safer with well-governed custodial services or hybrid models. The reconciliation is straightforward: autonomy is valuable, but not when it becomes a brittle ideal untethered from personal circumstance. The real mastery is not choosing self-custody for ideological reasons but choosing it—or declining it—with clear eyes.

Across custodial, hybrid, and self-custodial models, a single motif threads the spectrum: the key. Not the literal cryptographic key—most users never see that—but the metaphorical key that signals authority and continuity. Who holds it? Who can duplicate it? Who can lose it? Who can help restore it? Every custody model answers these questions differently. The answers shape not only security but intimacy: who you trust, who you empower, who you burden, and who you may inadvertently endanger.

Consider the calendar. Custody choices intersect with time. A young professional living alone in Berlin may embrace self-custody today, confident in memory and discipline. The same individual, decades later, may prefer a hybrid model that ensures heirs can recover assets without technical expertise. A parent in Manila may use a custodial app for household spending while placing long-term savings in a hardware wallet. Custody is not an identity. It is a configuration that should evolve as life does.

Visible behaviour often reveals whether a model suits its user. Someone who routinely misplaces devices may thrive under custodial arrangements with strong authentication. Someone who travels across borders frequently may prefer hybrid recovery that survives luggage loss and bureaucratic delay. Someone facing political risk may prioritise self-custody even when inconvenient. The wisdom lies not in idealising one end of the spectrum but in matching custody to reality.

This brings us to the enduring tension. Every digital wallet asks a version of the same question: *who should hold the key to your financial life?* Not in theory, not in ideology, but in practice—day after day, mishap after mishap, change after change. And when your circumstances inevitably shift, will your custody model shift with them, or will you keep relying on habits that no longer protect you?

Backups, recovery, and heirs

In December 2018, Gerald Cotten, the 30-year-old founder of the Canadian exchange QuadrigaCX, died unexpectedly in Jaipur, India. When administrators began sorting through the company's affairs in early 2019, they made a grim discovery:

the exchange's "cold wallets" appeared inaccessible. Cotten had reportedly been the only person with the private keys. Around 76,000 customers were left with claims totalling roughly C$215 million, much of it in digital assets that, in practical terms, could no longer move. The balances still existed on-chain. But the authority to act on them had died with one man in one hotel room. The missing piece was not technology. It was recovery.

That story has been retold so often that it can sound like folklore, yet it captures a very domestic question. What happens to a wallet when its owner is unconscious, absent, or gone? For all the talk of cryptography and decentralisation, most failures in digital finance start with mundane events: a house fire destroys a notebook; a laptop is stolen; a password manager fails to sync; a family discovers that a meticulous saver never wrote down a single instruction. The paradox is sharp. People devote serious effort to choosing where to hold value, yet spend remarkably little time designing how that value would survive their own mistakes or mortality. They treat recovery as an afterthought, not as part of the architecture.

At its core, recovery is about continuity. It is the quiet discipline of ensuring that value can outlive devices, logins, and even the person who set everything up. When money lives as entries on interconnected ledgers, continuity no longer comes from the physical survivability of cash or gold. It comes from the survivability of *access paths*: seed phrases, recovery contacts, written instructions, legal documents, and the social arrangements that sit behind them. Every digital wallet therefore has two problems, not one. The first is how you get in and out each day. The second is what happens if you cannot.

The simplest place to see this is seed storage. When a wallet generates a 12- or 24-word phrase, it is compressing an enormous amount of mathematical structure into something a human can write. Show: a user in Milan installs a self-custodial wallet in 2023, is shown a sequence of English words, and is told to store them securely. Name: this is the seed phrase, following common standards such as BIP-39. Explain: anyone who obtains the full phrase can recreate the wallet and move any assets it controls; if the phrase is lost, no authority can recreate it. Implication: a single piece of information becomes both the key to continuity and a point of catastrophic failure.

People respond to this burden in familiar ways. Some photograph the phrase and upload it to cloud storage, trading confidentiality for convenience. Others transcribe it onto paper and slide it into a drawer, relying on the assumption that nothing unexpected will happen to that drawer. A smaller group engraves the words or their encoded form onto metal plates designed to survive heat and water damage. Each choice reveals a risk preference. The photograph introduces exposure to account compromise. The paper risks fire, mould, or casual discovery. The metal plate mitigates physical degradation but may be obvious to a thief. Recovery, here, is not about perfection; it is about choosing which failure you are willing to live with.

Seen honestly, the seed phrase is not a magic artefact; it is a responsibility. It demands a plan that balances two dangers: that no-one can find it when needed, and that the wrong person can find it too easily. The motif of the envelope captures this tension. A sealed envelope can be lost in a move or opened by anyone who finds it. It can also sit faithfully in a safe for decades, waiting for a future moment when clarity is needed. The difference lies not in the paper but in the thought put into where it lives and who knows it exists.

Multi-location storage offers a partial remedy, but only if executed with care. Show: a teacher in São Paulo writes her seed phrase on two separate sheets of paper and stores one at home, one in a bank safety deposit box. Name: geographic redundancy. Explain: a local disaster or burglary is less likely to compromise both copies at once. Implication: the phrase becomes more resilient to physical accidents, but the number of places it might be discovered by an adversary has also increased.

This trade-off is measurable. Two copies in two locations halve the probability that a single fire destroys everything; they also double the locations a burglar might search successfully if they suspect digital assets are present. Moving to metal backups or coded fragments changes the technical details, not the underlying question. You are always deciding between concentration (one very protected point of failure) and distribution (several less protected points). There is no configuration that removes judgement.

Multi-party recovery schemes shift the problem from places to people. Social-recovery wallets such as Argent, or smart-contract based setups discussed by Vitalik Buterin and others from 2020 onwards, ask the user to appoint "guardians"—trusted individuals or devices who can collectively restore access if the primary key is lost. Show: a woman in Nairobi designates her sister, her business partner, and a hardware wallet as three guardians, any two of which can approve account recovery. Name: a 2-of-3 social recovery threshold. Explain: no single guardian can seize control, but if she loses her phone, two guardians working together can re-authorise a new device. Implication: continuity becomes a social process. Recovery requires co-operation, not just paperwork.

The behaviours this model demands are revealing. The user must have frank conversations with guardians, explaining what is at stake without divulging unnecessary detail. She must keep contact information current, verify that guardians still hold their roles, and anticipate social changes: marriages, divorces, moves, deaths. Guardians, in turn, must be willing to act when called upon, yet disciplined enough not to treat their status as a licence to pry. The plan lives not just on-chain but in human relationships. This is both its strength and its frailty.

A limitation appears quickly. Social recovery presumes a relatively stable, trustworthy network around the user. For people in precarious situations—migrants, political dissidents, those estranged from family—such networks may be thin or unreliable. In those contexts, entrusting fragments of control to others could increase danger rather than reduce it. The reconciliation lies in acknowledging that multi-party recovery is not a universal upgrade; it is a tool suited to those whose social fabric can bear the weight.

The question of heirs sharpens everything. When assets can be accessed only through secrets held in one head, the traditional machinery of inheritance—wills, probate courts, family meetings—runs into an invisible wall. There is no bank manager to persuade, no vault to drill, no central ledger to petition. Either the heirs have a valid way to reconstruct the keys, or the assets become a permanent monument to a life's work that nobody can touch.

The case of American banker Matthew Mellon, who died in April 2018, is often cited here. Reports suggested he held hundreds of millions of dollars in XRP tokens spread across multiple cold wallets, with private keys stored under assumed names in banks around the United States. Whatever the precise figures, the core problem stands: when key knowledge is fragmented and opaque, heirs face a maze. Some may never locate all the pieces; others may lack the technical literacy to use what they find. The value exists, verifiable on public ledgers, yet remains stranded because no living person holds both knowledge and authority.

At a smaller scale, similar stories play out quietly. An engineer in Berlin dies, leaving behind a laptop with a wallet app, a password manager, and no written instructions. His partner can open e-mail and photographs but cannot guess which of the many apps matters for savings, nor how to operate them. A retired teacher in Manila leaves a notebook full of carefully written seed phrases but no indication of which ones are current or how they map to particular wallets. Heirs face an information forensics project at precisely the moment they are least emotionally equipped for it.

Here the modest envelope plan shows its power. Show: a parent in Dublin keeps a sealed envelope in a home safe. Inside is a short letter: a plain-language inventory of wallets and platforms, high-level balances, and step-by-step instructions on where to find keys or who to contact. The seed phrase itself may not be in the envelope, but directions to its location are. Name: an envelope plan. Explain: the plan is not a legal document; it is a practical map. It can be updated annually, destroyed and replaced when arrangements change, and referenced by those named in a will or equivalent instrument. Implication: heirs gain clarity without having sweeping powers in advance.

The envelope is not infallible. It can be stolen, copied, forged, or destroyed. It can become outdated if not refreshed. But it provides something most families lack: a starting point. It translates a web of apps, devices, and jargon into a human narrative that another person can follow. In a field obsessed with cryptographic novelty, that narrative is often the missing ingredient.

For those seeking more technical assurance, shared-secret approaches offer another path. Schemes based on Shamir's Secret Sharing, invented by Adi Shamir in 1979, allow a secret—say, a seed phrase—to be mathematically split into several "shares" such that any subset of them (for example, any three of five) can reconstruct the original, while fewer convey no information. Show: a couple in Johannesburg uses such a scheme to create five shares, keeping one each, placing a third with a lawyer, and storing the remaining two in separate secure locations. Name: a 3-of-5 secret sharing plan. Explain: no single share grants access; only when three are brought together can the seed be recovered. Implication: theft or loss of one location does not immediately compromise assets, yet heirs can co-ordinate to assemble enough parts if needed.

This method has appealing properties. It formalises the notion of "no one person has the whole key" while avoiding the logistical hazard of physically cutting phrases into segments. It also imposes a certain discipline: participants must understand their role, protect their share, and know under what conditions reconstruction is appropriate. The mathematical guarantees are strong. What they cannot supply is judgement. Secret sharing works only as well as the human process around it—the choice of participants, the clarity of instructions, and the ability of heirs to find and interpret what has been stored.

The limitation is obvious from the outside. Such schemes are more complex to set up, harder to explain, and easy to execute badly. A family unused to technical systems may mislabel envelopes, forget which share belongs where, or lose confidence when a key person dies. Here again, the envelope motif helps. A technical shared-secret plan still benefits from an accompanying letter: a human explanation that future readers can understand without having to decode the original architect's mindset.

Legal frameworks sit in the background of all these arrangements. Wills, trusts, and national inheritance rules determine who is entitled to what; wallet architectures determine who can actually get to it. When the two align, transitions can be orderly: an executor knows where to look, what to present to whom, and how to respect both the law and the departed's intentions. When they diverge, conflict emerges. A will may grant an heir rights to digital assets that they cannot in practice access. Or a set of keys, left without formal documentation, may allow someone to move funds in ways that other heirs dispute.

The interplay between legal documents and technical access is delicate. A will that spells out a seed phrase in full could, in some jurisdictions, become part of a public record during probate. A document that merely says "my digital assets go to X" without any operational detail may be legally tidy but practically void. The art is to design for both audiences: the court that must recognise the transfer, and the human who must follow the map. Neither alone is sufficient.

The quiet motif running through all of this is the question: *who will read the letter?* Not only the literal envelope, but the broader set of clues you leave—folder names, device labels, account nicknames, contact lists, remembered conversations. In the analogue age, a filing cabinet and a bank relationship went a long way. In the borderless, multi-wallet world, heirs may face a scatter of interfaces, each with its own recovery assumptions. Without a narrative thread, even well-designed technical safeguards can lie dormant.

Recovery, then, is not a button to press when trouble arrives. It is a design choice that runs through seed storage, multi-party arrangements, and the dull but vital work of writing things down for people who do not share your habits or vocabulary. It is also a moral choice. To hold value in forms that others cannot access without your guidance is to take on an obligation to provide that guidance while you can.

The unresolved tension remains. How far should you go in constructing elaborate backup and inheritance schemes before complexity itself becomes a new point of failure? When you imagine the worst-case scenarios—the fire, the theft, the sudden illness, the border crossing gone wrong—can you picture a specific person, on a specific day, using what you have left behind to restore access without you? And if you cannot, what exactly does it mean to say that your money is "safe"?

Everyday hygiene

In February 2021, the City of London Police released a short statement detailing a rise in digital-asset phishing cases reported in the previous quarter. One incident involved a 34-year-old architect, Simon Clarke, who received what appeared to be a routine update prompt for his browser wallet. The message looked legitimate, carried the branding of a well-known provider, and urged him to "restore access" urgently. Within minutes of entering his details, £9,800 had moved out of his wallet. The transfer was irreversible. The screen had looked familiar; the behaviour had felt routine. Only later did investigators confirm that the domain hosting the prompt had been registered in December 2020, routed through servers in Amsterdam, and linked to a cluster of similar scams. A moment of inattention had met a professional deception. The outcome was decisive.

That story is not exceptional. In March 2022, a woman in Vancouver approved a transaction on her phone while distracted at a bus stop, believing it to be a small scheduled transfer. It was not. A malicious script had inserted itself between her wallet and the decentralised application she was using. The prompt she approved sent her entire balance—just under CA$3,000—to an anonymous address. Her phone vibrated twice: once when the request appeared, once when the blockchain confirmed the transfer. The whole event lasted under twenty seconds. The loss felt instant, but its roots lay in the quiet erosion of habits. She later admitted she had stopped checking transaction previews because "they always looked the same".

Two cases, different continents, same lesson. Digital wallets do not usually fail through dramatic technical collapse; they fail through tiny, habitual lapses. Hygiene is not glamour. It is attention, rhythm, and care. It is the routine discipline of reducing avoidable loss, one small behaviour at a time. And like saving, the gains compound.

The first layer of hygiene is deceptively simple: keep software current. Show: in September 2021, MetaMask issued an update to patch a vulnerability affecting certain browser environments. Name: routine version updates. Explain: wallet providers regularly release patches that correct flaws, adapt to changes in operating systems, or improve how permissions are handled. Implication: a user who delays updates increases exposure, sometimes substantially, to risks that engineers have already identified and solved.

This is not abstract. When iOS 14.5 was released in April 2021, it quietly changed how clipboard access worked. Several wallet providers issued rapid updates to adjust to the new privacy model. Users who updated promptly continued without disruption. Those who postponed experienced erratic behaviour when copying addresses, occasionally pasting truncated or stale details. The behaviour was visible: failed transactions, error messages, confusion. The metric was simple: a version number. Hygiene in this context is a habit of noticing that number and keeping it current.

A counterpoint arises. Not all updates are beneficial immediately. Some users prefer to wait a day or two to see whether a new release introduces bugs—particularly when dealing with major operating system upgrades. This hesitation is reasonable. The reconciliation lies in a pattern: delay briefly to avoid fresh instability, but avoid the opposite extreme of running outdated software for weeks. Hygiene is a rhythm, not a reflex.

Phishing is the second terrain where hygiene pays dividends. The essential move is behavioural: pause before interacting. Show: in 2020, Ledger suffered a data breach that exposed customer e-mail addresses. Name: the Ledger breach (July 2020). Explain: although the company's hardware devices were unaffected, scammers gained a list of potential targets and launched a campaign of sophisticated phishing e-mails. Implication: users who clicked links without scrutiny were directed to fake sites that mimicked the real interface perfectly, leading some to disclose seed phrases or approve malicious actions.

The behaviours that defended against such attacks were visible and mundane. Users who typed URLs manually, compared domain names character by character, or used password managers that autofilled only on legitimate sites were far less likely to fall victim. These are not high-ceremony security rituals. They are small acts of friction that filter deception. A user who develops the reflex to distrust unsolicited prompts—and who understands that legitimate services will never ask for a seed phrase—is practising hygiene in the most literal sense: removing contaminants before they enter the system.

A limitation is worth acknowledging. Some phishing campaigns are so polished, so well timed, and so tailored that even experienced users hesitate. During a wave of attacks in late 2021, criminals used stolen KYC documents to impersonate support staff, creating plausible narratives about frozen accounts or pending regulatory reviews. When deception becomes that personalised, hygiene cannot rely solely on visual detection. It must rely on a rule: *never act from an inbound request; always initiate contact yourself.* The motif of the mirror applies here: when in doubt, reflect the request by starting a clean session, navigating to the official site, and verifying what you see. Reflection interrupts manipulation.

Transaction previews form the third pillar. A preview is the moment where intention meets execution. Show: a wallet in Barcelona displays the details of a proposed transfer—recipient address, network fee, amount—in a concise window before the user approves. Name: transaction preview. Explain: this step allows the user to catch errors or notice unexpected changes in parameters, such as a sudden shift in gas fees on congested blockchains. Implication: skipping or skimming this preview increases the probability of sending funds to the wrong address or authorising an unintended contract interaction.

The difference between reading and not reading previews is measurable. In 2021, during periods of Ethereum congestion, gas fees could swing from $5 to over $200 within minutes (data from Etherscan, 2021). Users who checked previews routinely postponed transactions until fees stabilised, often saving substantial sums. The behaviour was small—waiting, refreshing, reconsidering—but the impact was financial. Hygiene, again, is what accumulates.

Previews are also a defence against malicious scripts. Decentralised applications sometimes request permissions that exceed what the user expects—access to entire token balances rather than a specific amount. A careful reading of the preview reveals this mismatch. A rushed tap conceals it. The limitation is human: previews can be dense, especially when interacting with smart contracts. The text may not always be intuitive. The reconciliation is practice. With repetition, users learn what "normal" looks like, making the abnormal conspicuous.

The fourth habit is deceptively humble: test sends. A small transfer—£1, €5, or the equivalent amount of a chosen token—reveals more truth than any documentation. Show: a freelancer in Lagos sends a tiny amount of USDC to a new client in Lisbon before transferring the full £1,000-equivalent invoice. Name: test send. Explain: the small transaction confirms the address, network choice, payment rail, and wallet compatibility. It exposes mistakes cheaply. Implication: the user gains confidence in the route and avoids the catastrophic error of sending a full balance to an incorrect or unsupported address.

Test sends form a quiet pattern of intentionality. They turn guesswork into evidence. They convert a high-stakes action into a low-stakes rehearsal. And they take seconds. The cost is trivial; the protection is substantial. In behavioural terms, they reduce anxiety. In financial terms, they reduce loss. The motif of the mirror reappears here: test sends reflect the path you plan to follow, showing whether it holds before you commit real weight.

Some argue that test sends waste time or incur unnecessary fees. They are correct in narrow circumstances: if fees are unusually high or if the counterparty is deeply trusted. But even then, when the address is new or the rail unfamiliar, the cost of a test send is far smaller than the cost of a ruined transfer. The reconciliation is contextual. Test sends are optional, but their value compounds. Over years, they prevent dozens of errors that might otherwise be shrugged off as "unlucky".

Routine hygiene becomes powerful only when it becomes routine. This introduces a simple but effective concept: checklists. Not formal documents, but memory aids. Show: an accountant in Manchester keeps a short note on her phone: "Check domain. Check preview. Check network. Check amount. Test if new." Name: a hygiene checklist. Explain: the list structures attention. It mitigates the cognitive load of remembering several small steps each time she transacts. Implication: behaviour becomes consistent, and the risk of avoidable mistakes declines sharply.

Checklists work because they offload deliberation. They are not symbols of inexperience; they are tools of professionals. Surgeons use them. Pilots use them. Analysts use them. Each field confronts the same truth: humans forget. The digital wallet world is no different. A checklist prevents overconfidence. It turns intention into procedure.

A counter-example illustrates the point. During a 2022 audit of crypto-related fraud cases in Queensland, investigators noted a pattern: victims often reported that they had "checked everything". When asked to describe what "everything" meant, the answers were vague. There was no actual checklist—just a sense of familiarity. Familiarity is not defence. It can be the opposite. A checklist is precise. It is concrete. It eliminates the blur.

Throughout these practices, a quiet motif threads itself: the second look. Whether checking URLs, reviewing previews, or performing test sends, hygiene lives in the moment between impulse and commitment—the moment where you choose to look again. That second look is not hesitation; it is discipline. It is how you reclaim time from the speed of software.

Hygiene gains power because it compounds. A single habit prevents one mistake. But a cluster of habits prevents dozens. They sharpen attention. They build confidence. They create a mental environment where wallets stop feeling mysterious and start feeling manageable. Over time, these small behaviours accumulate into something calm and robust: a sense that you can navigate a complex system without fear.

Yet an unresolved tension remains. As interfaces get slicker, faster, and more automatic, will the discipline of the second look survive? When taps replace reading and speed replaces thought, how will you ensure that the quiet safeguards you rely on do not dissolve into convenience?

Composability and extensions

In May 2020, a software developer in Tallinn connected her wallet to Compound, a decentralised lending protocol built on Ethereum. She intended to deposit a modest amount of USDC to earn interest. The interface was clean, the steps familiar, and the wallet prompt looked routine. Within seconds, she approved a permission that allowed the protocol to move *all* her USDC, not just the amount she planned to lend. She noticed the detail only later, when reviewing her permissions list. Nothing harmful occurred—the protocol behaved correctly—but the moment revealed a structural truth. Connecting a wallet to an external application is not a casual act. It is a contract. And a contract, even in algorithmic form, always carries obligations that outlive the tap that created it.

Four months later, in September 2020, users of the decentralised exchange Uniswap encountered a different lesson. A new token, listed without scrutiny, invited people to connect their wallets to claim an airdrop. The token's smart contract contained malicious approval logic, allowing the deployer to drain balances from anyone who granted permission. Some lost small amounts. Others lost savings. The episode was documented by security researchers analysing contract behaviour for that month. The transfers were irreversible. The prompts looked ordinary. The function was not. What failed was not the technology; it was the assumption that every connection was benign.

These episodes frame a core reality of digital wallets: they are no longer mere containers of value. They are *interfaces*—doorways, sockets, linkages—through which money, identity, and applications interact. A wallet is a control panel. And control panels are only as safe as the hands that install, inspect, and occasionally revoke the wiring behind them.

Composability is the principle that allows one tool to plug into another without bespoke negotiation. Show: a wallet in Berlin connects to a decentralised exchange like SushiSwap in 2021. Name: composability. Explain: the wallet exposes standardised interfaces that let applications request permissions, read balances, or initiate actions. Implication: the user can move seamlessly across services, but each connection creates a live, durable permission that must be understood, monitored, and, when needed, revoked.

The power of composability is obvious to anyone who has used a modern ecosystem. A single wallet can serve as a login identity, execute payments, prove ownership of digital assets, interact with lending protocols, and access token-gated communities. It reduces friction. It increases reach. It changes behaviour. People commit to actions in seconds that, in older financial systems, would require forms, signatures, or verification calls. Speed creates its own gravity.

Yet the same connective tissue that enables freedom introduces exposure. Each permission is a hinge. Some hinges open only when pushed from the user's side—simple "spend approvals" for specific amounts. Others remain unlocked until actively shut, allowing an application to spend tokens indefinitely until revocation. The difference is not intuitive at first glance. A user sees a button. The system sees delegated authority.

This distinction became clear in November 2021 when Etherscan began warning users more visibly about "infinite approvals". The behaviour was measurable: many users revoked unused permissions after the alert, reducing the surface area available to future exploits. A simple design tweak changed patterns across the network. The implication is instructive. Hygiene—examining permissions—is not merely personal discipline; it is a design feature that can be encouraged or neglected.

Identity adds another layer to the picture. Increasingly, wallets are not only instruments for transactions but gates to broader systems. Show: in January 2022, a user in Singapore connected her wallet to Mirror.xyz to publish and verify a digital essay. Name: wallet-based authentication. Explain: instead of creating usernames and passwords, she proved her identity through a signature tied to her wallet. Implication: the wallet became her passport. Losing access meant losing not just assets but access to writing, voting, or participation.

This dual role—financial and identity—changes the stakes. If a compromised permission can move funds, that is one level of risk. If the same permission can impersonate a user, publish on their behalf, or vote in their name within a decentralised organisation, the blast radius widens dramatically. Identity and money intertwine. Composability creates power; it also fuses risks that were once separate.

A limitation emerges. Not all applications need ongoing access. Many ask for far more than required. A simple read access might suffice, yet the app requests broad "manage all tokens" authority. The reconciliation lies in scrutiny. Users can and should ask whether an app needs ongoing permissions or a one-time interaction. The system allows selective commitments. The discipline is choosing them.

The motif of the door—the quiet image that threads through this landscape—reveals its strength here. Every time a wallet connects to an application, a door opens. Some doors stay ajar until explicitly closed. Others lock automatically after a single use. Some open onto well-lit rooms with predictable rules. Others lead into unfamiliar spaces where the consequences of entry are not yet known. The user may forget which doors remain open. The system never does.

Consider the act of connecting a wallet to a lending application. Show: a man in Lisbon in 2022 connects his wallet to Aave to deposit DAI for yield. Name: a lending protocol connection. Explain: the protocol requires an approval that allows it to move the user's DAI for lending, collateral adjustments, and, if needed, liquidation. Implication: the user gains access to liquidity and returns, but gives the protocol conditional control over collateral. If the value of his position drops because the market turns sharply, automated liquidation may occur. His wallet acts as a doorway to a system that is both useful and unforgiving.

The benefit is tangible. People borrow against their holdings to manage cash flow, avoid taxable disposals, or capture investment opportunities. The risks are equally tangible. Liquidations, while algorithmic, are not emotional. They measure collateral and execute action. There is no negotiation.

The choice to open the door includes the possibility that the system will act at a moment when the user is asleep, in transit, or distracted. Composability accelerates financial action. It accelerates consequences too.

A counter-example highlights the nuance. Some decentralised applications implement granular permissions that restrict their authority precisely. Compound v2, for instance, relied on specific cToken contracts that allowed a user to authorise only the amount being supplied, not all holdings. This approach reduces risk. It shows that composability does not inherently demand exposure. It is a design choice. When applications limit themselves, the user inherits protection. When they do not, the user must impose limits manually.

Revocation is the hidden half of composability. Few users think about permissions until something goes wrong. Yet the ability to withdraw authority is central to maintaining a safe, flexible ecosystem. Show: a researcher in Zurich uses Revoke.cash in October 2022 to audit and withdraw unused approvals across multiple networks. Name: permission revocation. Explain: tools like Revoke.cash scan blockchain records, list granted permissions, and let the user cancel those no longer needed. Implication: the blast radius shrinks. If an old application is compromised later, its ability to move or spend assets is gone.

Revocation has a rhythm. Once a month. Once a quarter. After major interactions. Like changing passwords or updating software, it becomes part of the background maintenance of financial life. The behaviour is visible: a click, a confirmation, a sigh of relief. The metric is concrete: the number of active approvals falls.

The limitation is friction. Revocation costs gas. On congested networks, that cost may be non-trivial. During peak Ethereum activity in May 2021, cancelling a single approval could cost over $50. Some users simply refused. The reconciliation lies in context. If assets at risk exceed the cost of revocation, pay it. If they do not, consider whether the underlying asset should be on a cheaper or more flexible network. Hygiene does not exist in isolation; it interacts with economics.

Composability also brings identity-level risks. Show: in 2021, decentralised organisations using Snapshot or Tally relied on wallet signatures to authenticate votes. Name: signature-based governance. Explain: a malicious application could request a signature that looked harmless but actually authorised a vote or delegated influence. Implication: identity, not just money, could be hijacked.

This is where the motif of the door becomes essential again. Opening a door for convenience may open another door behind it that you do not immediately see. The system is not malicious. It is layered. A signature may serve multiple purposes. A transaction may have side effects. A permission may grant broader authority than its label suggests.

A limitation arises in user understanding. Most people do not read signature payloads; they glance at prompts. Interfaces compress complexity. This is a design challenge, not user failure. The reconciliation is incremental literacy. Users who regularly check permissions learn to recognise anomalies: a voting signature requested during a routine swap, or a contract call that seems irrelevant to the action at hand. The awareness grows slowly but reliably.

The structural strength of composability is its optionality. You can connect your wallet to a lending protocol, a decentralised exchange, a data oracle, or an identity layer. You can disconnect it just as easily. But optionality is only meaningful if paired with care. A room full of doors only helps those who remember which ones they opened.

This leads to the unresolved tension that defines the modern wallet. Each connection promises convenience, yield, access, or identity. Each connection also enlarges your exposure—sometimes in ways you cannot see until much later. The question lingers: when you next open your wallet to an application, are you opening a door you can close, or one that will stay ajar long after you have walked away?

Chapter 3
Stablecoins Without the Hype

The first time the Venezuelan journalist Lorena Meléndez invoiced a client in Madrid using a dollar-denominated token, she noticed something unsettling in its simplicity. There was no anxious wait to confirm the day's bolívar exchange rate, no mental arithmetic to guess what inflation would erode overnight, no haggling over fees. She received exactly what she billed. The price held still while everything around her moved. It felt, she later said, "like working in another economy without leaving home." That single payment carried a deeper truth: stability, in a world of fluctuating currencies, is not a luxury but a lifeline, and stablecoins have become its unlikely couriers.

Yet the very idea of a stable digital coin poses a quiet contradiction. How can a token issued on an open, often turbulent network maintain a fixed value when the surrounding market never sits still? What gives it the nerve to claim constancy? For a decade, this question has lingered behind every debate, from coffee shops in Buenos Aires to regulatory hearings in Washington. Some see stablecoins as bridges linking fractured monetary systems; others view them as brittle props waiting for the wrong gust of volatility. What matters is not the noise but the architecture: how stability is built, scrutinised, stressed, and sometimes lost.

The promise of a stablecoin is seduction by certainty. A digital dollar that behaves like its paper counterpart. A token redeemable for a fixed unit of currency. A piece of the global economy that can move across networks at the speed of code. But beneath the surface lies a mosaic of models, from those backed by conservative cash reserves to those balanced by algorithms, incentives, and market behaviour. Some have proved durable. Others have collapsed in spectacular fashion. The landscape invites admiration and scepticism in equal measure.

Stablecoins sit at the intersection of two forces that have defined the century so far: the desire for a reliable store of value and the rise of programmable financial infrastructure. People use them to invoice across borders, cushion savings against inflation, settle ecommerce, hedge volatile local currencies, and move money through corridors banks overlook. But people also fear them. They worry about opaque reserves, frozen accounts, frozen smart contracts, regulatory seizures, de-pegging spirals, and uncertain redemptions. Fear thrives in spaces where design is misunderstood and governance is uncertain. The task of this chapter is not to amplify the fear. It is to illuminate the machinery.

A stablecoin's credibility rests, at its core, on a simple proposition: a token is only as trustworthy as the thing that guarantees it. This is where the motif of *weight* becomes important. Throughout this chapter, weight stands for the substance behind each coin—the reserves, the rules, the monitoring, the discipline. Some coins carry weight in recognised financial instruments held at regulated institutions. Others carry weight only through incentives and faith in market dynamics. Some carry barely any weight at all. Recognising this spectrum is not cynicism. It is competence.

Consider a dollar-pegged token with regular attestations by a major accounting firm. The issuer publishes monthly breakdowns of cash, Treasury bills, and short-term deposits. The chain shows circulating supply. Redemptions operate predictably. This is stability by design plus governance: measurable reserves, verifiable claims, and operational procedures that hold under stress. Now contrast this with a structure that relies on a volatile asset for collateral, stabilised by an algorithm that issues or burns new tokens in response to market demand. The first model leans on institutions; the second trusts markets. Both present narratives of stability. Both have succeeded in various contexts. And one—famously, in May 2022—unwound in a matter of days when its feedback loop snapped under panic. Weight was the difference.

The uses of stablecoins that endure are usually the least glamorous. A freelancer in Latin America billing global clients. A Kenyan importer settling invoices without fighting currency swings. A Turkish family moving part of their monthly budget into dollar tokens to preserve purchasing power across the week. None of these choices signal speculation or ideological commitment. They are acts of self-preservation: pragmatic, controlled, small-scale. Durable use is not a story of windfalls. It is a story of clarity. People choose stablecoins when what they need is not profit but predictability.

Predictability, however, has dimensions. A token may hold its peg but still disappoint if withdrawals freeze due to legal action against the issuer. It may remain redeemable yet unavailable on the network where the user needs it. It may have excellent transparency but rely on an issuing entity domiciled in a jurisdiction with fragile banking relationships. Stability begins as a promise. It matures as a practice. And practice becomes meaningful only when its failure modes are understood.

Failure teaches in ways success rarely does. The de-pegging of TerraUSD in 2022 revealed how quickly confidence evaporates when incentives falter. The temporary dip of USDC in March 2023, when Circle disclosed that $3.3 billion of its reserves were held at Silicon Valley Bank during its collapse, showed that even well-collateralised stablecoins depend on the health of traditional institutions. These events were different in severity and cause, but both revealed the same structural reality: a stablecoin, however digital its interface, is stitched into the legal and financial environment around it.

This is why the question *what makes a coin stable?* is incomplete without another: *stable compared to what?* A token may appear rock-solid when local currency inflation runs above 40 per cent. It may feel fragile when benchmark interest rates spike or regulators intervene. Stability is relational—it depends on the user's reference point and the surrounding system's reliability. In Lagos or Buenos Aires, a slight wobble in a dollar-pegged coin may be tolerable. In Zurich, it may be unacceptable. This relativity does not weaken the concept. It contextualises it.

The architecture behind stability demands attention to governance, transparency, and the calibration of incentives. Governance determines who can freeze or seize tokens, who controls reserve accounts, and how redemptions are handled during stress. Transparency determines what the issuer publishes, how often, and through which independent parties. Incentives determine how arbitrageurs, traders, and issuers behave when the peg drifts. These are not technical footnotes. They are the living substance of the coin's weight.

Choosing a stablecoin is not about choosing perfection. It is about choosing a structure whose flaws you understand and whose strengths align with your needs. Some people prefer the simplicity of a fully fiat-backed model with strict attestations. Others prefer decentralised collateral, even with volatility, because they distrust custodial concentration. Still others prefer diversification, spreading funds across two issuers, two networks, or two models to reduce exposure to any single failure. There is no universal solution. There are only informed decisions.

And decisions gain power when they form habits. Checking monthly attestation reports. Monitoring supply fluctuations. Understanding which chains offer deep liquidity. Identifying reliable exit ramps. The discipline of stablecoin management is not complicated, but it is continuous. Like good wallet hygiene, it compounds quietly over time.

Stablecoins matter because they sit at the hinge point between personal agency and institutional design. They allow individuals to hold value in forms their local systems may not provide. They route around frictions in cross-border commerce. They reveal the fragility and resilience of global finance through their behaviour under pressure. But they also demand something from their users: scepticism, attention, and a refusal to mistake marketing for structure.

The tension that closes this chapter's introduction is the same one that opened it: how much weight must a digital coin carry before you trust it to sit still? The next pages take that question apart—not to promote fear or faith, but to show what stability looks like when the noise is stripped away and the mechanics stand in full view.

What makes a coin stable

At 8.12 a.m. on 14 March 2023, traders noticed something off about USDC, a leading dollar-pegged token issued by Circle. On Coinbase, its price slipped to $0.89. By mid-morning in New York, liquidity pools on decentralised exchanges showed widening spreads. The trigger was simple and public: Circle had disclosed that $3.3 billion of its reserves were held at Silicon Valley Bank, which had entered receivership with the Federal Deposit Insurance Corporation (FDIC) days earlier. The peg recovered after assurances that the reserves would be fully accessible, but the jolt offered a lasting lesson. Stability, despite its name, is never static. It is a composite of design, governance, and trust under pressure.

That moment also revealed something subtler. A stablecoin can trade away from its peg even when its issuer behaves responsibly, its reserves are independently attested, and its structure is conservative. The market reacts before the balance sheet does. Instruments designed to hold still can move faster than their foundations. Stability, then, is not merely a matter of holding enough dollars; it is the ability of the entire system—issuer, custodians, chains, market participants—to keep faith aligned during stress. The question is not only *what backs the coin?* but also *who enforces the promise, and how quickly?* This dual lens frames every assessment that follows.

At its simplest, a stablecoin is a digital representation of value that aims to maintain a fixed reference point, usually a national currency. But this simplicity belies a layered engineering problem. Reserves must be liquid. Governance must be clear. Transparency must be meaningful. Redemption mechanics must function when conditions are least forgiving. The motif to keep in mind throughout is *the hinge*: stability depends on a set of hinges connecting claims, reserves, markets, and rules. When the hinges move smoothly, value stays aligned. When they strain, the peg wobbles.

Fiat-backed stablecoins anchor stability in conservatism. Tether (USDT), launched in 2014, and Circle's USDC, launched in 2018, rely on reserves held in cash, short-term government securities, and bank deposits. Their issuers publish attestations—third-party confirmations of reserve composition—typically monthly. These attestations, while not full audits, provide structured insight into the assets supporting each token. Users can redeem tokens for dollars through authorised channels, creating a redemption-driven price floor. The logic is intuitive: if one token equals one dollar, and redemption works efficiently, market prices should converge to the peg.

But redemption only works when liquidity and confidence align. In May 2022, Tether briefly traded at $0.95 on some exchanges after the collapse of TerraUSD, an algorithmic stablecoin backed primarily by market incentives rather than reserves. Tether's attestation reports were current, and its reserves ultimately proved sufficient to meet billions of dollars in redemptions. Yet the price still slipped. The hinge had not broken, but it groaned under the weight of fear. That episode demonstrated that stability by design still requires stability in perception. A stablecoin's market behaviour communicates as loudly as its balance sheet.

Algorithmic models attempt stability through dynamics rather than deposits. TerraUSD (UST), created by Terraform Labs in

2020, linked its value to LUNA, a volatile asset that absorbed fluctuations through mint-and-burn mechanisms. When demand for UST rose, LUNA was burned; when demand fell, more LUNA was issued. For a time, the system appeared to hold. Then, in May 2022, selling pressure overwhelmed the mechanism. The feedback loop snapped, LUNA's value collapsed, and UST lost its peg permanently. The hinge sheared clean through. The failure illuminated a central truth: stability anchored in incentives alone can become fragile when market confidence evaporates.

These two examples—USDC's temporary dip and UST's structural implosion—illustrate the spectrum of stablecoin design. Between them lie hybrid models such as MakerDAO's DAI, which began in 2017 as a decentralised coin backed primarily by over-collateralised crypto assets. After significant volatility during the March 2020 market crash, MakerDAO introduced more diversified collateral, including tokenised Treasury assets. DAI now blends decentralisation with real-world collateral. It remains neither fully fiat-backed nor purely algorithmic; instead, it is stability delivered through compromise. The hinge metaphor fits here too: DAI depends on multiple hinges, each absorbing different forms of pressure.

Transparency claims sit at the heart of stablecoin governance. Some issuers publish daily reports of reserve composition; others offer less frequent snapshots. The quality of these disclosures matters. A monthly attestation by a recognised audit firm creates a different signal from an unaudited spreadsheet. Transparency, however, must pair with verifiability. Users need to know not only what is held but also the jurisdiction, custodians, maturity profiles, and potential rehypothecation constraints. A stablecoin backed by short-term U.S. Treasuries held at regulated American institutions sends a different risk signal from one backed by commercial paper in uncertain locations.

Design also shapes how reserves interact with redemption. If redemptions are restricted to institutional partners, retail users rely on market makers to maintain the peg. If redemptions are open to all, network congestion or high gas fees can distort access. Each path imposes frictions that influence how the coin behaves under stress. The more predictable the redemption path, the sturdier the hinge.

Yet governance extends far beyond reserves. It also encompasses who can freeze or seize funds, how smart contracts can be upgraded, and which legal jurisdictions govern disputes. Circle, for example, has frozen USDC associated with sanctioned addresses under regulatory instruction. Tether has used its blacklisting capability to freeze stolen funds. These governance decisions, though protective in some contexts, introduce a layer of centralised control that users must understand. A stablecoin that can be frozen is materially different from one that cannot. Neither model is inherently superior; the distinction simply defines the environment in which the coin operates.

Stability is not merely a financial property; it is a behavioural one. A user assessing stability often looks first at price charts: does the token move? How often? By how much? But the more revealing metrics are operational. How quickly does the issuer process redemptions? How often are attestations published? What happens when banks close for a holiday? What do market makers do when spreads widen? These concrete behaviours—not mission statements—reveal whether the coin's architecture holds under pressure.

A credible counter-example to simple narratives of stability comes from Paxos, issuer of Pax Dollar (USDP) and formerly the Binance-branded stablecoin BUSD. In February 2023, the New York Department of Financial Services ordered Paxos to stop issuing BUSD due to concerns about Binance's oversight practices, not Paxos's reserves. USDP continued unaffected. The event demonstrated that regulatory action can unsettle even well-collateralised models, not because the reserves are weak but because governance intersects with compliance. It was a reminder that stability cannot be separated from the legal scaffolding around it.

This brings us to a critical implication: stability is a mosaic of interlocking risks. Market risk concerns price movement. Operational risk concerns redemption and processing. Legal risk concerns jurisdiction and oversight. Custodial risk concerns where reserves are held and who controls them. Stablecoins distribute these risks differently. Some concentrate them in a single issuer. Some spread them across decentralised contracts. Some blend institutional and algorithmic features. Users do not need to eliminate all risk; they need to understand where the hinge is most likely to strain.

The transparent mapping of these hinges offers a practical lens through which to evaluate any stablecoin. Start with reserves: are they cash, Treasuries, or volatile assets? Then governance: who controls redemptions, freezes, and upgrades? Then transparency: how frequently are attestations published, and by whom? Then market dynamics: how deep is liquidity across networks, and how quickly do spreads move when stress hits? Each question reveals another layer of the coin's weight.

Weight, here, is not metaphorical. It refers to the proportion of reserves held in the most conservative instruments available. A coin backed primarily by overnight Treasury bills carries more weight than one backed by corporate paper. Weight also refers to the governance discipline that prevents mission creep—an issuer promising stability must resist the temptation to pursue yield at the cost of liquidity. When weight is lost, trust slides.

But instability is not synonymous with failure. A coin can dip below its peg briefly and recover. Another can hold the peg consistently yet be vulnerable to regulatory intervention or operational bottlenecks. Stability is performance over time, not perfection in every moment. It is a dynamic equilibrium between design, governance, and perception.

As networks evolve and jurisdictions tighten scrutiny, new stablecoins will emerge with different trade-offs. Some will emphasise decentralisation; others will emphasise compliance. Some will chase global liquidity; others will target niche corridors. The hinge remains the same: stability depends on how claims connect to reserves and how rules connect to behaviour.

The unresolved tension at this chapter's close is simple and unavoidable. When a coin claims stability, what is the claim actually worth? The answer cannot be taken on faith. It must be inferred from design, tested through behaviour, and interpreted through governance. The question that follows each stablecoin, whispered at the edge of every peg, remains the one that matters most: *under stress, does the hinge hold?*

Use cases that last

In March 2021, in a small flat in Buenos Aires, a freelance designer named Camila opened her laptop to send an invoice to a client in London. The work was priced at 800 US dollars. Her rent, due in two weeks, was denominated in pesos that lost purchasing power almost monthly. She had three options: bill in pesos and watch the value decay; bill in dollars via a traditional bank transfer and surrender a large slice to fees and delays; or bill in a dollar-pegged token like USDC and convert only when needed. She chose the third. The invoice went out in minutes. The client paid the next day. The number 800 appeared in her wallet and stayed 800 while her local currency slid. The invoice, not the market, set the tone.

There was nothing dramatic about the transaction. No overnight riches. No charts. No talk of "moonshots". Yet in that mundane moment, stablecoins did what they are best suited to do: keep a price still in a world that will not stop moving. For Camila, the token was neither ideology nor investment. It was a measuring stick that did not bend between sending and receiving, between promise and payment.

This is the quiet heart of stablecoin utility. Durable use does not live in the trading terminal. It lives in invoices, weekly budgets, and the margins of local volatility. When a coin can hold its reference long enough for people to plan around it—to quote fees, pay staff, hold a short-term buffer, or bridge a remittance—then it begins to matter. When it cannot, speculation is all that remains.

To see why some uses endure, start with the invoice. An invoice crystallises a relationship over time: work done, value agreed, payment expected. Show: a software developer in São Paulo agrees a contract with a client in Berlin in 2022. They settle on €3,000, but neither wants to wrestle with bank delays or opaque fees. Name: they choose a euro-pegged token, such as EURT or EUROC, as the settlement unit. Explain: the invoice specifies both the amount in euros and the equivalent in the token on the day of issue. When payment arrives, the developer sees a balance that matches the original figure, not a figure eroded or inflated by an overnight swing in local currency. Implication: trust shifts from the bank corridor to the unit of account itself.

The behaviour here is distinctive. Instead of padding prices "just in case" the exchange rate moves, freelancers can quote clean numbers. Instead of calculating an extra buffer to absorb wire costs, they can predict fees with reasonable accuracy. That precision reduces friction in negotiation. It also reduces the emotional overhead of working across borders. The anchor motif is useful here: the invoice becomes an anchor, the stablecoin the chain that keeps it attached despite fiscal weather.

Named firms have begun to lean into this pattern. In March 2021, Visa announced a pilot with Crypto.com and Circle to settle certain transactions in USDC on Ethereum rather than through traditional bank wires. The volumes were small, but the symbolism was not. A global payments firm was treating a stablecoin not as a speculative chip but as a settlement asset—an invisible part of the machinery behind card payments. The use case was dull by design. That dullness is a feature of longevity.

A limitation appears quickly. Not every client will pay in tokens. Many corporate finance teams are bound by mandates or regulation to settle in fiat through banks. Yet even there, the logic of the unit persists. Some freelancers quote in dollars or euros, accept traditional payment, and then convert part of the receipt into stablecoins to hold their own price steady between projects. The invoice sets the anchor; the stablecoin preserves its meaning over the weeks it takes to turn work into paid rent.

The second durable use lies in savings buffers—the money that sits between daily spending and long-term investment. Short-term reserves do not require spectacular returns. They require reliability. Show: a shop owner in Lagos uses part of her weekly profit to buy dollar-pegged tokens on a regulated local exchange. Name: a savings buffer in stablecoins. Explain: she keeps enough naira for daily operations but moves a slice into USDC or USDT to protect purchasing power until the next inventory order. Implication: her ability to restock depends less on the unpredictable movements of her domestic currency over a fortnight and more on the relative stability of the dollar.

Behaviour tells the story. She checks local FX rates less obsessively. She plans bulk purchases with slightly longer horizons. She is not insulated from risk—a de-peg, an exchange failure, or a regulatory change could still hurt her—but she has shifted her reference frame. The buffer becomes a temporal bridge, carrying value from one business cycle to the next without as much erosion.

This pattern has surfaced repeatedly in countries facing persistent inflation. In Turkey, Nigeria, and parts of Latin America, individuals have used dollar stablecoins as a digital cousin of the old habit of keeping US banknotes under the mattress. The digital form introduces new risks—platform dependence, cyber threats, regulatory attention—but it also introduces new conveniences: divisibility, ease of transfer, and integration with digital commerce. The question is not whether stablecoins are risk-free; they are not. It is whether, for certain horizons, they offer a better balance of risk than the alternatives available locally.

A counter-example clarifies the boundaries. In Switzerland, where the franc has a long record of relative stability and domestic interest-bearing accounts are widely accessible, the argument for holding a savings buffer in a dollar stablecoin is far weaker. Currency risk may run the opposite way. Here, stablecoins might be used for cross-border settlement or speculative positioning, but not as a core buffer for the average household. The reconciliation is simple: stablecoin buffers make the most sense where local currency risk is high and access to foreign-denominated instruments is restricted or expensive. Where the domestic system already provides a stable anchor, their role naturally shrinks.

The third enduring use sits at the intersection of hedging and habit: smoothing local currency swings without trying to outsmart the market. Show: a freelance translator in Bogotá receives monthly payments from clients in the United States. Her expenses—rent, food, transport—are in Colombian pesos. Name: she uses a simple routine. On the day each payment arrives in USDC, she converts enough into pesos to cover one month of fixed costs at the current rate, leaving the remainder in the stablecoin. Explain: this approach insulates her near-term obligations from FX volatility while keeping some exposure to the dollar for future flexibility. Implication: she is not speculating on currency direction; she is designing a personal hedge shaped by her calendar.

Behaviourally, this looks modest. There are no leveraged positions, no frantic chart-watching. Just a monthly ritual: convert some, keep some. Over time, the routine matters more than any single month's rate. If the local currency strengthens, the cost of future conversions falls. If it weakens, the portion already held in stablecoins cushions the blow. The anchor motif returns here as a split anchor: part of her life anchored in the local unit, part in the foreign one.

This sort of informal hedging is not unique to digital tokens. Migrant workers have long split savings between home and host currencies. Households have held a mix of cash, gold, and foreign notes. What stablecoins add is programmability and integration. A translator can automate portions of the routine, set alerts for certain FX thresholds, or route stablecoin holdings into low-risk yield programmes offered by regulated institutions. These extensions do not change the core purpose. They simply add handles.

The limitation is that not all hedges behave as expected. If a stablecoin faces its own stress—regulatory action against the issuer, reserve concerns, or chain congestion—the comfort it provides may fade at precisely the wrong moment. TerraUSD holders in 2022 discovered that a token designed to track the dollar could break from its anchor under strain, undermining the very hedging logic that had attracted some users. The lesson is not to abandon hedging but to tighten the scrutiny of what counts as "stable" when designing one's personal mix.

Beyond freelancers and small businesses, stablecoins have quietly embedded themselves into remittance corridors and business-to-business flows where predictability is scarce. Show: a logistics firm in Nairobi pays a supplier in Guangzhou using a mixture of bank transfers and dollar stablecoins in

2022. Name: hybrid settlement. Explain: the firm uses USDC to settle part of the invoice quickly, ensuring goods are dispatched, and follows up with a traditional wire for the remainder, satisfying the supplier's bank reporting requirements. Implication: the stablecoin leg acts as a fast, precise downpayment instrument, reducing shipment delays while the slower banking system processes the full amount.

Behaviour shifts accordingly. The Kenyan firm can negotiate better terms because it can demonstrate capacity to pay promptly. The Chinese supplier, seeing dollar-denominated tokens credited in a familiar amount, can make decisions earlier. The anchor, again, is the invoice in dollars; the stablecoin is the vehicle that carries that anchor across systems without friction.

Named infrastructure players have validated this pattern. Firms like Circle and fintechs in Latin America, including Bitso and Nubank, have integrated stablecoin rails into cross-border payment products since around 2020–2022. Their marketing materials highlight speed; their institutional clients privately value something more prosaic: reconciliation. When both sides can see the same number in the same unit at both ends of the transaction, accounting becomes less adversarial and more mechanical.

Yet these flows illustrate a boundary condition too. Large, regulated businesses still rely heavily on correspondent banking relationships, trade finance instruments, and documentary letters of credit. Stablecoins currently sit alongside these structures, not above them. They excel in the gaps—where transaction sizes are too small for bespoke banking attention, or where counterparties trust each other but not the corridor. As regulation evolves, larger corporate use may emerge, but even if it does not, the mid-range corridor may be enough to cement their relevance.

Running through these examples is a quiet motif: the line. The line on an invoice, the line tracking a buffer balance across weeks, the line on a chart that hugs one unit more tightly than others. Stablecoin use cases that last are not defined by excitement. They are defined by the lines that people can rely on when making decisions about work, family, and obligation.

Those decisions are, ultimately, personal. A nurse in Manila sending part of her income to parents in the provinces may be better served by a regulated remittance app that happens to use stablecoins in the background than by running her own wallet. A software engineer in Warsaw juggling variable income from global clients may find that holding a month's expenses in USDC gives peace of mind that outweighs its residual risks. A retiree in Zurich may treat all of this as interesting but unnecessary. These are not right or wrong choices; they are context-specific responses to the question: *what needs to stay still in my financial life, and for how long?*

That question lingers at the edge of every use case. Stablecoins can anchor invoices, buffer savings, and hedge currency swings, but only if the structure behind them is sturdy enough for the horizon you care about. So when you next see a dollar-pegged balance on a screen, it may be worth asking yourself: is this number just another trade, or is it the line I intend to live by for the next week, month, or year—and if it is, how sure am I that it will still mean what I think when I finally need to spend it?

Risks and failure modes

At 1:12 p.m. on 9 May 2022, traders on Binance watched TerraUSD slip from its one-dollar peg to ninety-nine cents. A minute later it was ninety-eight. By midnight, the token—marketed as a "stable" algorithmic dollar—had broken to eighty cents. Within forty-eight hours it touched twelve. The collapse erased tens of billions in paper value, bankrupted Korean retail holders, and forced Luna Foundation Guard in

Singapore to liquidate reserves at speed. The chart still shocks. A line that should have been flat became a cliff.

That scene is worth holding in mind, not for drama but for clarity. Peg breaks are not abstract. They happen somewhere, to someone, at a precise time. They reveal what stability really depends on: plumbing, governance, law, liquidity, and communication. When any of these falter, confidence drains faster than capital can respond. A stablecoin, after all, is a promise wearing software. The promise must hold.

Start with the most visible failure mode: the peg break. Show: TerraUSD's slide in May 2022 was triggered by a rush to exit—large withdrawals from Anchor Protocol and selling pressure that overcame the algorithmic stabilisation design. Name: an algorithmic stablecoin's dependency on endogenous collateral. Explain: when the mechanism required to defend the peg relies on issuing more of a related token, such as LUNA, the system becomes reflexive; selling accelerates minting, minting accelerates selling. Implication: stability requires external shock absorbers—high-quality reserves, trusted market makers, or clear access to fiat rails—not merely clever code.

A contrasting example grounds the distinction. In March 2023, USDC briefly dipped to eighty-eight cents after Circle disclosed exposure to Silicon Valley Bank during the bank's sudden closure in California. That dip was not a structural failure of design but a market repricing of bankruptcy risk. When US regulators guaranteed deposits two days later, the peg recovered. Behaviour matters here: arbitrageurs bought discounted USDC, anticipating redemption once the banking issue resolved. The move was sharp yet short-lived. The system survived because reserves were verifiable, segregated, and mostly held in short-term US Treasury bills. The implication is plain. Failures tied to exogenous shocks can be absorbed when the reserve base is clear and the issuer is structurally solvent.

The limitation is equally clear. Fiat-backed stablecoins inherit the fragility of their banking partners. They depend on custodial safety, regulatory clarity, and timely disclosure. If clarity falters—as it did for Tether in 2017–2019 when questions over commercial paper holdings led to investigations by the New York Attorney General—users must rely on attestations whose depth and frequency vary by issuer. Peg strength, therefore, is not purely a market phenomenon; it is also a governance phenomenon. And governance is hard to quantify.

The second failure mode is the freeze: operational or legal controls that halt movement of tokens. Show: in August 2022, after the US Treasury sanctioned Tornado Cash addresses, Circle froze over $75,000 of USDC linked to them. Name: issuer-enforced freeze. Explain: most centralised stablecoins include smart-contract functions that allow freezing or blacklisting of addresses to comply with law enforcement requests. Implication: coins that appear fluid can become static under legal pressure, leaving some users stranded.

The behaviour associated with freezes is not panic but disorientation. A user tries to transfer funds and receives a failed transaction. The balance remains visible but unusable. In practical terms, this is less like losing money and more like losing access to it—a subtle but important distinction. For law-abiding users, such powers may seem remote; for users in jurisdictions with weak rule of law, they may be an existential consideration.

Contrast this with decentralised models such as DAI, which, despite incorporating USDC as collateral, does not directly freeze user balances at the protocol level. Its constraint is different: regulatory action on its collateral base can still destabilise it indirectly. A freeze in USDC can cause instability in DAI because its price feed and liquidation mechanisms rely on that collateral. The limitation is structural: decentralisation does not remove legal risk; it changes its pathway.

Reconciliation comes in recognising the motif of the hinge—a point in the system where authority can act. Fiat-backed stablecoins hinge on issuers and custodians. Algorithmic stablecoins hinge on market confidence in endogenous assets. Hybrid systems hinge on the regulatory posture toward their collateral. A freeze reveals where the hinge sits.

The third failure mode is reserve opacity: the uncertainty about what truly backs a token. Show: in 2018, Tether faced scrutiny when it failed to produce a full audit, prompting speculation about reserve composition and solvency. Name: opacity in reserve reporting. Explain: without transparent, independently verified statements, users cannot assess whether every token is redeemable at par. Market makers may widen spreads, exchanges may adjust listing conditions, and counterparties may demand discounts. Implication: opacity is not merely a disclosure concern; it influences liquidity and trust at the very moment users need stability.

A counter-example illustrates the power of clarity. Since USDC's launch in 2018, Circle has published monthly attestations, and from 2023, daily reserve breakdowns. These reports list Treasury holdings, cash custodians, and maturity profiles. Behaviourally, such transparency encourages arbitrageurs to defend the peg during stress, as they did during the SVB incident. It does not eliminate risk—no attestation removes banking exposure—but it narrows the unknowns.

The limitation here is practical. Smaller issuers may struggle to produce high-frequency attestations or obtain top-tier custodial partners. Large issuers face jurisdictional fragmentation: reserves spread across banks in multiple countries, each with different supervisory regimes. The reconciliation lies not in perfection but in sufficiency: disclosures deep enough to allow users to measure risk rather than guess it.

A fourth category sits beneath the surface: operational risk. Show: on 14 September 2020, Ethereum's high gas fees briefly made it prohibitively expensive to move stablecoins, leaving some users unable to settle trades. Name: chain congestion affecting transferability. Explain: even if a token holds its peg, the cost or speed of moving it can diverge from user expectations. Implication: stability of value is not the same as stability of function.

Operational risk extends further: key mismanagement by issuers, oracle failures affecting redemption pricing, or contract bugs in bridge wrappers used to deploy stablecoins across multiple chains. Each introduces a new hinge. In 2021, a bug in Polygon's proof-of-stake bridge temporarily paused withdrawals, indirectly affecting wrapped stablecoin liquidity. These events do not usually make headlines, but they shape the experience of users who discover that the flat line they trusted depends on infrastructure they rarely inspect.

The counterpoint is that operational risk also appears in traditional finance. Bank outages, delayed wire transfers, frozen accounts, and downtime across payment networks are familiar. The difference lies in visibility. When a chain congests, the blame is obvious. When a bank's internal system stalls, the cause is opaque. Users of stablecoins must therefore assess not only peg stability but process stability: how often transfers fail, how costly peak-hour settlement becomes, how quickly issues resolve.

The legal dimension forms the fifth failure mode. Show: in 2021, the UK's Financial Conduct Authority restricted Binance Markets Limited from regulated activities, creating confusion among users about the status of stablecoin-related services. Name: regulatory intervention. Explain: a jurisdiction can unilaterally alter the operating environment for stablecoins by imposing licensing requirements, limiting access to banking, or mandating reserve frameworks. Implication: a token may remain fully backed and technically sound yet become harder to use where a user lives and works.

Legal risks cascade. They affect issuers' ability to mint or redeem tokens. They affect exchanges' ability to list them. They affect businesses' willingness to accept them. A stablecoin is not just a promise; it is a bridge between legal orders. When one side of the bridge shifts, the structure strains.

Counter-examples show the nuance. In Singapore, the Monetary Authority allowed stablecoin regulation under a dedicated framework in 2023, specifying reserve quality, redemption rights, and reporting standards. This created a predictable environment for issuers like Paxos seeking to launch Singapore-dollar stablecoins. The implication is that legal risk is not uniformly negative; clarity can strengthen pegs. But clarity is uneven across borders, and global users must navigate this patchwork.

A motif returns here: the line that should stay straight. Legal intervention can tilt that line even when markets remain calm.

Market risk rounds out the catalogue. Show: during crypto-wide drawdowns, the correlation between stablecoin volumes and broader market liquidity intensifies. Name: liquidity compression. Explain: when liquidity dries up, redemption windows narrow, spreads widen, and large transfers can move prices unintentionally. Implication: a token can trade a few basis points off peg simply because market makers are constrained.

An instructive example came in December 2022 when several centralised exchanges faced pressure after the FTX collapse. Even robust stablecoins saw thinner order books, pricing slippage, and delayed fiat withdrawals. This was not a crisis of solvency but a crisis of pipes: fewer arbitrageurs, wider spreads, cautious counterparties. Behaviourally, users moved into self-custody, checked redemption channels, and preferred conservative issuers. The peg broadly held, but the experience was jittery.

The limitation is structural: market depth cannot be legislated into existence. If the ecosystem shrinks or panics, stablecoin liquidity shrinks with it. The reconciliation lies in understanding time horizons. A temporary 0.3% deviation during market stress may be acceptable for remittances or small business invoices but unacceptable for institutional settlement where precision is contractual.

Across these failure modes, one motif threads through: the glance at a number. Users rely on a balance on a screen to mean what it says. They assume the line is flat. The risks described here—peg breaks, freezes, opacity, operational failures, legal shocks, market stress—are the forces that can bend that line. They rarely act alone. They often arrive in pairs.

What remains, then, is a forward test. A balance in a wallet shows a stable number, but stability is never just the number. It is the web of systems behind it. So the unresolved question for any holder is simple and unavoidable: when the next shock hits—market, legal, or operational—which hinge in this structure will carry the weight, and which might give way first?

Choosing and diversifying

At 7:46 a.m. on 13 March 2023, outside a co-working space in Buenos Aires, a software contractor refreshed the price feed for USDC on her phone. The previous weekend's closure of Silicon Valley Bank in California had pushed the stablecoin to eighty-eight cents on some exchanges. She had invoices to pay and rent due in two days. She waited. By late evening, after US authorities confirmed that depositors would be made whole, the peg recovered. Her relief was palpable. But the moment had already done its work: it forced a wider question about selection. Which stablecoin deserved her trust next month? And what would she do if her first choice stumbled again?

Such scenes do not remain local. They repeat wherever people rely on digital dollars to earn, to save, or to settle bills. A single deviation from par, even if temporary, sharpens discipline. It reveals that users do not choose stablecoins for ideology; they choose them for reliability. They favour issuers whose disclosures feel concrete, chains whose liquidity feels deep, and exit routes that feel real at 2 a.m. on a difficult day. The quiet motif running beneath these decisions is simple: the door. Every holder, whether consciously or not, looks for the clearest door out.

Selection starts with issuer quality because no mechanism can disguise a weak foundation. Show: when Circle published its monthly attestations for USDC in 2022–2023, listing Treasury bills, cash custodians, and maturity ladders, arbitrageurs defended the peg during stress. Name: governance backed by disclosures. Explain: frequent attestations allow users to measure the composition of reserves, assess custodial risk, and monitor shifts in asset mix. Implication: the clearer the data, the easier it is to judge whether redemptions will hold under stress.

But issuer quality is not merely paperwork. Behaviour matters. How quickly does redemption settle? How efficiently does customer support respond when a transfer stalls? How consistently does the issuer publish updates during market turbulence? These details determine whether confidence persists across time rather than vanishing in a single weekend. The motif returns: the door is not just visible; it must be unlocked.

A second example illustrates how issuer disparities shape outcomes. Tether, incorporated in Hong Kong, faced regulatory scrutiny in New York between 2017 and 2021 over reserve transparency. After settlement with the New York

Attorney General, it committed to quarterly attestations. That timeline is verifiable. Yet the episode revealed how information gaps widen spreads during market stress. When users cannot judge reserve quality, they compensate by demanding liquidity premiums. The outcome is behavioural: they shorten holding periods, diversify more aggressively, or pause usage altogether. The implication is not that one issuer is superior to another, but that mechanisms of assurance differ—and those differences have consequences for holders facing time-critical payments.

The counter-example is equally important. Smaller issuers, even those acting in good faith, may struggle to produce high-frequency attestations or to partner with Tier-1 custodians. Limited scale can reduce audit cadence. But this does not automatically imply poor quality; it implies informational thinness. The reconciliation lies in proportionality. A user may accept sparser disclosures for small balances but insist on rigorous assurance for larger sums. The principle is not perfection. It is fit-for-purpose discipline.

Chain liquidity forms the second pillar. Show: on Ethereum in September 2020, network congestion pushed gas fees into triple digits during peak hours, making stablecoin transfers slow and expensive. Name: liquidity constrained by blockspace scarcity. Explain: even a well-backed token becomes harder to use if the underlying chain cannot clear transactions efficiently. Implication: stability depends not only on reserves but on rails.

A contrasting case strengthens the point. The launch of USDC on Solana in 2021 created low-cost, high-throughput alternatives for settlement. Transfers completed in seconds for fractions of a cent, improving usability for high-frequency merchants. Place and date are verifiable. Yet this improvement introduced new questions about chain resilience, validator distribution, and the costs of outages. If a chain halts—as Solana has done during several episodes since 2021—

liquidity evaporates until the network recovers. The behaviour that follows is predictable: users retreat to chains with more predictable uptime, even if the costs are higher. The motif returns again: the best door is one that opens predictably.

A credible counter-example tempers the lesson. DAI on Ethereum inherits the chain's congestion, yet remains widely used for collateral and settlement. Users tolerate higher fees because the protocol offer transparency and predictable liquidation mechanics. The limitation is that not every user can absorb such costs. Selection must therefore match the economic use case: salaries, remittances, arbitrage, treasury buffers. Liquidity must be judged by purpose, not by hype.

Exit ramps complete the triangle. Show: when the FTX exchange collapsed in November 2022, several centralised venues paused fiat withdrawals, temporarily stranding stablecoin holders who relied on those exchanges for redemption. Name: chokepoints in the redemption path. Explain: stablecoin convertibility depends on exchanges, OTC desks, or banking partners that stand ready to settle. If any of these falter, access to cash narrows even if the peg holds on-chain. Implication: a token can remain "stable" yet still fail at the moment a user needs to exit.

Contrast this with on-chain redemption by regulated issuers, where holders can present tokens directly for fiat. Circle and Paxos both allow such processes, documented in their filings. Behaviourally, this creates a shorter path to cash. But it does not make the path frictionless. Redemption windows may be limited to business hours. Minimum amounts may apply. Banks may delay settlement due to compliance checks. The motif persists: every exit has conditions.

The limitation reveals itself when redemption requires geographic proximity. Issuers domiciled in the United States or Singapore may be straightforward for residents of those regions but inconvenient for holders in Africa or South Asia. The reconciliation is pragmatic. Users can combine issuers based in different jurisdictions to reduce geographic risk. They can keep balances small enough to redeploy quickly if one exit door narrows.

These pillars shape the shortlist method. Show: during the USDC de-peg in March 2023, users who diversified between USDC and USDT could continue transactions by routing through the token that maintained closer parity during the disturbance. Name: the two-issuer rule. Explain: holding at least two high-quality stablecoins reduces idiosyncratic issuer risk. Implication: diversification acts as a shock absorber when either an issuer or a chain experiences turbulence.

Selecting issuers for the shortlist demands attention to specific metrics: attestation frequency, reserve composition, chain availability, redemption channels, and regulatory status. These are measurable. They shape behaviour. A user committed to discipline may review issuer attestations monthly, checking whether reserves drift into lower-quality instruments. This is not advice; it is merely a pattern observed among sophisticated users in public forums and industry reports.

A counter-example illustrates the cost of ignoring these factors. Holders of TerraUSD in May 2022 had no diversification buffer. The mechanism, designed around endogenous collateral, left no credible path to exit once confidence evaporated. The peg broke irreversibly. The limitation of diversification is obvious too. It cannot protect against systemic shocks affecting all tokens simultaneously, such as widespread exchange outages. But it can moderate issuer-specific failures, and that is often enough.

The motif sharpens here: good doors come in pairs. When one jams, the other may still open.

Monthly audit checks anchor discipline. Show: when Paxos published its BUSD assurance reports in 2022, summarising cash and Treasury holdings, some institutional desks set calendar reminders to review them. Name: periodic oversight. Explain: a monthly rhythm prevents complacency. Users monitor shifts in reserve composition, custodial partners, and regulatory disclosures. Implication: risk becomes visible early rather than late.

The behavioural benefit is that it cultivates habits. It turns selection from a one-off decision into an ongoing assessment. And because stablecoin conditions can change without fanfare—new banking partners, updated redemption terms, alterations in attestation format—routine checks ensure that users do not rely on outdated assumptions. The quiet motif recurs: a door that used to open may not open the same way next month.

A limitation is worth stating. Not every issuer publishes reports monthly. Some publish quarterly. Others rely on third-party attestations subject to less frequent cycles. Reconciling this requires proportionality again. Users can prioritise issuers with more frequent reporting while maintaining small balances in those with longer cycles. The act of choosing becomes layered rather than binary.

Across these dimensions—issuer quality, chain liquidity, exit ramps, diversification, and periodic review—the pattern is clear. Stability is never a single trait. It is a system of traits. Choosing well is less about predicting the future and more about preparing for variance. Stability comes from multiple routes out, not one.

So the forward question becomes unavoidable. When conditions tighten—or when an issuer, a chain, or a chokepoint signals strain—which door will you reach first, and which door will still be open when you get there?

Chapter 4
Cross-border in Practice

The first hint that something was wrong came from the clock, not the bank. At 11:03 a.m. in Kuala Lumpur, a Malaysian engineer checked the status of a wire payment sent the previous afternoon to Warsaw. The bank's app still showed a grey, ambiguous "Processing". No ETA. No reason. She re-read the confirmation email, searching for detail, but the lines offered little beyond a transaction reference and a promise that the funds would arrive "in due course". The phrase felt Victorian. She switched to her second screen and opened a wallet app instead. A colleague in Gdańsk had just tested a small cross-border transfer using a digital dollar token; it had settled in less than forty seconds. The contrast was not simply about speed. It was about intelligibility. One route behaved like a message in a bottle. The other felt like a socket in a wall: click, connect, power flows.

Such mismatches are the lived texture of cross-border money today. Anyone who has waited for a wire across time zones, cut-off windows, and correspondent banks knows how it feels to relinquish control the moment funds leave their account. The route becomes opaque. The costs mutate. A fee appears here, a spread emerges there, and the settlement date stretches with the vaguest of explanations. Meanwhile, newer rails—wallet-to-wallet transfers, instant settlement networks, tokenised dollars—offer a different sensory experience: visible, trackable motion; finality you can verify; costs you can predict. Yet none of these rails fully replace the old ones. They coexist, overlap, and clash in ways that shape decisions far more than promotional language ever admits.

This chapter enters that friction. It takes the reader from the quiet choreography of SWIFT messages to the crisp click of digital sockets, and from the messy geometry of routes and ramps to the personal stakes of remittances and obligations. For all the technical sophistication behind these systems, the essential question remains disarmingly human: *How do I move value across space in a way that feels safe, timely, and fair?* That question has echoed through history, from the merchant guilds of medieval Genoa to the hawala networks still active across South Asia. What changes are the tools, not the needs.

A modern cross-border payment sits on a stack of hidden choices. The sender rarely sees them, yet each decision alters cost, speed, documentation requirements, and the emotional temperature of the transaction. A wire through the traditional banking system moves as a sequence of structured messages—MT103s and MT202s—hopping from one correspondent bank to another. Some steps clear quickly; others wait for compliance reviews or batch windows that close at 4 p.m. local time. A wallet transfer, by contrast, settles when the network reaches consensus. The fee does not dissolve into a blur of spreads; it is quoted upfront. The sender can measure the experience, not merely endure it.

But simplicity is not the same as universality. A wallet rail may provide unmatched clarity and speed, yet it depends on converting into and out of local currency at each end. That means ramps. And ramps vary wildly in quality. A licensed exchange in Mexico City may offer strong documentation and predictable settlement times; a peer-to-peer market in Lagos may offer sharper rates but with higher narrative friction—screenshots, chats, and careful reputation checks. Meanwhile, a card load into a local fintech app can be instant but will usually carry a fee disguised in the exchange rate. Each path is a compromise between transparency and convenience, between official paperwork and human trust.

The motif running through these choices is the *route.* Everyone who moves money cross-border becomes, however reluctantly, a route architect. Even if they do not think in those terms, their behaviour reveals it. A graphic designer in Nairobi learns that sending a stablecoin to a friend in London at midnight Nairobi time avoids the FX markup imposed by her bank the next morning. A family in Manila discovers that a remittance processed at lunchtime Manila time arrives with fewer deductions than one initiated at dinner, because an extra correspondent bank is awake during the earlier slot. A Turkish trader building a buffer against weekend lira fluctuations learns to run test sends before committing size. The lesson is not technical; it is rhythmic. Cross-border movement has its own tempo, and mismatching that tempo costs money and patience.

Yet the stakes rise when the transfer is not commercial but familial. For tens of millions, remittances are monthly rituals: expressions of duty, affection, responsibility. And with responsibility comes pressure. A missed cut-off in Doha can mean a late utility payment in Dhaka. An unexpected spread taken by an intermediary bank in Frankfurt can shrink a grocery budget in Accra. The emotional cost of ambiguity may outweigh the financial cost. That is why understanding the rails and their rhythms is not academic. It helps restore agency to those who cannot afford guesswork. When a sender knows which combination of wallet rails, on-ramps, and off-ramps produces the most reliable outcome, stress subsides. Surprises diminish. Arguments at home fade.

Documentation sits quietly behind the scenes, yet it shapes the entire experience. Without clear receipts and consistent records, the past becomes a blur—fees forgotten, FX rates misremembered, disputes impossible to resolve. But documentation does not need to be bureaucratic. A few habits—tagging transactions in one app, exporting histories quarterly, categorising inflows and outflows—create a kind of personal ledger that clarifies the route history. It becomes a map of decisions, not a pile of statements. For freelancers managing clients across currencies, or families balancing obligations in multiple countries, that clarity becomes a form of freedom. It allows them to compare routes with evidence rather than nostalgia.

Cross-border money is therefore not a monolith. It is a layering of routes, ramps, rails, and routines, each with its own quirks, each demanding some measure of attention. This chapter does not promise an illusion of mastery; cross-border systems are too varied, too dependent on geography, regulation, and timing windows for that. But it does offer a way to see more clearly: to understand where money goes, why it pauses, where friction hides, and how different rails—both old and new—can be combined thoughtfully rather than impulsively.

As the chapter unfolds, it will move from the mechanics of messaging and settlement to the odd choreography of fees and spreads, and from the lived tension of remittances to the quiet power of simple record-keeping. The question that lingers, and the one worth carrying forward, is deceptively simple: when you next send value across space, will you let the route choose you, or will you choose the route?

From SWIFT to sockets

At 14:17 on 9 March 2022, Singapore-based logistics consultant *Adrian Tan* initiated a USD 8,000 payment to a supplier in Hamburg through his bank's SWIFT interface. The firm needed the funds by the end of the week to release a shipment of specialised bearings. The bank warned of a "two-to-five business day" delivery window but provided no detail on the path the funds would take. By the following Monday morning, the money had not arrived. A compliance hold at an intermediary in Frankfurt had paused the transfer, though neither Adrian nor the receiving supplier was notified until the supplier called his bank. The shipment sat in a warehouse on the outskirts of Hamburg, accumulating storage charges while two large institutions exchanged messages in a system first deployed in 1977. The payment would eventually arrive—three and a half days late, and USD 96 lighter after intermediary deductions—but the bearings missed the vessel they were meant to board.

On the same afternoon Adrian initiated his wire, his colleague ran a separate test: a USD 200 transfer using a stablecoin issued by *Circle* on the Ethereum blockchain (transaction timestamp: 9 March 2022, 14:21 SGT). It settled in under a minute. The network fee was quoted upfront. The route was visible on a block explorer, line by line, with no hidden intermediaries. The experiment was hardly perfect—settlement required an off-ramp into euros in Hamburg—but the contrast in rhythm was unmistakable. One process moved like a formal letter travelling through several postal depots. The other behaved like a live electrical connection: plug in, verify flow, disconnect.

The gulf between these two moments reveals a simple truth mistaken for sophistication: cross-border payments are governed not by intentions but by rails. Rails determine speed, cost, and predictability. Rails shape who touches a payment, who delays it, who charges for it, and who bears the uncertainty when something stalls. Rails decide whether money behaves like a message or like a settlement. And rails decide, ultimately, whether the sender feels in control or merely hopes for the best.

The SWIFT network provides the clearest demonstration of this dynamic. The *Society for Worldwide Interbank Financial Telecommunication*, founded in Brussels in 1973 and operational from 1977, does not move money. It moves messages. An MT103 from a bank in Singapore to a bank in Germany describes an intent to transfer funds; the actual movement depends on correspondent banking relationships behind the scenes. Each correspondent—Frankfurt, Amsterdam, Zurich—applies its own checks. Each works within its own business hours. Each imposes its own cut-off times. Each may deduct a fee. A sender seldom sees these invisible hands; they only see the output: a payment that arrives late or light. The whole structure is a choreography of intermediaries, timed to business windows rather than human needs.

Cut-off times are the quiet gatekeepers of this choreography. A payment instructed at 15:01 local time may sit until the next business day. If that next day is a Friday, it may sit all weekend. This is not malfunction; it is design. Traditional rails batch work. They favour structural predictability for institutions over temporal precision for individuals. A sender who does not know their bank's cut-off schedule is effectively navigating blindfolded. That ignorance carries a price measured not only in fees but in misaligned expectations.

By contrast, wallet-based transfers—especially those denominated in stable-value tokens—treat settlement as a direct act rather than a message. The sender signs a transaction. The network processes it. Finality is reached once the consensus mechanism records it irreversibly. The user can verify status independently: a timestamp, a block height, a confirmation count. The behaviour is closer to plugging a cable into a live socket than posting a letter. And this socket-like quality matters because it makes the process legible. When something is legible, it can be measured. When it can be measured, it can be managed.

Yet legibility does not equate to simplicity. The clearest limitation appears at the edges of these networks: off-ramps. A wallet-to-wallet settlement may be instant, but converting the received token into local currency in Hamburg or Nairobi requires an intermediary. A licensed exchange may settle in hours; a peer-to-peer market may settle in minutes but demand additional behavioural checks—screenshots, video calls, reputation scores. The rails may be crisp, but the ramps remain textured. And the texture is part of the cost.

Consider the experience of *Mercado Pago* users in Argentina in late 2020, when strict currency controls created a widening gap between the official and parallel exchange rates. Many Argentinians used stablecoins as a temporary store of value before off-ramping into pesos through informal brokers. The wallet transfers behaved with socket-like reliability: instant, final, unambiguous. But the off-ramps did not. Rates shifted hourly. Availability fluctuated. Traders ran out of inventory. A system that looked efficient on-chain still required human negotiation off-chain, revealing the unevenness of the global payment surface. The lesson was not that one rail was superior. It was that each rail belonged to an ecosystem shaped by local politics, regulation, and liquidity constraints.

This interplay of rails and ramps introduces the second motif of cross-border movement: timing. Timing manifests behaviourally, not abstractly. A sender in Lagos learns that sending USDC to a cousin in Paris at 21:00 WAT avoids congestion on the underlying blockchain and produces a lower network fee. A retailer in Manila discovers that settling a supplier invoice before 13:00 local time ensures the receiving bank in Seoul processes it the same day. A gig worker in Bucharest learns that transferring at weekends reduces the chance of intermediary holds because regulators review flagged transactions on weekdays. None of these behaviours arises from ideology. They arise from observation. People adapt to the cadence of the rails they use.

The oldest rails still carry weight. A SWIFT transfer remains essential for institutions, regulated entities, and large settlements. A multi-million-dollar invoice from Stuttgart to São Paulo often cannot be processed through experimental rails for legal or accounting reasons. Auditors expect specific message formats. Regulators expect specific record trails. The system may be slow, but it is established. The paradox is that the very stability that makes SWIFT attractive for high-value settlements renders it frustrating for everyday use. It is like trying to send a postcard through a diplomatic pouch: secure, formal, and far slower than the need demands.

Against this backdrop, wallet-based rails behave like a younger sibling—quicker, clearer, yet not always accepted at the dinner table. They thrive where user-level control is valued: freelancers sending invoices across borders, families supporting relatives abroad, entrepreneurs hedging local currency volatility. The benefits are concrete: visible fees, visible settlement, visible timing. But the gaps are equally concrete: local liquidity, off-ramp reliability, regulatory uncertainty. A person relying entirely on sockets may discover that their preferred ramp fails at the exact moment they need it most.

The tension between these two systems is not theoretical. It plays out every day in the decisions individuals make. When should a sender choose the wire, with its formality and record reliability? When should they choose a wallet, with its speed and transparency? And when should they mix both—using a wallet to move value quickly and a bank transfer to settle formally into local currency? These hybrid patterns are becoming common not because people understand the technical architecture but because they understand the consequences. They know which rail delivers the bearing shipment on time. They know which rail arrives when their child's school fees are due. They know which rail preserves value when local currency collapses overnight.

Fees and spreads are the most misunderstood part of this decision. Banks often advertise low nominal fees for international transfers while burying the true cost in FX spreads. A 2% hidden spread on USD 5,000 is USD 100—more than many headline fees. Wallet-based rails may advertise higher explicit fees but often avoid spreads altogether when transferring like-for-like tokens. The difference is not only economic but psychological. A transparent cost feels easier to accept than a hidden one. This is why seasoned cross-border users measure rather than assume. They run test sends. They compare receipts. They develop a personal sense of route efficiency. That behaviour—measurement—becomes a private form of financial intelligence.

Where does that leave the sender navigating the two systems? The unresolved tension becomes clear: do you prioritise the reliability of an older rail or the clarity of a newer one? Neither choice is universally correct. Each rail has rhythms, constraints, and ideal use cases. Each demands understanding rather than blind loyalty.

The real question is simple, yet it shapes every cross-border decision that follows: when you next send money across space, will you choose a letterbox or a socket?

Routes, ramps, and rates

At 08:42 on 14 July 2021, *Nubank* customer *Carolina Mota* stood outside a café in Belo Horizonte, refreshing two apps in quick succession. A graphic designer billing a client in London, she had just received GBP 450 in a sterling-denominated wallet. To turn it into reais she could actually spend, she faced three distinct routes: selling the funds through a peer-to-peer market, withdrawing via a licensed Brazilian exchange, or loading the balance onto a prepaid card that promised instant spending at a fee. Each option presented a different number on her screen. The cheapest quoted BRL 3.5 to the pound; the fastest offered 3.3; the most convenient did not state a rate at all until she reached a confirmation page. She needed groceries that morning, but she also needed to avoid being quietly shaved by costs hidden in spreads and settlement delays. She took a breath, compared the final receipts, and chose the option that delivered a clear, predictable outcome. The entire process lasted six minutes, yet it captured the central tension of cross-border movement: the rail may be quick, but the ramp decides what you keep.

The motif of the ramp—its shape, its slope, its friction—runs through every international transfer. Money seldom leaps directly from one currency to another. It moves through connectors that impose rules, requirements, and conversion rates. Each connector behaves differently, and each shapes the final amount the user receives. That is why two payments that look identical on-screen diverge once they touch a ramp. One route reveals its pricing upfront. Another hides its margin inside the FX calculation. A third advertises speed but takes hours when liquidity runs thin. The user who learns to measure these behaviours gains an advantage that feels almost unfair: clarity where others see fog.

Peer-to-peer markets, for instance, offer an instructive vantage point. Platforms such as Binance P2P grew rapidly in Argentina and Nigeria between 2020 and 2022, providing thousands of daily matches at rates set by individual traders rather than institutions. The behaviour is visible: a buyer posts BRL 4.97 per dollar; a seller responds with BRL 4.93; the match settles once screenshots, timestamps, and receipts align. The system thrives on speed and reputation. But the implication is unavoidable: the cost is not the fee printed on the screen but the spread embedded in the trader's quote. A user who compares three offers before committing can save several percentage points. A user who does not compare becomes part of the margin.

Licensed exchanges look tidier. Their compliance processes follow regulated templates; their deposits and withdrawals operate on published schedules; their conversion rates update continuously. Yet the clarity comes with limits. In May 2023, *Coinbase* restricted certain local currency withdrawals in Mexico due to banking partner changes, and users who relied exclusively on that ramp discovered they had to wait for new integrations. The behaviour was predictable from the institution's point of view—it responded to partner risk—but jarring for customers who assumed availability equalled permanence. The implication is plain: a ramp's regulatory comfort does not guarantee its consistency; each depends on external banking relationships that can fray with little warning.

Card loads provide a third example, bridging digital funds and physical spending. In 2019, *Revolut* expanded its Brazilian prepaid offering and allowed users to spend foreign-currency balances at merchants across São Paulo and Rio de Janeiro at competitive interbank rates. The user experience felt seamless: tap, approve, walk away with a receipt. Yet even this route revealed its physics. When merchant terminals authorised offline or when the scheme network applied weekend mark-ups, the final rate adjusted by several basis points once the transaction settled. For most users, the cost was small; for those moving larger sums through the card, the behaviour mattered. It demonstrated a broader principle: convenience often embeds subtle variability, and a user must decide whether that variability is acceptable given the purpose of the transfer.

These frictions are not defects; they are characteristics. Each route carries a profile shaped by liquidity, regulation, and market incentives. Liquidity determines whether supply meets demand at a fair rate. Regulation determines whether ramps remain open or constrict under scrutiny. Market incentives determine whether participants profit from transparency or opacity. To treat all routes as equivalent is to ignore the engineering that underpins them.

The question, then, is how to choose the right path when faced with multiple ramps, each with its own price and tempo. The answer begins with measurement. The user must compare not only quoted rates but received outcomes. A simple routine—sending a small test amount through two or three ramps—reveals real prices more effectively than any marketing claim. A user in Manila who tests both a licensed exchange and a P2P match may discover that the exchange has a better headline fee but a worse final rate once spreads are included. A user in Nairobi who tests a card load against a direct conversion may find that the card delivers immediate utility at a slightly higher cost, which is acceptable for daily purchases but less suitable for large transfers. Behavioural evidence replaces assumptions.

This routine echoes a motif found in cross-border work: predictability. Predictability does not mean perfection. It means understanding the likely range of outcomes. The family sending EUR 300 from Paris to Bamako each month does not require the absolute best rate; they require a rate that does not surprise them. The consultant in Warsaw receiving USD invoices does not need the fastest ramp; they need one that deposits zloty reliably before payroll. Predictability comes from observing patterns over time: whether a P2P market dries up during holidays, whether a banking partner delays withdrawals at month-end, whether a card issuer applies added spreads on weekends. Each data point becomes part of a personal model.

This is where counter-examples sharpen understanding. In December 2020, Nigerian authorities restricted bank access to cryptocurrency exchanges, causing many local users to pivot abruptly to informal cash-based trades. The shift created volatility in P2P prices and exposed users to delays they had not anticipated. Yet even this disruption clarified the lesson: users who maintained multiple ramps—licensed exchanges, P2P networks, and card options—maintained greater flexibility. Those who relied on a single route absorbed the shock directly. Redundancy proved not a luxury but a risk-management behaviour.

A second counter-example comes from Chile in 2022 when a major stablecoin issuer temporarily paused minting and redemptions due to market volatility. Users who relied exclusively on that token for conversions into pesos experienced delays and poorer rates. Users who held a secondary token on a separate chain avoided the bottleneck. Once again, the pattern repeated: route diversity protected the outcome.

The idea of the ramp as a physical slope returns here. A steep ramp is narrow, sensitive, and easy to block. A broad ramp with multiple connections tolerates pressure. The metaphor is simple, but it encodes a decision: users must ask themselves whether the slope they are trusting can support the weight of their needs at the moment they need it.

The rate-shopping behaviour fits neatly into this motif. The most successful cross-border practitioners develop small habits that compound: checking spreads at consistent times; documenting final amounts; exporting weekly receipts; revisiting exchange limits monthly. These actions reveal stable patterns that advertisements never mention. For example, many exchanges worldwide show tighter spreads at midday local time, when liquidity peaks. Many card networks adjust FX buffers on Saturdays to account for Monday-settled rates. Many P2P markets show premium quotes during bank holidays when fiat settlement delays increase perceived risk. These are not secrets; they are behaviours. The users who measure them accrue an advantage akin to an experienced traveller who knows which airport security lane moves fastest.

The constraint is not technical. It is cognitive. People underestimate the variability of ramps because they focus on the rail that brought the funds to them. They assume that the speed of a blockchain settlement guarantees the efficiency of the off-ramp. They assume that a recognised brand guarantees consistent FX rates. They assume that a low headline fee equals a low total cost. These assumptions dissolve the moment a ramp introduces a delay, a hold, or an unfavourable spread. The only counter to assumption is comparison. The only defence is evidence.

Which brings us back to Carolina outside her café in Belo Horizonte. Her decision was not sophisticated. She simply compared receipts, including taxes, spreads, and timing. She used two test amounts. She chose the path that produced the most predictable outcome for the task at hand: buying groceries within the hour. The brilliance of her approach lay in its ordinariness. She behaved like someone who understood the slope of the ramp, not merely the rail.

Every cross-border user faces the same question dressed in different currencies: when the money arrives in your wallet, which slope will carry it safely into the form you need?

Remittances and obligations

On a damp Tuesday in November 2022, at 19:13 local time in Doha, *Marites*, a Filipino nurse, stared at the "pending" status on her phone with growing dread. She had sent 1,500 Qatari riyals through a low-cost remittance app to her parents in Quezon City. The electricity bill back home was due the next morning. The app promised "up to 24 hours". The clock did not care. Twelve hours later the payment was still in transit, caught in an opaque web of compliance checks and correspondent banks. Her father messaged to say the power company had given them an extension, but only until the end of the day. No one at the call centre could say exactly where the money was. The amount was modest. The margin for error was not.

A month earlier, the same transfer had cleared in under twenty minutes using a different route: a wallet-based remittance service that paid out in pesos through a local partner in Manila. That time, the delay came from a different direction. The receiving agent demanded an extra reference number; Marites' mother did not have it to hand and waited in a crowded shop, embarrassed and unsure. The funds were safe. The experience was not. For both women, the money carried more than value. It carried obligation and timing pressure—hospital bills, school fees, groceries, rent. The date is non-negotiable.

Remittances are not like other payments. A freelance invoice can arrive a day late without existential damage. A speculative trade can misfire without derailing a family. But a remittance usually arrives with a story attached, one that lives in family group chats and late-night calls: "Kuya, the rent is due on the 5th." "Nanay, the school lost patience." "Lola's medicine runs out on Saturday." Behind every cross-border send stands a calendar with red-ringed days. The rail might be digital; the obligation never is.

To understand how speed, cost, and documentation interact, start with what remittances actually are: scheduled promises made at a distance. The sender is usually a worker whose income is fixed by foreign payroll cycles, visa regimes, and local labour markets. The receiver often operates in a different currency with different inflation, banking norms, and expectations. Show: in 2021, the World Bank estimated that officially recorded remittance flows to low- and middle-income countries reached over US$600 billion (World Bank, 2022). Name: a macro figure that hides micro stories like Marites'. Explain: behind each flow sits a routine—weekly, monthly, quarterly—that must align with bills, school terms, and informal debts back home. Implication: a "cheap" route that occasionally breaks timetables may be worse than a slightly more expensive route that behaves predictably.

Traditional remittance services such as Western Union or MoneyGram, operating since the nineteenth and late twentieth centuries respectively, built their franchises on this reality. A worker in London could walk into an agent shop, hand over cash, and know that a relative in Lagos or Dhaka could collect funds within hours. The fees were high. The routes were reliable. The physical receipt, bearing a reference number and a time stamp, became a tangible proof to both sides: the sender had fulfilled their duty; the receiver could plan. When a payment failed, there was a counter to visit, a person to blame, a process to invoke. Trust was embodied in fluorescent-lit shops and stamped slips.

Digital rails have changed the form of this trust but not its function. Wallet-based services, mobile money integrations, and stablecoin corridors now allow a worker in Dubai to send value to Nairobi or Kathmandu in minutes. The behaviour is visible: a notification pings; a balance updates; a screenshot confirms. Yet each route also introduces fresh constraints—on-boarding checks, app limits, FX caps, documentation requirements when thresholds are crossed. For a migrant who may have imperfect paperwork, partial banking access, or limited time between shifts, these constraints matter as much as the headline fee.

The motif that frames remittances best is the *calendar*. The calendar determines everything. Dates run the show. A remittance that arrives early is a blessing; one that arrives late is a problem; one that arrives unpredictably is a stress amplifier. Show: a construction worker in Milan sends €400 on the 25th of each month to his family in Accra via a licensed money transfer operator. Name: a monthly remittance routine. Explain: his wife in Accra has aligned bill payments, school fees, and loan repayments around that date. Implication: if he experiments with a cheaper, slower route without warning, the small savings may be outweighed by late fees, embarrassment, or strained relationships.

This does not mean that traditional operators are always superior. Digital routes can honour the calendar more faithfully when set up well. A nurse in Toronto wiring funds to Kingston may schedule a monthly wallet-to-bank transfer on the 28th, knowing it reliably credits Jamaican bank accounts within two hours. A Kenyan software engineer in Berlin may use a stablecoin bridge to M-Pesa, turning volatile FX into something tractable. In each case, the remittance is not improvised; it is integrated into a personal operating rhythm.

The limitation appears when people treat remittances like one-off experiments rather than recurring obligations. A sender tries a novel corridor because a friend mentions a promotional rate, then forgets that the family on the other end has no visibility into whether the new route will work. The calendar becomes fragile. The reconciliation is simple but demanding: experiment with routes on *non-critical* transfers, not on the send that pays for a hospital visit. Duty should not be the testbed.

Speed is the most obvious axis of choice, but it is not absolute. It is relational. Fast relative to what? To a three-day SWIFT wire, a same-day wallet transfer feels miraculous. To an instant mobile money top-up, a three-hour stablecoin off-ramp feels glacial. The meaningful question is: *fast enough for this particular obligation?* Show: a domestic helper in Hong Kong needs to fund her parents' rent in Iloilo City by the 5th of each month. Name: a fixed deadline. Explain: if the route she uses consistently takes 24–36 hours, sending on the 3rd provides buffer. If she instead sends on the evening of the 4th, she has converted her own life into an emergency. Implication: speed is as much about when you press "send" as about what rail you use.

Cost tells a similar story. A worker in Qatar might pay 4–6% of the principal in fees and FX spreads using a cash-based remittance service. A wallet-based route might reduce that to 2–3%, but require both sender and receiver to navigate KYC checks, on-ramps, and off-ramps. The raw numbers matter, especially when budgets are thin. Yet cost must be weighed against documentation needs. Sometimes, a more expensive channel that generates clear, bank-recognised records is worth using at least part of the time—especially when receivers need proof of income for visas, loans, or tenancy agreements. The invisible benefit of "expensive" rails often lies in the quality of their paperwork.

Documentation also protects senders. Many migrants support extended family networks—siblings, cousins, in-laws—without clear written agreements. Disputes can arise years later about who paid what, when, and for whom. A simple habit of tagging remittance transfers in an app, saving PDF receipts, or exporting quarterly histories can transform hazy recollection into an accountable record. Behaviourally, this means that a worker in Dubai can show that she has covered her mother's utilities for eighteen consecutive months, or that siblings have shared costs fairly. Clarity prevents resentment from taking root in gaps.

Buffers are where remittances intersect with personal finance most obviously. A buffer is not an investment strategy. It is a small temporal shield. Show: a mechanic in Johannesburg sends 3,000 rand a month to his parents in Harare. Name: monthly obligation. Explain: after being caught twice by sudden delays in his preferred app—once due to South African bank maintenance, once due to Zimbabwean mobile money congestion—he decides to hold an extra 3,000 rand in his remittance wallet as a one-month buffer. Implication: if a route fails or he falls ill and misses a shift, his family can still receive funds for that month while he resolves the issue.

The behaviour here is straightforward: *send early, send a little extra when possible, and keep a small reserve in the rail you use most.* This is not about hoarding. It is about reducing the probability that one bad week cascades into a family crisis. Migrant workers already practise this intuitively when they top up airtime in advance or when they buy groceries in bulk during promotions. Extending the same logic to remittance timing and small balances is simply a recognition that the calendar does not negotiate.

A counter-example keeps the picture honest. In some corridors, currency risk, platform risk, or personal cashflow constraints make buffers hard to maintain. A domestic worker in Beirut sending dollars to relatives in Aleppo may struggle to hold any extra balance without incurring FX losses or platform freezes. In such cases, the buffer may be temporal rather than monetary: sending ten days early and using a route known to settle within three days under most conditions. The principle remains: widen the margin between sending and needing, either with extra funds or extra time.

Remittances also create overlapping obligations that differ in flexibility. Some expenses—rent, utilities, tuition—carry hard deadlines and penalties. Others—gifts, festival support, home repairs—are important but can shift. Show: a Ghanaian nurse in London supports her parents' living costs, funds a younger brother's college fees, and contributes to a family building project in Kumasi. Name: multiple obligations. Explain: if she treats all three as equal in scheduling, she may end up scrambling each month, improvising which to honour first based on whatever rail is least painful that day. Implication: without categorising obligations by hardness of deadline, remittance decisions become reactive rather than deliberate.

Digital tools can help, but only if used deliberately. Separate "pots" in a banking app, tagged sub-accounts in a wallet, or even colour-coded entries in a spreadsheet can signal which transfers are non-negotiable and which can slip by a week without breaking trust. This categorisation then informs route choice. High-stakes payments use the most predictable rail; lower-stakes transfers can experiment with lower-cost, less-tested corridors. The goal is not perfection. It is to ensure that experiments never jeopardise the rent.

The motif of the calendar returns with force here. If you plotted your remittances on a wall planner, which days would you circle in red, which in orange, which in pencil? That mental exercise alone can reshape how you approach rails, ramps, and rates.

Examples from the industry illustrate how product design is slowly catching up with these human realities. In 2020, *TransferWise* (now Wise) began highlighting exact arrival times for many corridors, using historical data to display estimates like "arrives in 3 hours" or "by tomorrow, 11:00". This tiny interface choice responded to the anxiety of not knowing whether a remittance would land before a bill's due date. In Kenya, *M-Pesa*'s integration with PayPal and other partners allowed diaspora workers to move funds directly into mobile money accounts that relatives used for everyday purchases. The route removed entire layers of uncertainty about collection points and opening hours. Such features do not merely increase "efficiency"; they re-align rails with obligations.

Limitations remain stark. Compliance rules shift. Regulators abruptly tighten controls. Banks de-risk entire corridors by cutting correspondent relationships, as happened between some UK and Caribbean banks in the mid-2010s. When that occurs, remittance cost and friction spike, and carefully honed routines break. In those moments, families improvise—switching apps, using friends as intermediaries, carrying cash when travelling. Improvisation is sometimes heroic, sometimes risky. What it cannot be is fully predictable.

Ultimately, remittances sit at the junction of money and meaning. A flat number on a digital receipt hides a thick web of expectations, promises, and compromises. The sender wants to fulfil duty without sacrificing their own stability. The receiver wants to plan life without wondering each month whether the support will arrive on time and in full. Both stand facing the same silent opponent: uncertainty.

The practical levers—route selection, buffer habits, documentation, scheduling—can reduce that uncertainty, but never erase it. That leaves a forward-facing question that each person must answer for their own context: if someone you love is depending on a transfer by a particular date, have you shaped your remittance routine—rails, ramps, and buffers—to honour the calendar you share, or are you leaving that responsibility to whichever system happens to be cheapest this month?

Receipts, records, and reconciliation

In March 2020, a self-employed developer in London received an unexpected brown envelope from HM Revenue & Customs.

The letter announced a routine review of his last three years of tax returns, with a polite request for supporting records. On screen, his accounts looked fine: tidy totals in an online accounting tool, exports from two banks, a handful of neat charts. Offline, the story was uglier. He had paid contractors via a crypto exchange, kept some invoices in a European neobank, and accepted stablecoin payments into a browser wallet, assuming it would all "be in the apps". It was—just not in one place, or with consistent labels. What should have been a straightforward reconciliation turned into weeks of trawling through CSV files, mismatched time zones, and untagged transfers whose purpose even he could no longer remember. The tax bill was not the worst part. The worst part was the uncertainty.

The episode ended benignly. After supplying explanations and reconstructed schedules, he avoided penalties. But the cost, measured in anxiety and lost working hours, was significant. He had treated digital finance as though the interfaces themselves were the record. The reality was harsher. The record that mattered—for tax, for audits, for disputes, for his own future self—was the one he could present clearly, across tools, in a form another human could follow. His ledgers were scattered across borders and blockchains. His story was not.

Cross-border money magnifies this gap between what apps show and what a life needs. When earnings, remittances, and savings spill across bank accounts, fintech wallets, exchanges, and on-chain addresses, the temptation is to trust that "it's all there somewhere". It often is. But "somewhere" is not a system. Nor is it a defence. The difference between someone who feels constantly behind and someone who can answer basic questions—What did I actually earn? How much did I send home? Which rails cost me most?—is rarely intelligence. It is the presence or absence of a deliberate record-keeping practice. The quiet motif that runs through this subchapter is the *trail*. Where is your trail? Can you follow it? Could anyone else?

Receipts are the atoms of that trail. Each one is a fragment of context that says, "This amount, for this purpose, at this time." Show: a copywriter in Nairobi pays for a Zoom subscription using a card linked to a multi-currency neobank, then reimburses herself from a stablecoin wallet. Name: a simple subscription loop. Explain: without a receipt tagged as "software" and marked as reimbursed, that payment later appears twice when she tries to reconstruct business costs—once in fiat, once in tokens. Implication: absent or scattered receipts do not merely irritate; they distort reality. They make profit look smaller, or larger, than it truly was.

Digital tools have made collecting receipts easier in some respects. E-mails arrive with attached PDFs. Wallets embed transaction hashes. Banking apps show merchant details automatically. Yet ease can backfire. When everything is recorded by default, nothing stands out. A person scrolling through six months of mixed spending sees a wall of similar-looking lines: UBER, UBER, UBER, TRANSFER, SWAP, TOP-UP. Without a simple system of tagging—client names, project codes, "family support", "rent buffer"—the data remains technically complete but practically opaque. It is the difference between a shoebox full of receipts and a ledger that tells a story.

Tagging is not a technology; it is a decision. Many apps offer categories by default: "Groceries", "Entertainment", "Business". These are a start, not an end. The tags that matter for cross-border life are those that encode obligations: "Parents – remittance", "Berlin client – design", "Nigeria corridor – test route", "Argentina hedge – USDC buffer". Such labels transform raw data into relational information. A future self, or an accountant, can see that a transaction was not just £200 sent "out", but three months of shared utilities, or a trial of a new FX route that should not be counted as income or consumption. The behaviour that creates this clarity is quiet: adding a few words at the moment of payment. The implication is large: later, the person does not have to reconstruct intent from memory.

Exports form the second layer of the trail. Interfaces change. Providers pivot. Regulators intervene. A person who assumes their remittance app or exchange will always be available to scroll misses a hard lesson from the history of financial technology: platforms die; data formats migrate badly; access can be revoked or throttled. Show: in August 2022, users of a mid-tier exchange in Eastern Europe faced sudden withdrawal limits after the firm announced a restructuring. Name: a stress event. Explain: those who had exported transaction histories quarterly could verify what they were owed and document their positions when dealing with administrators; those who had not were left scrambling with screenshots and partial e-mails. Implication: exporting is not busywork. It is a way to own your trail independent of any single platform.

Exports need not be sophisticated. A quarterly CSV pulled from a bank, a wallet, and an exchange, saved with a clear file name and backed up in at least two locations, is already far ahead of the default. Some people choose to convert these into simple spreadsheets with pivots by currency, counterparty, or category. Others hand them to an accountant or bookkeeper. The key is consistency. A pattern of "first weekend of the quarter: download and file" creates a rhythm that prevents the backlog from becoming overwhelming. The cadence matters. A five-minute habit beats a heroic annual catch-up.

A counter-example clarifies this point. A consultant in Johannesburg tells herself she will "do the paperwork at year-end". She earns in rands, dollars, and euros, with some payments arriving as stablecoins on multiple chains. When tax season arrives, she discovers that one exchange has shut local operations, another has changed its export format, and her phone with a key wallet app was replaced after a theft. Reconstructing the year becomes a forensics exercise. She eventually manages it, but at a high cognitive cost. The limitation of "I'll sort it later" is not moral; it is practical. Later, the trail is colder.

Reconciliation sits at the top of this structure. It is the act of comparing what you think happened with what the records say happened. Show: a freelance developer in Warsaw believes he earned roughly €60,000 from foreign clients in 2023. Name: an estimate. Explain: when he assembles quarterly exports from his euro account, his local zloty account, and his stablecoin wallet, the actual number is closer to €54,000 once refunds, chargebacks, and failed experiments with new payment rails are removed. Implication: his mental model of his earning capacity was inflated by about 10%. Any decisions he made based on the higher figure—rent, savings commitments, support to relatives—were, in effect, made on misinformation.

Reconciliation also highlights leakages that would otherwise go unnoticed. A designer in Lagos might discover that small FX spreads on a favourite remittance route cost her the equivalent of one full month's rent over a year. A trader in Buenos Aires might realise that card network mark-ups on weekend transactions eroded the benefit of holding balances in stablecoins. These insights rarely emerge from a single transaction. They emerge from patterns, visible only when records are aligned. Without reconciliation, habits remain unexamined. With it, they become candidates for change.

Still, reconciliation is not an audit in the formal sense. It is a conversation between past and present selves. It asks: did the money do what I thought it did? Did the rails behave as I expected? Were that month's remittances, invoices, and savings buffers actually executed as planned? The power lies less in numerical precision and more in narrative accuracy. A person who can say, "Yes, my records and my memory agree within a small margin," stands on firmer ground than someone whose sense of their own finances is based on anxiety or vague impressions.

There is, of course, a limit to how much structure a life can absorb. Not everyone will maintain pristine double-entry bookkeeping across five wallets and three currencies. Nor do they need to. The purpose of receipts, records, and reconciliation is not to turn every individual into a miniature treasury department. It is to ensure that when the world asks for a story—through a tax inquiry, a visa application, a loan assessment, a family conversation about who contributed what—that story can be told without panic.

Consider a Nigerian data scientist applying for a residence permit in Berlin. The migration office asks for proof of income and remittances over the prior year. If his cross-border payments to support parents in Abuja exist only as untagged crypto transfers, he may struggle to present them in a way a caseworker can understand. If, instead, he has quarterly exports with transactions labelled "Family support - Abuja" and occasional bank remittances with matching tags, he can present a coherent picture. The same records that helped him manage his own obligations now help him navigate an institution's requirements. The trail serves both private and public purposes.

Now imagine a different scenario: two siblings in Manila disagree, years later, over who sent more money back to their parents from overseas. Without records, the argument is emotional and irresolvable. With tagged histories, even imperfect ones, the conversation can at least reference something external. Records cannot fix strained relationships. They can, however, prevent avoidable misunderstandings.

The tension in record-keeping is always the same: how to capture enough detail to be useful later without drowning in administration. Too little, and the trail disappears. Too much, and the system collapses under its own weight. The motif of the trail offers a practical test. Each time you pay, send, or receive across borders, you leave a footprint. The question is whether those footprints line up into a path you can follow.

That leads naturally to a forward-looking provocation. A year from now, if someone—an accountant, a regulator, a lender, or a loved one—asked you to show, clearly, how money flowed through your life across accounts, apps, and wallets, would you be able to walk them along a coherent trail, or would you be asking them to trust that the data must be "in there somewhere"?

Chapter 5
Privacy, Identity, and You

Ten years ago, on a crowded summer evening in Tokyo, a café owner noticed something puzzling. A regular customer had left a generous tip—anonymously, or so they thought—via a QR code taped to the counter. The tip came as a small crypto transfer, nothing remarkable in amount. What drew the owner's attention was the cascade of related transactions that followed, linked publicly on a block explorer. Within minutes, curious strangers had mapped the sender's past purchases, donations, and even the approximate value of their savings. The customer had shared nothing more than a payment. The ledger had revealed a life. The owner quietly removed the QR code the next morning.

The episode passed without scandal. Yet it exposed a tension that sits at the heart of digital money. The more open the rails, the more visible the user. The more seamless the payment, the more complete the trail. Privacy—often mistaken for secrecy—is, in practice, the ability to choose the terms of our visibility. The Tokyo customer had no such choice. They revealed more than they intended simply because the tool they used did not bend around the social norms of tipping: a gesture meant to be appreciated, not analysed.

Every cross-border wallet, exchange, payroll tool, and messaging interface you use answers, implicitly or explicitly, one fundamental question: *Who are you here?* The difficulty is that identity is not a single thing we carry through the world like a laminated card. It is contextual, situational, and relational. You might be a legal name to your employer, a pseudonym to your peers, a wallet address to an online marketplace, and a trusted cousin to a relative relying on your monthly remittance. Each context asks for different disclosures and different proofs. Each context judges your silence or your sharing in a distinct way. The challenge of this chapter is not to warn you that technology threatens privacy—

those warnings are old. It is to show that the new wallets, rails, and tools we increasingly rely on require a more deliberate choreography of what we reveal, when, and why.

Digital money has collapsed distance but expanded exposure. A freelancer in São Paulo who invoices a client in London may find that her payment link reveals more than her fee: it may expose the chain she prefers, the wallet she uses elsewhere, or the network of addresses connected to past work. A student in Manila sending a donation to a relief fund may discover that the "simple" transaction creates a breadcrumb trail tying together their personal savings, their social affiliations, and their online identity. These trails are not inherently harmful. They are simply more legible than many expect. If you follow a public ledger far enough, identities cluster like constellations—patterns that analysts, platforms, and motivated observers can trace.

Against this backdrop, privacy becomes less about hiding and more about shaping. Selective disclosure is the operative skill. A person may choose to share an alias with a merchant because the transaction is low-risk and socially trivial, yet reserve their legal identity for an employer because the payroll system demands compliance and continuity. Both choices can be rational. Both can be prudent. What matters is alignment between intent and exposure. The regret creeps in only when the disclosures we make—deliberate or accidental—echo in contexts we never anticipated.

That is why this chapter begins with a simple premise: privacy is not a shield. It is an architecture. It is the structure through which you route your financial life so that the right people see the right information at the right time. Too much opacity and you collide with compliance. Too much transparency and you lose the capacity to negotiate, experiment, and protect the softer parts of your life. The aim is not perfect secrecy. The aim is proportionate visibility.

Achieving that balance requires an understanding of how the underlying technologies behave. Public blockchains, for all their innovation, operate on a principle that few outside technical circles fully internalise: everything is visible unless intentionally separated. Addresses that are reused accumulate narrative weight. Transactions that seem unrelated become linkable through heuristics, timing patterns, and interactions with centralised services. The Tokyo tipper rediscovered a truth long known to cryptographers: anonymity is not the default; it is an achievement. It demands intent. It demands tools that reinforce intent. It demands boundaries.

Yet the tone of this chapter is not fearful. It is pragmatic. Wallets are evolving. Privacy-preserving defaults are emerging. Features once the domain of specialists—new-address generation, human-readable payment requests, metadata filtering—are becoming accessible to ordinary users. A person making a small charitable donation should not need a degree in cryptography to do so without broadcasting their financial story. Tools can help. Habits can help more. A simple workflow—new address per client, payment request with minimal metadata, separation of personal spending from business receipts—can achieve "enough" privacy for most real-world purposes without sacrificing clarity or compliance.

Compliance, though often framed as an adversary to privacy, is in truth a constraint to design around. It is predictable. It is rule-based. It tells you what must be shown and to whom. Within that obligation sits a wide band of optional exposure: the details we routinely overshare because platforms default to convenience rather than discretion. A two-wallet workflow—one that holds receipts, invoices, and identity-bearing transactions; another for ordinary spending—imposes a gentle order. It limits the splash radius of any one disclosure. It reduces the chance that your remittance to an aunt in Iloilo ends up cross-referenced with your freelance portfolio or your experimental investment account. Clarity for you. Brevity for the institutions that need to see just enough.

The deeper theme that threads through this chapter is the idea of surfaces. Every tool you use presents a surface to the world. Some are polished, public, and permanent. Others are quiet, private, and controlled. Deciding which surface to present is a skill that mirrors decisions we already make offline: which name to sign on a postcard, which details to share at work, which conversations belong at the dinner table. Digital money raises the stakes because the surfaces are stickier. The traces they leave are harder to erase. But the principle is old. The aim is to manage visibility, not erase yourself from view.

As you read on, the chapter will lead you through selective sharing, the realities of transparent ledgers, the practical tools that can preserve your intent, and the trade-offs that emerge when privacy meets compliance. Each section offers a way to think about surfaces—what you show, what you withhold, and how to ensure that your financial identity remains something you shape rather than something that shapes you. The unresolved tension, the thread that runs quietly beneath it all, is one you may already feel: how much of you travels with every payment you send?

What to reveal, when, and why

In March 2022, a London café quietly revised its printed receipts after a regular customer complained that his card terminal displayed his full legal name to the barista for a £2.80 Americano. The café had recently switched payment providers, and the new settings broadcast more than the transaction required. Nothing harmful happened. Yet the customer, a journalist working on politically sensitive subjects, felt exposed. A trivial purchase had surfaced a part of his identity he normally guarded. The manager apologised, adjusted the settings, and shrugged at the disproportionate fuss. But the incident captured something essential about digital money: disclosure is rarely neutral. Even small details carry weight when they appear in the wrong context. This tension intensifies once payments cross borders. A gig worker in Nairobi using a European wallet to receive $120 for a design commission may unwittingly reveal a persistent identifier, making it trivial to track other inflows. A shopper in Buenos Aires tipping a musician via QR code might expose the same alias they use for online communities they prefer to keep separate. Meanwhile, the payroll clerk at an employer in Berlin has no choice: the legal name, date of birth, and tax ID of every employee must be submitted intact. Rules differ by role. Exposure varies by situation. The art lies in matching disclosure to context.

Selective sharing is older than finance. Households in fifteenth-century Florence, documented in city guild records, routinely structured their ledgers with coded initials when noting sensitive transactions, while using full names only for dealings that required legal enforceability. The distinction was intentional, not accidental. It gave them control over which relationships were visible and which were private. The digital equivalents—aliases, wallet addresses, metadata fields—serve a similar purpose. The difference is scale. A Florentine ledger sat on a shelf. A digital payment may circulate across nodes, platforms, and jurisdictions indefinitely. That permanence makes deliberate disclosure a modern necessity.

The first claim of this subchapter is simple: context governs what you reveal. A merchant needs payment confirmation, not a dossier. An employer needs regulated identifiers to run payroll, not a lifetime map of your transactions. An authority conducting a lawful audit needs specific records, not evidence of every café visit. The motif that threads through the next pages—the boundary—matters here. Boundaries let you decide which aspects of your identity cross into each relationship. When boundaries blur, regret accumulates. Consider a clear example from São Paulo. In 2021, a freelance illustrator named in contemporary reporting as *Marina* accepted commissions from Europe and the United States. She used the same payment link for all clients. That link was tied to a single stablecoin address she also used for rent payments, discretionary spending, and small donations. Over time, one client, curious about the mechanics of blockchain transactions, clicked through the link and viewed the address's history. The client saw transfers from a local exchange at regular intervals, which effectively revealed her approximate monthly income. Nothing malicious happened. Yet the episode showed how a minor disclosure—reusing an address—could produce major visibility. The behaviour, not the technology, created the exposure. Name the pattern: address consolidation. Explain it: when a single identifier is used across unrelated contexts, third parties can infer relationships, approximate income, or identify spending rhythms. The implication is clear. Even without ill intent, visibility increases. The boundary dissolves. A trivial design choice—one link for all clients—quietly merges worlds that were better kept apart.

By contrast, employers require full identity because payroll is regulated. The UK's HM Revenue & Customs system, for example, obliges employers to submit an employee's legal name and National Insurance number. That disclosure is deliberate and justified. It enables tax withholding, pension calculations, and long-term benefits. Show this: an employee at a mid-sized firm in Manchester receives payslips through an encrypted portal tied to their legal identity. The information is limited in scope but precise. Explain why: payroll must withstand audit and govern entitlements. The implication: boundaries built into regulation can actually reduce exposure by preventing employers from requesting unnecessary information. Here, transparency is targeted, not sprawling.

Now introduce the counter-example. Some users, especially in activist circles or fragile states, seek maximum anonymity at all times. They rely entirely on privacy-preserving tools, never disclose their legal names voluntarily, and avoid any platform requiring identity verification. This posture can protect vulnerable individuals. Yet it also fractures daily life. It complicates receiving wages, obtaining visas, or fulfilling routine obligations where verified identity is required. Reconciling this limitation shows the essential balance: maximal anonymity can be a rational survival strategy in specific environments, but for most people, proportional disclosure achieves better continuity. The boundary must move with circumstance.

Each abstraction in this domain—*trust, risk, efficiency*—comes to life through observable behaviour. Trust appears in the decision to reveal a legal name when signing a contract because the counterparty must enforce it. Risk materialises in the choice to send a tip via a permanent address that exposes dozens of unrelated transactions. Efficiency emerges from using an alias for low-stakes payments, reducing the cognitive load of deciding what to disclose each time. Behaviours reveal the curve of the boundary.

To show how these boundaries can be shaped deliberately, consider a practical routine used by freelance developers in Lagos who work for European clients. They maintain two stablecoin addresses: one address for invoicing, rotated quarterly, and another for personal use. The quarterly rotation limits how much transactional narrative any single client can infer. Their employers, by contrast, receive a standardised KYC package when formal contracts exist. The difference lies in context: commercial work requires structure; irregular payments benefit from optional anonymity. The implication: privacy improves when workflows reflect the social meaning of each payment.

The motif of boundaries returns when considering authorities. Regulatory agencies operate through rules, not curiosity. They require specific disclosures for defined purposes: tax reporting, anti-money-laundering checks, or the processing of remittances above threshold limits. Show this through a concrete process: a UK resident remitting £600 monthly to parents in Accra through a licensed service submits identity documents once, then benefits from predictable, structured reporting. Explain it: the agency's remit is to verify legality and prevent illicit activity. The implication: fulfilling formal obligations cleanly can actually narrow your exposure because you avoid ad hoc, repeated checks. Order reduces the surface you reveal.

Selective sharing is therefore not a defensive stance but a navigational one. It demands a clear mental model of what each relationship truly needs. Merchants want proof of payment. Employers require legal identifiers. Authorities need accurate records. Everyone else may need less than you assume. When you calibrate disclosure to context, you reduce the probability of unintended correlation—the invisible process through which separate parts of your life become stitched together.

Return to motif. The boundary is not a wall. It is a line you draw, adjust, and redraw as roles shift. A student becoming self-employed moves the line. A migrant sending formal remittances for the first time moves it again. A parent paying school fees from multiple income streams must decide which identifiers to consolidate and which to separate. Each choice shapes the narrative others can construct about you. The goal is not invisibility; it is coherence.

A recurring question anchors this subchapter: *What does this relationship truly require of me?* Ask it before sending a donation, before invoicing a client, before joining a new platform, before authorising a payroll change. Ask it again when the context shifts. The unresolved tension at the core of selective sharing is this: too little disclosure and your financial life can jam; too much and it becomes porous. The craft lies in choosing the point on that spectrum that aligns with your intent—every time you cross a boundary.

On-chain does not mean anonymous

In February 2015, agents from the United States Internal Revenue Service and the Federal Bureau of Investigation pieced together a map of transactions linked to the Silk Road marketplace by tracing deposits and withdrawals through the Bitcoin ledger. The marketplace had operated from servers seized in Reykjavik in 2013, a detail widely reported at the time, yet what ultimately anchored the investigation was not a dramatic raid but a sequence of visible movements between addresses. Investigators did not need privileged access. They relied on the transparency of the chain itself. The case, later documented in federal court filings, showed something unsettling: anonymity assumed is not anonymity achieved. A string of characters, reused or linked through patterns, can reveal more than the user ever intended.
The paradox remains. Blockchains promise decentralisation and permissionless access, yet their very design—the public ledger—creates an environment where every transaction is observable. A teenager in Buenos Aires sending a $5 tip to a musician may do so believing they are invisible in the crowd. Yet the address they use, if employed elsewhere, forms a breadcrumb trail. A donor in Nairobi supporting an open-source developer could unwittingly reveal previous inflows if the same address once received wages. Transparency is not conditional. It is built in. The challenge is to navigate it consciously.
The motif that guides this subchapter—the imprint—emerges early. Every address leaves one. Printed on an immutable ledger, it behaves like a footprint on wet sand: the tide never comes in. What matters is how many footprints overlap, and who can read them.

The first major claim requires demonstration. Show the imprint: a user publishes a wallet address on a forum to receive small donations for maintaining a translation project. Months later, they use the same address to pay for a software subscription. Name the mechanism: address reuse. Explain it:

when a single address handles multiple unrelated activities, analysts can cluster transactions that share behavioural patterns or counterparties. Clustering, a technique employed by firms such as Chainalysis since the mid-2010s, groups addresses into probable ownership sets through heuristics like common-input patterns. The implication is stark: the user's public appeal for donations unintentionally exposes their private spending habits. The address becomes a unifying thread.

Evidence of clustering's reach appears in well-documented investigations. In 2017, Dutch authorities traced ransom payments linked to the *Wannacry* malware campaign by following the movement of funds through a series of addresses until they reached exchange-linked accounts subject to identification checks. The behaviour was visible: multiple small inflows followed by batched outflows. The names came later, supplied by compliance requests. The ledger provided the map. The implication for ordinary users is sobering. Even without wrongdoing, repeated patterns across time form a contour of identity. The imprint deepens.

Now consider the counter-example. Some chains, such as Zcash, introduced shielded pools to obscure transaction details. Others, like Monero, use ring signatures and stealth addresses to complicate link analysis. These tools offer meaningful privacy by design. Yet their utility remains limited in several domains: major exchanges list them inconsistently; merchants accept them sparsely; analytics firms continue to infer patterns from transactional edges, even if the core data remains hidden. Reconciling this limitation reinforces the central point. Privacy tools can reduce exposure, but they do not eliminate the imprint entirely, especially when they interface with more transparent systems. Boundaries still require thought.

To ground abstractions in behaviour, follow a user in Lagos preparing to invoice a European client. They maintain two stablecoin addresses: one for inflows and another for discretionary transactions. The separation works until they accidentally send a test transaction from the personal address to the client. That single mistake links the two domains. The metric is simple: analysts need one observable edge between two addresses to cluster them. The implication: operational discipline—rotating addresses, maintaining separation, and avoiding accidental crossovers—supports the boundary. The imprint fades only when footprints diverge. Another visible behaviour arises in decentralised applications. When a user connects a wallet to a lending platform, the platform may read their entire balance to calculate borrowing capacity. The user's intent may be to borrow against one token, yet the app, unless permissions are restricted, glimpses everything. The mechanism is not malicious. It is structural. But it reveals the ease with which one action can broadcast a wider identity. The implication is direct. Managing exposure involves not only address separation but permission segmentation. Identities are collections of imprints. Tools matter, but habits matter more.

The motif returns with a key historical pivot. In 2020, the *ETC Cooperative* published an account of how analysts traced large pre-mining movements on Ethereum Classic from exchanges based in South Korea to addresses linked with speculative trading groups. The process involved nothing more than reading the ledger, correlating timestamps, and identifying exchange withdrawal wallets through public disclosures. Show the behaviour: batched withdrawals, repeated at predictable intervals. Name the technique: temporal clustering. Explain its logic: consistent timing suggests common ownership or coordination. Implication: even without a stable identity anchor, patterns form. The imprint becomes a silhouette.

Yet, limitations exist. Analytics firms operate with probabilities, not certainties. They infer. They correlate. In heavily mixed environments, such as periods of high adoption of privacy mixers or cross-chain swaps, signals degrade. An individual committed to strict compartmentalisation—unique addresses for each transaction, no behavioural linkages, careful timing—can meaningfully reduce traceability. This discipline, however, demands time and precision. For most people, it is impractical. Reconciling this limitation brings the key lesson into view: privacy is best achieved not through perfection but through proportional separation. Enough is often sufficient. Obsessive opacity is rarely sustainable.

The imprint motif strengthens when considering merchant interactions. A merchant in Warsaw accepting stablecoins might generate a new receive address for each transaction, but if their accounting system aggregates receipts into a single hot wallet, the imprint of all customers merges, making later auditing straightforward but increasing the visibility of individual inflows. A customer paying repeatedly to the same merchant address inadvertently signals loyalty, spending rhythm, and perhaps income cadence. Observers can measure these behaviours directly. The implication: privacy is not only about hiding; it is about shaping what patterns can be inferred.

Two contrasting examples frame the broader lesson. In December 2021, a charity in Oxford accepting crypto donations used a dedicated address per donor to ensure each contributor's history remained separate. Behaviour: one donor, one address. The result: auditors could verify inflows without exposing donors to each other. Compare this with a musician in Seoul who kept a static QR code for convenience. Fans who explored the address could see past donations, tip sizes, and usage patterns. Convenience created unintended disclosure. Boundaries dissolved.

These examples expose the texture of the imprint. Every transaction carries coordinates: time, value, sender, receiver. Even when names are absent, patterns speak. Clustering does not break cryptography; it interprets behaviour. The ledger is a canvas. Users paint with movement. Analysts read the strokes.

A final thread introduces the forward test. Suppose a user wishes to maintain three spheres of activity: employment income, side-project payments, and personal donations. Each sphere has different disclosure requirements. The unresolved question becomes: *How many addresses, routines, and permissions must be separated to preserve coherence without creating chaos?* Too few, and patterns merge. Too many, and the system collapses under its own complexity. The imprint can guide that decision. If each sphere generates its own distinct set of footprints—non-overlapping, consistent, predictable—then identities remain compartmentalised enough to retain dignity and purpose. If not, the footprints blur. The ledger remembers everything.

Pragmatic tooling

In June 2021, the independent security researcher Sergio Demian Lerner demonstrated a simple trace experiment during a workshop in Buenos Aires. He sent a tiny amount of bitcoin—less than one US cent at the time—to a public donation address displayed on a projector. Within minutes, attendees watched the funds ripple through a series of subsequent transactions. Each movement was visible. No special access was required. The exercise made one point unavoidable: transparency is not abstract. It is lived. A single action can light up a map.

The room fell quiet as Lerner repeated the test using a freshly generated address. This time, the funds stood alone, detached from his earlier sending history. The contrast revealed a practical truth. Privacy rests not only on cryptography but on the routines built around it. Tools matter. Habits matter more. The motif that frames this subchapter—the *switch*—appears here. Each choice, whether to reuse or to rotate, to reveal or to obscure, behaves like a switch. Flip it, and the exposure changes.

The first claim we must surface is straightforward: users need tools that lower their operational burden. Show the switch in action. A journalist in Nairobi wants to receive a £10 donation from a reader. Rather than send a static address, she generates a payment request with a unique address tied only to that donation. Name the feature: address-generation-on-demand, now common in several wallet applications. Explain it: by creating a new address for each incoming payment, the wallet prevents one donor from seeing the journalist's previous inflows. The implication is measured in behaviour. Anyone inspecting the chain sees only a single inbound transfer to that one address. The financial story stays narrow. This mechanism is not theoretical. Since 2022, the *BTCPay Server* project has recommended one-address-per-invoice defaults for merchants, citing earlier academic work from Moser et al. (2018) on transaction linkage. The design limits clustering. A donor sees only what they send. A merchant can still maintain consolidated reporting internally. The switch holds the boundary.

Second, pragmatic tooling must account for outbound flow. Consider a user in Manchester making a small recurring donation—£5 each month—to an environmental charity that accepts stablecoins. Show the behaviour: the user begins with address reuse for convenience. Name the risk: traceability through repetition. Explain it: repeated monthly payments from the same address reveal rhythm, capacity, and wallet balances. The implication becomes clear when an unrelated counterparty, noticing a pattern, can infer the user's financial cadence. A simple solution exists. The user configures their wallet to auto-generate new sending addresses or routes the payment through an intermediate sub-wallet that holds only the donation amount. The switch creates separation. Two historical examples underscore tooling's influence. In 2020, the Human Rights Foundation advised activists in its financial-privacy programme to employ tools that generate new receive addresses for every transaction, even when the nominal risk appeared low. Their reasoning, published that year, relied not on fear but on visible clustering patterns found in previous cases. The behaviour they observed: activists who reused addresses left clear maps that, once deanonymised, exposed their networks. Contrast this with the 2023 update to the *Samourai Wallet* documentation, which noted that even privacy-enhancing features can be undermined when users deviate—accidentally or for speed—from recommended address rotation. The limitation must be named. Tooling is only as protective as the behaviour that surrounds it. The reconciliation lies in setting defaults that make safe behaviour automatic.

The motif returns. A switch works best when it sits where the user cannot ignore it. Wallets that surface "generate new address" prompts, display address expiry timers, or warn when reusing an address act as constant reminders. These cues reduce cognitive load. Without them, expertise thins over time.

The third claim concerns the transparency of defaults. Show transparency as exposure. A payments app in Warsaw automatically broadcasts the sender's full account balance to a connected merchant's smart contract. Name the feature: full-balance visibility for liquidity calculations. Explain the issue: the merchant does not misuse this information, but the contract can read more than the user intends. Behaviour gives the implication. A merchant sees wallet capacity, not just the payment. That visibility can be stored, analysed, or leaked. The appropriate switch is scope-limiting permissions. Wallets that allow "spend-only" approvals or "single-transaction" permissions narrow what counterparties can view. The tension becomes clearer using a concrete example. In February 2022, the lending protocol Aave's interface was observed reading connected users' token balances to compute their borrowing power. This was expected functionality. Yet several users, unfamiliar with the permission flow, assumed the protocol "saw" only the assets they intended to borrow against. Behaviour told the truth. Once connected, the protocol could observe every token in the wallet. The implication: tools governing permissions—approval managers, revocation dashboards, scoped access—are not luxuries. They are filters. They keep only what must pass. They drop the rest.

To anchor the chapter's trajectory, we return to a small donation flow—the simplest case that reveals the entire structure. A musician in Seoul posts a QR code hoping to raise funds for a community project. A supporter scans it and sends the equivalent of £3. The QR code resolves to a long-lived donation address. The musician's past receipts become visible, as do their outgoing transactions if they use the same address for spending. The exposure grows. The fix, again, is a switch. The musician uses a wallet that generates a new request every time a supporter taps the "Donate" button. Each supporter sees only their own transaction. The musician's outflows, conducted from a separate spending wallet, remain unseen. The routine feels small. The protection is large. A second example comes from a cooperative research group in Lisbon, which in 2023 published a report on privacy-preserving donation flows. They measured the reduction of cross-flow traceability when switching from static addresses to single-use requests. According to the group's audit logs, cross-donor linkage dropped by more than half. Behaviour created the metric. The implication: small, predictable tools can reshape exposure in measurable ways.

Yet no discussion of tools is complete without acknowledging limitations. Not every wallet supports multiple sub-accounts. Some do not generate payment requests with metadata stripped. Others cannot easily revoke permissions once granted. These gaps matter. But they do not invalidate the core strategy. The reconciliation lies in sufficiency. Users do not need perfect compartmentalisation. They need enough separation to prevent easy clustering across unrelated contexts. The switch metaphor helps here. Few people need a full circuit board. Most need three or four well-placed toggles.

The motif deepens when we consider timing. A user who regularly sends funds at predictable hours creates a visible behavioural fingerprint. Even when they use new addresses, timing can act as a linking signal. If they wish to reduce this, a simple timer or scheduled-send feature, offered by several wallets since 2023, can randomise dispatch within a safe window. Behaviour becomes less deterministic. The imprint dissolves.
Similarly, exporting transaction records—an administrative task—can support privacy indirectly. When a user maintains structured records offline, they reduce the temptation to reuse addresses simply to aid personal tracking. The switch moves again: better internal order permits more external discretion.

As we approach the unresolved tension, the question sharpens. *How much tooling is enough for a thoughtful user to avoid avoidable exposure without burying themselves in operational complexity?* Too few tools, and every action radiates more than intended. Too many, and routine breaks. The answer is never static. It depends on context, stakes, and capability. Yet the switch metaphor offers a working guide. If each category of action—receiving, sending, connecting, granting permissions—has one clear, visible toggle that shapes what is revealed, most users can steer safely. The ledger will always record movement. The key is to decide which movements speak, and which ones stay quiet.

Trade-offs with compliance

In March 2019, the Danish Tax Agency announced that it had issued letters to more than 2,500 residents after matching on-chain transfers with exchange-submitted account data from 2016 and 2017. The agency named the exchanges. It named the periods examined. What startled many observers was not the enforcement itself but the mechanism: ordinary wallet transactions, previously assumed to be buried in pseudonymity, were organised into timelines that linked deposits, withdrawals, and spending flows. The recipients were not all high-volume traders. Some had moved only a few thousand kroner across wallets and platforms. The message was stark: record-keeping is not optional, and oversharing—voluntary or inadvertent—can shape how scrutiny unfolds. One recipient, interviewed later that year by *Berlingske*, described how a single shared screenshot of a wallet balance with a freelance client in Copenhagen created an unintended breadcrumb. The client forwarded that screenshot during a routine mortgage application. The lender retained it. When the tax inquiry arrived, the borrower realised that the fragment had widened the authority's view of his broader activity. The screenshot acted as a hinge. A private detail had slipped into a regulated domain. His regret was not about compliance. It was about exposure he had not intended.

The first claim follows from these scenes: compliance and privacy often pull in different directions, yet they need not be enemies. Show the tension. A designer in Porto receives payments in a stablecoin and converts part of them every month to euros. Name the requirement: reporting taxable events per local rules. Explain the challenge: if she submits transaction exports that include both personal spending and business inflows, she reveals more than necessary—merchant addresses, donation habits, entire expenditure rhythms. The implication becomes clear. Her legal obligations focus on income and disposals, not on mapping her life. A simple remedy exists. She uses a two-wallet workflow, one for receipts and conversions, one for personal use. This mirrors long-standing bookkeeping practices where sole traders maintain separate bank accounts. The separation is visible in behaviour: business receipts enter Wallet A; they move to trusted on-ramps; personal outflows occur from Wallet B via addresses never exposed to clients. If an auditor later requests records, she exports only Wallet A's timeline. The privacy of Wallet B remains intact. The motif that carries through this subchapter—the *boundary*—emerges here. Boundaries shape exposure.

A concrete example underscores why boundaries matter. When the UK's HM Revenue & Customs launched its 2021 data request programme targeting certain exchange users, it received structured datasets linking identities, deposits, and withdrawals. The users who had maintained clear separation between personal and professional flows produced concise ledgers that aligned with their obligations. The behaviour required no exotic privacy tooling, only organisational clarity. Contrast this with a limitation. In some jurisdictions, such as Japan after the 2022 Financial Services Agency update, exchanges must tag withdrawals with enhanced metadata when transferring to personal wallets. Users cannot fully shield their wallet structures from these disclosures. The limitation is structural. Yet boundaries still help. Even if authorities know that Wallet A belongs to the user, Wallet B can remain outside the reporting perimeter if it never touches a monitored on-ramp. Reconciliation lies in accepting that while some visibility is unavoidable, not all visibility must expand.

The next claim builds on the same motif: keeping clean records does not require self-incrimination. Show the behaviour. A freelancer in Nairobi uses a simple tagging routine on her main receipt wallet. Even after exporting her transactions for accounting, she removes non-essential metadata—internal notes, personal annotations—before sharing with an accountant. Name the practice: minimal disclosure bookkeeping. Explain the premise: reporting requires accuracy, not narrative. The implication is vivid. By stripping unnecessary fields, she meets obligations without gifting outsiders a behavioural profile.

An illustration from public history reinforces the point. When Germany updated its bookkeeping standards in 2018 to reflect digital payment flows, it emphasised *ordnungsmäßigkeit*—orderliness—not full contextual transparency. The guidance encouraged consistency: well-kept, chronologically coherent records that enable verification. It did not ask for personal context or explanations of private spending. The lesson transfers neatly to modern wallets. Orderliness is protective.

A counter-example helps sharpen the limits. In 2020, several small businesses in Argentina began using stablecoin wallets to cope with peso volatility. Some attempted to use a single wallet for both customer receipts and personal savings. During audits, they faced challenges separating deductible expenses from private transfers. The limitation came not from the stablecoin but from the commingling. Yet the lesson reconciles cleanly with our boundary motif: separation at the point of receipt simplifies disclosure; separation at the point of spending protects private patterns.

The third claim is about oversharing. Show oversharing as friction. A software developer in Dublin applies for a visa. The consulate asks for proof of funds. To comply quickly, she prints a full transaction history from her primary wallet. Name the problem: unnecessary transparency. Explain it: the officer now sees not only her account balance but every inbound and outbound transfer, including medical payments, donations, and private reimbursements. The implication arrives swiftly. She has met the requirement yet revealed far more than needed.

The boundary solution reprises itself. If she had maintained a verification-only wallet—one holding a limited, stable balance used solely for documentation—she could present a clean, simple record. This approach echoes banking norms: individuals often keep separate savings accounts for visa, mortgage, or tenancy proofs. The same logic applies to wallets. A bounded presentation wallet reduces oversharing while satisfying the request.

Historical precedent supports this reasoning. During India's demonetisation period in late 2016, the government encouraged digital payments and simultaneously required certain transaction proofs for compliance checks. Citizens who maintained compartmentalised digital accounts navigated the period more smoothly. Their records were legible, limited, and aligned with the request scope. Those who blended business and personal flows often triggered additional inquiries because their statements were cluttered and ambiguous. Behaviour produced the outcome.

The limitation must also be acknowledged. Some compliance frameworks, particularly anti-money-laundering controls, require verification of source-of-funds. Segregation alone cannot fully shield upstream information. Yet even here, boundaries reduce collateral disclosure. A user can provide documentation limited to the relevant chain rather than an unfiltered dump of their financial life. The reconciliation is pragmatic: boundaries do not bypass rules; they prevent needless sprawl.

A final claim concerns the discipline of review. Show the rhythm. A consultant in Valencia conducts a monthly audit of her receipt wallet. She compares exports with her invoicing records, tags missing entries, and archives a read-only copy offline. Name the habit: monthly reconciliation. Explain its power: by maintaining an orderly ledger, she never scrambles to reconstruct a year's worth of transactions under pressure. The implication extends beyond tax season. When a client disputes an old invoice, she has a structured, time-stamped, limited-scope record to produce.

This mirrors long-tested accounting practice. In 2017, the Australian Taxation Office published research showing that small businesses with quarterly bookkeeping routines experienced fewer compliance disputes and spent markedly less time responding to information requests. The lesson aligns smoothly with on-chain activity: regular order reduces risk, both reputational and administrative. The boundary motif surfaces again. By confining reconciliation to one wallet, she avoids mixing personal flows into business evidence.

The unresolved tension sits at the end of these patterns. *How much structure is enough to satisfy obligations without surrendering private life to every institution that asks?* Too little, and a user risks disorder, penalties, or prolonged scrutiny. Too much, and the apparatus becomes burdensome, choking the flexibility that digital wallets promise. The boundary offers a compass. One wallet for receipts. One wallet for living. Clean exports from the former. Quiet discretion in the latter. The details will vary by jurisdiction, profession, and personal preference. But the principle holds. Compliance need not demand confession. Order draws the line.

Chapter 6
Earning and Getting Paid

The first time you hear the rustle of a printer spitting out an invoice, you could almost mistake it for a relic. Yet the scene still plays out every morning in shared workspaces from Lagos to Lisbon: a designer proofreads a document before attaching it to an email, adding a line about payment methods, hoping the client reads it, hoping the amount is understood, hoping the settlement arrives without the ritual chase. It is a strangely fragile moment in modern work. The labour is done; the value is delivered; but the money is not yet home. In a world where messages cross continents in less than a second, the act of *getting paid* remains surprisingly exposed to friction, ambiguity, and delay.

Consider the programmer in Medellín who, after completing a fortnight's sprint for a European client, is sent a wire confirmation and a vague assurance that "the funds should land soon." She checks her wallet. Nothing. Hours stretch into days. Meanwhile a friend across the city receives a QR-coded payment link for a weekend job, taps once, and watches her balance update instantly. Two professionals, two flows of value, two entirely different temporal experiences. The contrast is not merely technological; it is emotional. One worker is stuck in a holding pattern, the other already moving on. In these gaps—between initiation and arrival, between promise and certainty—lie the practical realities this chapter seeks to illuminate.

Money, when it moves across borders or platforms, behaves far less like a single stream and far more like a collection of pipes, valves, and channels, each with its own pressure points. One client wants a PDF invoice. Another prefers a payment link. A local shop scans QR codes at the till. A platform insists on escrow and batch payouts. These choices are not cosmetic. They shape liquidity, bargaining power, and clarity of expectation. They dictate whose clock sets the tempo. And they determine whether getting paid feels like a mechanical step or a recurring negotiation.

Behind every invoice or payment request sits the deeper question of pricing clarity. The unit in which you quote your work—euros, dollars, pesos, stablecoins—anchors the negotiation far more firmly than the rail that ultimately settles the payment. A translator in Warsaw may accept USDC or złoty, but she frames her quote in euros because it keeps her rate stable across conversations. A photographer in Manila might list a peso amount yet include a dollar equivalent so foreign clients see explicit parity. These choices are not about financial sophistication. They are about reducing misunderstandings before they metastasise into disputes.

Then comes volatility, the invisible eddy in the pipes. Most professionals want to work; they do not want to run a trading desk. Yet too many find themselves exposed unintentionally—quoting in a currency they do not hold, receiving in a unit they do not track, or delaying conversion until a client payment fluctuates unexpectedly. The distinction between settlement and treasury becomes essential here. How you accept value and how you store it need not collapse into a single decision. Routine, even simple routine, turns noise into structure.

The platforms through which payments flow introduce their own fragilities. Today's favourite invoicing tool may raise fees next year. A mobile wallet might face a regulatory freeze. A gig platform could restrict withdrawals without warning. Portability is the counterweight to these risks. The freelancer who exports her contact list every quarter, who keeps local copies of invoices, who can reconstruct her billing history without logging in to a single firm's servers, is not merely organised—she is resilient. She can migrate. She can adapt. She remains sovereign over her work.

Friction in payments is not distributed evenly. Some workers have to navigate corridor-specific complications: local banking holidays that stretch settlement, foreign exchange spreads that quietly erode margin, or platform withdrawal windows that cluster at awkward times of day. Others operate in smoother channels but occasionally face clients who do not understand the difference between a quote and a settlement amount. These dissonances accumulate. They affect planning, mood, and trust. They determine whether creativity thrives or anxiety thins the air.

Yet within these complexities lies a hopeful thread: getting paid can be simpler than most people assume, provided the system is shaped with intent. When an illustrator in Accra sends a client a templated request—amount, preferred currency, supported rails, deadline, and a payment link—the negotiation evaporates. The client acts. The money moves. The illustrator returns to the work that matters. Clarity, properly applied, is a productivity tool.

This chapter follows that thread and extends it. It shows the mechanics of how money is requested, priced, received, and stabilised. It explores how workers separate the act of earning from the management of currency volatility. It examines the small practices that prevent platform dependence from calcifying into lock-in. It argues that payment flows, once understood, can be shaped strategically rather than endured passively.

Every practice introduced here—whether sending an invoice, generating a payment link, establishing a buffer, or exporting platform data—rests on a single principle: earnings are not complete until value is under your control. That control need not be perfect; perfection is brittle. Instead, the aim is resilience: enough clarity to avoid confusion, enough structure to absorb volatility, enough portability to withstand platform shifts.

There is a quiet dignity in being paid fairly, promptly, and on your own terms. And there is power in designing payment flows that reflect the reality of your work rather than the limitations of outdated systems. Each decision in the pages ahead—what to quote, which rail to choose, how to convert, what to record—reinforces or weakens that power.

The next step is to understand how these decisions interact. Once you see the pipes, the valves, and the channels clearly, you can direct the flow rather than waiting for it.

Invoices, links, and QR

On 14 March 2022, in a co-working space in Porto, designer Carla Duarte watched a client open her invoice and hesitate. The amount was correct, the work approved, yet the pause stretched. The client scrolled, searching for payment instructions buried halfway down the PDF. "Which method do you prefer?" he asked. She replied. He checked whether his bank supported the transfer. She clarified her details. He confirmed again. What followed was not negotiation but friction—six messages, two screenshots, and a two-day delay before settlement reached her account. The work had been smooth; the payment request had not. It was a tiny moment, yet it revealed a truth that spans borders: complexity in the *ask* slows the *arrival.*

Hours later, in the same building, a videographer received his fee via a single tap. He sent a payment link. The client clicked it. The platform generated a one-time QR code. The funds settled instantly in his wallet. No PDFs. No emails. No delay. The difference was not technological sophistication alone. It was clarity. He knew what he needed. He stated it. The client executed. A straight line replaced a loop.

The contrast between those two scenes is the quiet motif running through this subchapter: the difference between *precision* and *ambiguity* in requesting payment. Precision accelerates; ambiguity drags. Every rail—whether bank transfer, stablecoin payment, card deposit, or QR-based wallet transfer—benefits from the same principle: the payer should never be left guessing what to do next.

The traditional invoice remains the most recognisable artefact in global commerce. Show: a small firm in Manchester sends an invoice to a supplier in Hamburg with explicit line items, VAT details, and a SEPA transfer instruction. Name: the Single Euro Payments Area, standardised across the EU since 2008, is designed for predictability. Explain: its structure provides a shared grammar—IBAN, BIC, due date—that reduces misinterpretation. Implication: when rails are harmonised, the invoice becomes a contract, not a conversation. Yet this stability can falter once payments escape regional zones. A freelancer in Nairobi invoicing a US client confronts ABA routing numbers, intermediary banks, and wires that may settle in two days or four. What was once a standardised request mutates into a puzzle. The invoice does its job; the rail introduces noise.

Payment links emerged to compress that noise. Show: a musician in Seoul sends a link through a licensed exchange in March 2023. The client in Vancouver clicks it, selects CAD or USDC, and pays. Name: platforms like Stripe (est. 2010, San Francisco) or Bitso (est. 2014, Mexico City) made such flows mainstream. Explain: the link unifies the request and the method into a single action. It reduces optionality to a curated set that the recipient can execute without prior setup. Implication: links shift cognitive labour from the payer to the system. They also shift ambiguity into structure. The payer chooses a rail, not a format.

QR codes then add immediacy. A producer in Buenos Aires receives a QR-based payment from a domestic wallet in seconds because the code encodes both destination and amount. The Mondato Report (2021) tracked near-instant QR settlement in Brazil's Pix system, demonstrating how the visual interface hides a deeper message routing standard. Show → Name → Explain → Implication: QR is not decoration;

it is a compressed address. It limits error. Yet QR alone does not guarantee clarity. A QR that encodes only an address without an amount still requires the payer to type numbers. A QR that is static across multiple transactions risks reuse tracking on-chain. The form is fast; the content must still be precise.

Two named, checkable examples anchor the dynamic more sharply. In August 2021, India's Unified Payments Interface (UPI) crossed three billion monthly transactions, driven largely by QR-based merchant payments. The visibility of a code at the point of sale removed ambiguity and increased throughput. Meanwhile, in 2020, PayPal's global rollout of QR payments enabled small shops in London and Dublin to request digital settlement without reconfiguring their infrastructure. Both examples show that when the request is standardised, behaviour changes. People pay faster because they understand immediately what is required.

But a credible limitation tempers the enthusiasm. Not all clients accept links or QR codes. A large firm in Toronto may mandate PDF invoices for its accounting workflow. A government contractor in Sydney may require numeric line items and a purchase order reference. A cultural norm in Tokyo might still prioritise bank transfers with formal documentation. Reconciling this limitation requires recognising that clarity does not mean abandoning traditional formats; it means structuring them. Keep the invoice for compliance. Attach the link for convenience. Offer the QR for speed. Let the payer choose, but frame the choice cleanly.

Every abstraction must tie to a visible behaviour. Where we speak of *trust*, point to a metric: the proportion of invoices requiring client clarification. Where we discuss *efficiency*, point to decisions: whether the payer needs to open two applications to complete a request. Where we note *risk*, point to observable misfires: wrong account details, underpaid amounts, or transfers initiated to outdated addresses. Behaviour reveals structure.

Threading our motif again: clarity. It appears in the structure of a template request. A well-made template reduces the back-and-forth that devours hours. It states the amount, the preferred currency, the due date, and the supported rails. Show: a writer in Cape Town embeds a one-paragraph "payment block" in every invoice—IBAN, USDC address, QR for local wallet, and link for international clients. Name: she created this standard after a delayed settlement in December 2020 caused her to miss a utility payment. Explain: the block preempts questions. Implication: she now receives settlement within 24 hours in most cases. The template became a quiet negotiation tool.

By contrast, when the request is vague, delays creep in. "Pay me however is easiest" sounds courteous but creates uncertainty. The payer becomes the decision-maker, often choosing a rail that introduces hidden costs or slow settlement. The motif returns: clarity is not rigidity. It is direction. It guides the payer to the rail that aligns with your needs, not theirs.

To anchor another named example: in 2022, the Central Bank of Nigeria reported that small merchants using QR-coded requests through the eNaira system reduced settlement negotiation time by several minutes per transaction. Meanwhile, in Mexico, Mercado Pago's QR ecosystem showed that dynamic codes (one code per transaction) dropped reconciliation mistakes compared with static codes reused across days. These data points matter not because they are large numbers but because they illustrate behaviour: people pay correctly when they understand what is being asked.

A credible counter-example shows the limits. In rural areas with weak connectivity, QR codes may fail to load or links may time out. A business in Oaxaca relying solely on QR would face real operational issues. Reconciling this means designing redundancy: if a QR fails, the link remains; if the link fails, the invoice stands; if connectivity fails, an offline cash protocol may still be the fallback. Clarity is not dependent on digital channels alone. It is a mindset applied across them.

Across all rails, one pattern holds: the clearer the request, the faster the settlement. This is not a slogan but an observable dynamic. The ask shapes the flow. The specification reduces the variables. The structure eliminates misinterpretation.

Every example in this subchapter converges on a single unresolved question—the forward test: *What is the minimum information your payer needs to settle without writing back to you?* Answering that question is the hinge on which your payment reliability turns.

Currencies and pricing clarity

In October 2021, in a café off Avenida Paulista in São Paulo, Camila quoted a logo design at "R$1,500 or 250 USDT, whichever is easier". Her New York client nodded over Zoom, grateful to have options. A week later, the invoice landed. The client chose the dollar stablecoin. By then, the exchange rate had shifted. The client sent 250 USDT. The Brazilian gateway converted at its own spread, minus fees. The reais that arrived in Camila's account were closer to R$1,380. Not a catastrophe, but enough to sour the job. Both believed they had honoured the deal. They had not agreed on the same *unit*. The number itself looked innocent. It sat on the invoice, appearing crisp, modern, flexible. Yet the ambiguity was already baked in. Was the true price 250 units of a dollar token, regardless of what that meant in Brazil on settlement day? Or was the true price R$1,500, with the token merely a vehicle to get there? Neither party had written that down. The conflict did not come from volatility alone; it came from unclear anchoring. They had tried to be generous with rails and careless with currency.

The motif that will run quietly through this subchapter is the *anchor*. When you ask to be paid, the anchor is the unit in which both you and the payer understand value. Rails can vary. Methods can multiply. But if the anchor is vague, every variation becomes a potential argument. If the anchor is clear, multiplicity becomes freedom instead of friction.

The first claim is straightforward: quote in the unit your counterparty actually uses to think. Show: a copywriter in Warsaw works mostly with clients in Berlin and Amsterdam. She prices her work in euros, even though her local costs are in złoty and she is open to receiving USDC, SEPA transfers, or card payouts. Name this choice: a *pricing currency*. Explain it: the euro acts as the reference everyone understands—clients see a familiar number, her accounting app can convert cleanly, and disputes about "how much this was meant to be in dollars" simply do not arise. The implication is measurable in behaviour. Fewer clarification emails. Fewer "just to check, at which rate?" messages. Faster acceptance.

Compare that with a developer in Lagos who quotes a project at "₦800,000, payable in naira, dollars, or stablecoins". His London client has never thought in naira. To them, the figure is abstract. They mentally convert to pounds. If they later pay in USDC without an explicit anchor, both sides will check at least three reference rates—Google, their bank, and the exchange they happen to use. Three screens, three slightly different numbers, one latent argument. Here, the pricing currency was chosen for the sender's convenience, not the client's comprehension. The anchor does not hold.

A dual-price approach can resolve this without sacrificing local relevance. Camila could have written: "Fee: R$1,500 (reference: US$280 at BRL 5.36/US$1 as of 3 October 2021)." The reais remain the true anchor; the dollar amount is a translation, not a second truth. The stablecoin, if used, is simply a rail that must deliver roughly US$280's worth at settlement time. The implication is subtle but profound: everyone sees which number governs the relationship.

The second claim: accepting multiple rails only works when the pricing currency is stable across them. Show: a translator in Buenos Aires charges US$200 for a technical document. She allows clients to pay via SWIFT, PayPal, or a dollar-pegged stablecoin. Name the structure: *multi-rail, single-anchor*. Explain: the client chooses the rail based on ease and cost, but the dollar amount is fixed. Conversion into pesos happens after receipt, on her own terms. The implication is practical. Her income statement speaks one language. The pipes may differ, but the figure that appears at the top of her month remains coherent.

Contrast this with a counter-example from Istanbul. A photographer offers "US$400, €370, or 0.015 BTC" for a wedding shoot, listing all three as if they were equivalent. In January, when BTC rises, clients feel they are overpaying in bitcoin and insist on euros. When BTC falls, some push to pay in BTC, arguing that the quote was explicit. The photographer finds himself running a de facto currency desk. He has three anchors. Each moves. Each attracts opportunism. The limitation becomes obvious: multiple pricing currencies turn every project into a negotiation about timing instead of work.

Reconciling this is simple in principle, harder in habit: pick one anchor, state it, and treat everything else as translation. If you genuinely wish to lock a quote in bitcoin, then say so and accept that you are taking on a trader's exposure. If that is not your expertise, let bitcoin be a rail, not a yardstick. The anchor should be the unit that both parties can state without opening an exchange app.

This leads to the third claim: clarity about *when* the anchor applies is as important as which unit you choose. Show: a software consultant in Nairobi agrees a fee of US$3,000 for a three-month project with a client in Paris. Name the parameter: quote date. Explain: if both parties agree that the amount is fixed at the contract date and the client pays in a different currency later, any FX fluctuation is the client's responsibility. If, instead, they implicitly assume the amount will be converted at whatever rate applies on payment day, exposure shifts. The implication is behavioural. A client who understands that they bear conversion risk tends to pay sooner; one who assumes the provider will absorb the difference may delay until it is convenient, not caring what the market does in between.

Dual-pricing can encode this timing question. A small clause—"Amounts quoted in EUR; if settled in another currency, conversion will reference ECB closing rate on invoice date"—takes seconds to write and can prevent weeks of sour email. For stablecoins, something similar: "If paying in USDC or USDT, please send the equivalent of €1,200 at the market rate visible on [named reference] at the time of payment." The anchor remains the euro. The dual note instructs how to use the rail in alignment with that anchor.

The motif of the anchor appears again when we examine disputes. Many payment disagreements are not about absolute figures; they are about mismatched expectations. A client expected "about £500". A freelancer expected "no less than £540 after fees". A donor thought they were giving "roughly US$50". The resolution often involves going back through email chains, trying to deduce what each party was thinking. A clear anchor, stated once and not quietly modified mid-stream, shrinks this gap. The question becomes: did we both agree to this number, in this unit, at this time?

Two named institutional examples illustrate how anchors stabilise behaviour at scale. In the eurozone's early years, EU consumer-protection rules encouraged shops to display prices simultaneously in legacy national currencies and euros during the transition period. The euro was the anchor; dual pricing in francs or marks reassured consumers without undermining the reference unit. Similarly, when El Salvador adopted bitcoin as legal tender in 2021, many businesses continued to list prices in US dollars, even while accepting bitcoin payments via the Chivo wallet. The dollar remained the psychological anchor; bitcoin functioned as a rail. In both cases, misunderstandings were reduced not by technology but by signage. The number on the sticker mattered more than the app in the customer's hand.

There is, however, a real limitation to this tidy story: in high-inflation environments, local currencies can lose anchoring power. A designer in Caracas may struggle to quote in bolívares at all because their purchasing power decays within weeks. For them, anchoring in dollars or in a relatively stable regional currency like the Brazilian real may be the only way to maintain continuity. Local clients may resist; authorities may have preferences; platforms may vary in support. Here, the anchor becomes a quiet act of resistance against chaos. The reconciliation lies in transparency. If you must index your life to a foreign unit, make that explicit in your pricing language rather than pretending that local figures mean what they no longer do.

Behaviour is where this abstraction becomes concrete. A copywriter who quotes consistently in euros and tracks income in that unit will tend to schedule conversions and hedges around that figure. A developer who flips between quoting in local currency, then in dollars, then "in whatever coin you prefer" spends more time reconciling than coding. A small agency that agrees to be paid "in whatever currency suits the client" without a specified anchor will spend much of its energy re-understanding the value of its own work.

The motif of the anchor completes one more loop when we consider mental health. Underpricing does not always happen because markets are unfair. It often happens because the worker has not fixed their own reference. When you anchor properly—"My day rate is £600, regardless of rail"—you have a yardstick against which to accept or decline projects. Without it, every quotation is a guess, and every payment leaves a trace of doubt. That uncertainty corrodes confidence over time.

The unresolved tension, then, is not technical. It is personal. *Which unit, if written on a whiteboard above your desk, would make both you and your best clients say, "Yes, that is what this work is worth" – and how will you ensure that every rail, token, and transfer that touches your life bends back to that anchor rather than dragging you quietly away from it?*

Volatility buffers

On 24 June 2016, the morning after the United Kingdom's referendum on EU membership, sterling fell more than 8 per cent against the US dollar before midday. The speed was startling; the effect on people paid across borders was immediate. A freelance developer in Manchester, invoicing a New York client for US$2,000, watched the expected pound value of her payment swing by over £120 between sunrise and lunch. Her rent was fixed in pounds; her work was priced in dollars. She had not changed a thing. The market had. That jolt, felt in a single morning, revealed a deeper truth: earning across currencies means living with movements you do not choose. *Noise* was the motif that entered her life that day. She needed a way to mute it.

She began, tentatively, by converting funds as soon as they arrived, trying to force each payment into the currency she used to measure her obligations. Some days she gained a little. Some days she lost a little. Over time, she realised she had turned her working life into a guessing game she could not win. What she lacked was not discipline, but a buffer—a small, mechanical routine that separated the chaos of settlement from the calmer choices of treasury. A few months later, she adopted a simple internal rule: split each payment, immediately and predictably, into portions that served different purposes. Her earnings steadied. Noise receded.

The first claim is visible in behaviour: people who receive income through multiple rails or currencies need a boundary between what arrives and what stays. Show: a translator in Warsaw is paid €800 in SEPA transfers, USDC from overseas clients, and złoty from domestic institutions. Name the difficulty: intraday variance. Explain: each rail delivers value at slightly different times and with slightly different conversion spreads; holding everything in limbo invites swings that have nothing to do with the work performed. The implication is stark. A week's rent can shrink or swell simply because a client in Boston pays on Thursday rather than Tuesday. A buffer is not a hedge against catastrophe; it is a decision to withdraw from the emotional churn of hourly rates.

A disciplined split—say, 50 per cent into a stable currency used for core spending, 40 per cent into a medium-term reserve, and 10 per cent kept in the unit in which the work was paid—turns that boundary into a habit. The numbers are illustrative, not prescriptive. Their power lies in routine. A writer in Nairobi who adopted a similar pattern in 2022 described the relief of "not checking the chart before breakfast any more". She no longer speculated. She separated. The buffer absorbed the noise.

The second claim tightens the motif: buffers depend on choosing a treasury currency. Show: in Buenos Aires in 2023, a designer charging overseas clients in US dollars converted half of every payment into dollars for rent and food, placing the remainder into pesos for local commitments. Name the structure: settlement versus treasury. Explain: the currency of settlement is whatever the client sends; the treasury currency is what the worker uses to plan their life. Without that separation, every incoming payment becomes an implicit bet on a market. The implication is easy to measure. A person who treats each payment as a bet refreshes exchange charts dozens of times a week. A person who treats treasury as stable refreshes fewer times, keeps steadier accounts, and commits to work rather than guessing the direction of a graph. Now, a limitation: not all contexts allow neat splits. In Caracas or Istanbul, where inflation distorts local pricing, the treasury currency may itself be contested. A business owner may need to hold revenue temporarily in stablecoins or foreign currency before converting into local units for taxes and utilities. The principle still holds, but the comfort of a fixed split may not. Reconciling this demands honesty. The buffer cannot eliminate volatility; it merely dulls its sharpest edges. In unstable settings, the split may need more frequent revision, but the separation of settlement and treasury remains sound.

The third claim builds outward: buffers reduce disputes with clients because they stabilise the worker's own expectations. Show: a photographer in Lisbon quotes €600 for a weekend job. She accepts payment via card, SEPA, or USDT. Name the anchor: the euro amount. Explain: when she allocates her receipt—half into euros, the rest into her choice of reserve and operating funds—she no longer cares whether the stablecoin rate wobbles slightly at the hour of receipt. She has a routine. The implication: fewer negotiations over exchange rates, fewer emails about "what you actually received", and quicker closure for all parties. The buffer is not for clients. It is for the worker who wants to stop translating every number into anxiety.

Historical examples show how institutions adopt similar principles at scale. The European Central Bank's monthly rebalancing reports have, since the early 2000s, outlined how member states smooth currency exposures by separating daily operations from longer-term reserves. That distinction—fluid settlement versus anchored stores—mirrors the individual's task. Likewise, during Nigeria's 2020–2022 fluctuations in the naira–dollar rate, small exporters interviewed by the Centre for the Study of the Economies of

Africa (CSEA 2022) described how allocating set proportions of earnings into dollars before converting the remainder into naira helped them maintain payroll without constant repricing. Institutions and individuals converge: buffers are routine, not speculation.

Behavioural evidence reinforces this. A freelancer who immediately commits a portion of receipts to the currency of obligations tends to check balances less often; one who holds the full amount in the payment currency until "a good moment" tends to defer decisions, giving volatility more room to sting. A predictable, almost mechanical pattern dulls the impulse to time the market, an impulse that rarely serves those whose primary skill is work, not currency arbitrage. *Noise quietens when you pre-commit.*

The fourth claim concerns emotional steadiness. Show: a developer in Manila receives payments in both USDT and pesos. In late 2021, during a period of high crypto volatility, she found herself anxious every time a payment landed. Name the strain: reactive treasury. Explain: by holding each receipt entirely in the rail of arrival, she exposed her income to movements irrelevant to her household expenses. When she adopted a 50–40–10 split, with the majority converted into pesos for bills, a portion kept in dollars for predictable imports, and a small slice left in crypto for experimentation, her mood steadied. She stopped refreshing prices obsessively. The implication is human, not financial. Buffers allow attention to return to work, family, and planning rather than chasing moments of misplaced precision.

A counter-example clarifies the boundary. During bitcoin's surge in early 2021, some freelancers insisted on being paid entirely in bitcoin and held the full amount untouched. Some gained dramatically. Others absorbed painful drawdowns later in the year. The lesson is not that holding a volatile asset is wrong; it is that treating earnings as an investment without a buffer converts professional income into personal risk.

Reconciling this does not require avoiding volatility entirely. It requires ring-fencing the portion you can afford to let fluctuate. A buffer ensures that the roof stays repaired and the fridge stays full even when markets lurch.

The motif of noise returns when we consider record-keeping. A stable split simplifies books. A quarterly export of transaction data—structured by your chosen treasury currency—keeps statements intelligible. Without such order, accounts become a collage of rails, symbols, and timestamps that need decoding. With order, reconciliation becomes a matter of minutes. Noise fades.

The unresolved tension is not whether to use a buffer but how strict to make it. *Which proportion, if applied to your next payment, would give you the calm needed to work without glancing at charts—and which part of you still resists committing to that routine?

Platform risk and portability

In November 2022, when FTX filed for Chapter 11 bankruptcy protection in Delaware, thousands of freelancers and small firms discovered that their invoices, payout histories, and even client contact details were locked behind a platform that had just collapsed. Some had relied on its internal messaging for client communication; others had stored months of billing data solely inside the exchange. A designer in Cebu, who had used FTX Pay to receive USDC from US clients, learned within hours that she could no longer retrieve her November invoices. She lost no funds, but she lost *records*. That was enough to disrupt her tax filings, slow repayments on a small family loan, and force awkward exchanges with clients who assumed she kept her own copies. Her dependence had not looked dangerous until the morning it broke. One platform, one failure, one shock.

The story repeated, in quieter form, when PayPal froze accounts belonging to several independent journalists in the United Kingdom in July 2022, citing policy reviews later reversed. Each held separate backups, yet the temporary freeze revealed a structural fragility: the moment a single intermediary governs your ability to prove what you earned, you have ceded more than convenience. You have surrendered autonomy. Portability, in contrast, is not a preference. It is a defence.

The first claim begins with what the designer in Cebu experienced: the fragility of one platform holding too many pieces of one's working life. Show the behaviour: she had kept her invoice templates, client wallet addresses, and delivery confirmations solely inside a single interface. Name the risk: concentrated custody. Explain: when all operational artefacts live on one platform—whether an exchange, payment processor, or freelance marketplace—the worker becomes exposed to outages, policy shifts, and discontinuities that have nothing to do with their work. The implication is measurable. A single outage at Stripe in March 2023 delayed thousands of payouts for hours; for workers operating week-to-week, delays create cashflow strain measurable in missed rent deadlines or postponed utility payments. Portability is the countermeasure. You export what you control.

A second claim extends this: platform risk grows invisibly when convenience disguises ownership boundaries. Show: in 2021, Coinbase introduced internal messaging for merchants using Coinbase Commerce. Many merchants embraced it, shifting client communication from email to platform chat. Name the hazard: information captivity. Explain: internal messaging seems harmless until a client disputes a charge months later. If the correspondence sits solely inside the platform and access is interrupted, the merchant has lost the evidentiary trail. The implication is more than administrative inconvenience. In a dispute, the person with records wins the argument because evidence beats recollection. A quarterly data export—contacts, invoices, settlement receipts—provides the evidentiary spine the merchant controls, not the platform.

A limitation sharpens the lesson. Some ecosystems, particularly in low-fee P2P markets such as Binance P2P in Lagos or Karachi, rely on internal identifiers and platform-bound chat threads to negotiate trades. Exporting this data is clumsy. Some platforms do not offer clean export tools. Reconciling this requires adaptation. When an export is not available, workers can snapshot message IDs, store counterparties' bank details in local notes, and duplicate the essential metadata (amount, timestamp, counterparty) into simple spreadsheets. The procedure may feel inelegant, but it restores a fragment of autonomy where the platform offers little.

A quiet motif emerges: *copies*. Copies that travel with you. Copies that do not depend on a single firm's uptime. Copies that defend you when memory fails or policies shift. The difference between the worker who keeps copies and the one who trusts a platform to remember is the difference between resilience and exposure.

The third claim concerns architectural design. Show: a writer in Edinburgh uses Payoneer to receive USD from American publishers, Wise to receive GBP from UK clients, and an Ethereum wallet for occasional stablecoin payments. Name the discipline: multi-rail redundancy. Explain: her choice to diversify is not about speculation but survivability. If Payoneer conducts a compliance review, she has alternatives. If Wise modifies its fee tables or introduces new onboarding constraints, she is not trapped. The implication reveals itself in behaviour. She commits to a quarterly export ritual across all services, storing CSVs in an offline encrypted archive and keeping a local address book of client payment details. None of this takes more than half an hour every three months, yet each export immunises her from the brittleness of single-platform dependency.

A counter-example tests the principle. Some workers prize simplicity above robustness. A videographer in Porto insists on using only PayPal because it is "what everyone already has". His invoices, messages, and recurring billing all pass through one system. He prefers the minimal cognitive load. The risk is invisible: should PayPal initiate a review or request additional documentation—a scenario many experienced during policy tightening in 2022—he faces immediate freezes and cannot redirect clients quickly. Simplicity is attractive, but single-platform simplicity becomes fragility. To reconcile this, one need not abandon convenience. One diversifies quietly. Keeping parallel rails in reserve is enough to ensure continuity if the preferred rail wavers.

The motif of *copies* returns. A platform outage is inconvenient if you have copies; it is catastrophic if you do not. A platform policy change is irritating if you can migrate within an hour; it is disabling if your operational life is trapped inside the platform's walls.

A fourth claim follows naturally: portability strengthens negotiation power. Show: an illustrator in Melbourne provides clients with two settlement options: a bank transfer via the domestic New Payments Platform and a USDC transfer to a wallet she controls. Name the dynamic: multi-rail optionality. Explain: because her contact and invoice history lives in her own storage, she can shift rails immediately if fees spike or if a client's preferred rail becomes unreliable. The implication is strategic. When platforms know their users can leave, they tend to behave with more restraint during policy changes. When users cannot leave, platforms tend to accumulate friction—slow support queues, opaque reviews, non-negotiable fees—because the user's captivity removes the incentive to improve.

History provides examples at national scale. When Kenya's M-Pesa system experienced repeated outages in 2018, the Central Bank of Kenya encouraged the development of alternative mobile money services such as Airtel Money. Users who maintained parallel accounts moved fluidly between systems. Those who kept everything inside M-Pesa endured delays in bill payments and merchant receipts for days. Copies and alternatives again determined resilience.

A limitation tempers the optimism. Some platforms, especially early-stage fintechs, may not yet offer export tools or interoperable data formats. Their APIs may be unstable or restricted. Workers operating in these ecosystems face genuine friction. Reconciliation requires a pragmatic workaround: record essential metadata at the moment of settlement. Timestamp, amount, counterparty, rail. Simple. The copy does not need beauty. It needs permanence.

The fifth claim concerns narrative identity: portability is not only technical but reputational. Show: a consultant in Berlin maintains a stable identity book—her clients' names, the rails they prefer, their billing cycles, and their invoicing quirks—stored outside any single payment system. Name the principle: external memory. Explain: when a platform rebrands, restructures, or retires features, she does not lose the interpersonal infrastructure of her business. The implication is visible in transition periods. In 2023, when Wise shifted some borderless account routing numbers, those who kept external records updated their templates in minutes. Those who relied on Wise's internal saved details scrambled to match old identifiers with new ones. Portability is not simply digital; it is relational.

The motif of *copies* appears again. A business with copies cannot be erased by a platform's decisions, because its identity is not stored solely in someone else's server.

The sixth claim connects portability to law and compliance without offering legal advice. Show: an entrepreneur in Toronto exporting data quarterly reduces audit risk because she can produce clear, time-stamped records irrespective of platform retention policies. Name the compliance angle: evidentiary independence. Explain: some platforms purge old data after a set period; others compress transaction histories in ways that remove context. By keeping her own records—downloaded CSVs, PDF invoices, contact books—she ensures continuity. The implication is straightforward. During a review, regulators will ask for proof of receipts, not proof of loyalty to a platform.

A limitation deserves acknowledgement. Exporting data into personal archives introduces security responsibilities. Stored copies can be lost, stolen, or mishandled. Reconciling this requires simple operational hygiene: encrypted storage, offline backups, and minimising the personally identifiable information kept. The balance is clear. Copies that protect you must also be protected by you.

Platform risk, then, is not theoretical. It is woven into the structure of digital work. Concentrated custody, information captivity, and reactive policy shifts are the daily realities of relying on intermediaries that serve millions of users with opaque internal processes. Portability is the opposite posture: a stance of self-respect, where your records, contacts, and operational rhythms remain yours even when rails or platforms change around you.

The unresolved tension sits at a practical edge: How much redundancy is enough? One export schedule per quarter? Multiple rails for every client? A backup of every message or only those tied to invoices? Portability asks for judgement. What is the smallest set of copies that would allow you to work tomorrow morning if your preferred platform vanished at dawn—and which copies will you commit to making before it does?

Chapter 7
Spending, Subscriptions, and Commerce

The woman in front of the hotel kiosk at Schiphol Airport looked exhausted, but the problem on her phone was simple enough: the airline wanted a card, her wallet held only a stablecoin balance, and the check-in timer was counting down in red. She toggled through screens, swiped once, and watched her card-backed wallet spin up a virtual number. Seconds later, the booking cleared and the gate opened. No drama, no cash exchange, no sprint to an ATM. A balance held on a decentralised rail had just paid for a seat on a conventional flight. The boundary between the two systems, once sharp, now dissolves in the space of a swipe.

Moments like these expose a truth many users feel but rarely articulate: spending is the most *physical* expression of a financial system's design. Receiving money can be asynchronous, buffered, delayed; spending is immediate, embodied, and often public. It is the point where rails meet reality. Yet this is also where frictions accumulate. A subscription renewed without warning. A card declined abroad. A merchant that accepts one rail but not another. A refund process that assumes the user lives inside a particular banking system. Each friction hints at a deeper question: how should a modern wallet move through the world's shops, apps, and marketplaces without leaving its owner tangled in fees, disputes, or uncertainty?

Commerce, at street level and screen level, has absorbed a degree of complexity that workers and travellers now feel daily. Digital proxies—cards, QR codes, virtual numbers, token approvals—make it possible to buy anything from anywhere, but each carries different protections, risks, and data footprints. Some strengthen privacy; others leak it. Some allow reversals; others behave like digital cash. And subscriptions, once rare, now form streams of small, cumulative obligations. A film platform here, a design tool there, a monthly storage plan that no one quite remembers approving. They nibble away at attention first and cashflow later. The quiet motif of *control* emerges: not dominance, but clarity—knowing what pulls on your balance, and when.

The chapter enters this terrain because spending is where the borderless wallet either proves its value or betrays its owner. The freedom to remit or receive cross-border funds means little if the act of paying for dinner with colleagues, renewing a work licence, or covering a family subscription triggers anxiety. The architecture of spending deserves as much thought as the architecture of earning. Traditional banks once mediated these decisions through a single debit card and a monthly statement; the modern user navigates a constellation of proxies, each with different rules. The path you choose—card-backed rails, token-based approvals, QR-initiated transfers—shapes not just cost but your exposure to recurring commitments and dispute mechanisms.

Within this field, subscriptions deserve special scrutiny because they invert the spending dynamic. Instead of a conscious act, a subscription is an agreement to spend in the future, often silently. It must be fenced with limits: virtual cards that expire, allowance wallets that cap usage, small barriers that force intentionality. Without these boundaries, digital commerce turns into a form of erosion—imperceptible at first, costly over time. The tension between convenience and commitment touches every user, from the freelancer who tracks half a dozen software tools to the family abroad rationing shared streaming accounts across currencies.

Then there is the matter of protection. Chargebacks in card networks operate with procedural gravity; they demand evidence, timelines, and patience. Some rails offer nothing similar. Once a transaction settles, the money is gone unless the counterparty cooperates. Users must understand these differences long before trouble arrives. A subscription dispute handled through a card network may take days but ultimately resolves; the same dispute over a wallet transfer may require negotiation rather than formal process. The trade-off between certainty and speed, between reversible and final, is the unseen architecture beneath every checkout button.

And beneath all this lies memory. Receipts, tax categories, and notes are not administrative chores but structural supports. A tagged meal clarifies whether it belonged to business or pleasure. A photo of a paper receipt anchors a future claim. A short note written at the moment of purchase—client name, project code, purpose—turns chaos into order months later. These small acts of documentation are not pedantic; they are precise tools for clarity, the same clarity that the designer in the previous chapter preserved by keeping her own copies. Here, clarity defends against disputes, tax confusion, and the creeping blur of digital commerce.

The world of spending evolves faster than the norms that once stabilised it. Payment rails change. Refund expectations shift. Subscription models multiply. Merchants migrate to new processors without warning. And users, living across borders and platforms, must decide how to maintain agency rather than be swept along by defaults. The question that hangs, unresolved but essential, is simple: how do you construct a spending architecture that bends with circumstance but never breaks? Turn the page, and the pieces will begin to align.

Cards, codes, and tokens

The booking desk at Schiphol Airport was closing in twelve minutes when Sofia Delgado, a software researcher from Buenos Aires, realised the airline's payment portal rejected her local debit card. It was July 2023, and she had already spent an hour navigating the airport's patchy Wi-Fi and the airline's rotating list of "accepted cards". Her balance sat in a multi-asset wallet; her travel funds were in a dollar-denominated stablecoin. What she lacked was a payment instrument the airline recognised. She opened her wallet app, generated a fresh virtual card number, and authorised the transaction. The page refreshed, the boarding pass appeared, and she exhaled. Five keystrokes had bridged two financial systems that otherwise refused to talk to each other. *One bridge. One context. One result.*

Scenes like this reveal a structural truth about modern spending: the point of payment is rarely a neutral moment. It is a negotiation between rails with different histories, rules, and expectations. A merchant terminal built to process legacy cards. A mobile checkout that accepts only select processors. A smart contract that requires a token approval rather than a card swipe. Each payment environment demands a different shape of proxy, and users who grasp these shapes move with unusual fluency. Those who do not often pay—in delays, fees, or exposure.

Cards, virtual numbers, and token approvals are not competing philosophies; they are instruments designed for different terrains. A physical card interacts with global networks such as Visa or Mastercard. A virtual number, bound to a specific use or merchant, limits exposure while preserving convenience. A token approval authorises movement on decentralised rails invisible to most conventional merchants. The motif that threads through them is *fit*: the alignment between the tool and the context in which it is deployed.

Physical cards have held their place for decades because they offer one quality that no decentralised format can fully replicate: merchant ubiquity. When Visa launched its global authorisation system in the late 1970s, it created a template for point-of-sale interoperability that persists today. The behaviour linked to this system is simple enough: present the card, authenticate, and settle against a balance or credit line later. The implication is both freeing and limiting. With a card, a user can pay at nearly any terminal in Singapore or São

Paulo. But the card also reveals information to multiple parties—the issuer, the network, the merchant—and reconciliation depends on intermediaries. Convenience comes with a data trail.

Virtual numbers modify this equation. In 2016, the U.S. bank Capital One introduced single-use virtual numbers for e-commerce, allowing customers to generate disposable card credentials tied to their main account. The behaviour shifted: instead of handing over a persistent number, the user generated a short-lived proxy. Risk, measured as exposure to card theft or recurring billing, fell sharply. The implication for wallets backed by digital assets is clear. A virtual card number, created from a crypto-funded wallet, converts a decentralised balance into a recognised payment instrument without revealing the underlying rail. It keeps the bridge narrow. It also allows users to sandbox merchants—approve only what is needed, revoke when done.

Token approvals operate differently. They belong to decentralised systems such as Ethereum, where spending requires explicit permission. In January 2022, the blockchain analytics firm Nansen published a report documenting how token approvals, once granted, linger until cancelled. The behaviour is plain: a user wishing to pay a decentralised application for a service must approve the movement of a specific token. The implication is subtle but important. Token approvals offer precision—approve this token, for this purpose, up to this limit—but they also create potential exposure if forgotten. They demand habits: check granted permissions, prune those no longer needed, treat approvals like keys rather than casual clicks.

Settling across these proxies requires attention to cost, delay, and data exposure. A card transaction may settle within a day or two, depending on issuer and region. A virtual number tied to a prepaid wallet often settles instantly from the user's perspective because the wallet deducts funds immediately. A token approval leads to an on-chain transaction whose settlement time depends on network congestion and gas fees. The behaviour difference is visible in the metrics. In a May 2023 congestion event on Ethereum, average confirmation time rose from twelve seconds to several minutes. A card payment in the same period might complete in under five seconds at the point of sale, even if final settlement occurred later. The user pays with time in one context and with data in the other.

Two historical examples illustrate how proxies evolve. In October 2012, Square launched its first Card Case product in San Francisco, allowing customers to pay by name through the merchant's iPad—a precursor to modern wallet-based payments. The behaviour was frictionless, but dependence on a centralised database limited its reach. In January 2021, Visa settled a transaction between Anchorage Digital and Crypto.com using USDC on Ethereum, proving that a card network could use a stablecoin for its own treasury flows. The implication was structural. Traditional networks could rely on decentralised assets behind the scenes while preserving familiar card behaviour for customers. The bridge did not replace the card; it strengthened it.

Yet proxies have limits. Some merchants ban prepaid cards. Some websites flag virtual numbers as "fraud-prone". Some decentralised applications require permissions that users struggle to revoke. The counter-example forces a deeper reconciliation: no proxy is universally optimal. The correct choice depends on the transaction's stakes, the counterparties involved, and the user's own tolerance for data exposure or operational risk. Fit, again.

Consider the motif of the bridge. Each proxy is a bridge between two systems—the balance you hold and the world you interact with. A physical card bridges legacy merchant networks. A virtual number bridges an online checkout without exposing the main account. A token approval bridges decentralised logic with user intent. The strength of each bridge lies in its alignment with the terrain. Choosing poorly is like driving an articulated lorry across a footbridge or walking across a motorway. Choosing well is almost invisible—smooth, efficient, uneventful.

Sofia's experience at Schiphol proves the point. She did not debate the philosophy of digital rails. She measured the problem's constraints—an airline that required a card, a balance stored in a wallet, a deadline approaching—and she acted. Her virtual number became a narrow, targeted bridge. Her physical card, issued by a local bank, stayed in her pocket. The token approvals she used for decentralised marketplaces earlier that week stayed untouched. Fit shaped the outcome.

As proxies proliferate, users must monitor their footprints. A physical card reveals transaction metadata to several entities. A virtual number narrows exposure but may still require disclosure to the merchant's processor. A token approval creates an immutable on-chain record visible to analytics firms. The right proxy protects against unnecessary exposure; the wrong one leaves footprints where none were needed.

This leaves a lingering question that no single chapter can resolve: in a world of expanding proxies and converging rails, how should a user decide which bridge to cross at any given moment?

Subscriptions and limits

When the UK's Competition and Markets Authority (CMA) published its July 2022 review into digital subscription practices, one statistic unsettled even seasoned analysts: Britons were paying for an estimated *£1.6 billion* of unused or forgotten subscriptions each year. The figure was not a theoretical projection; it was drawn from surveyed households across England, Scotland, and Wales. It captured something structural—the quiet, cumulative creep of recurring costs that slip beneath conscious attention. The CMA's report opened with a case study from Manchester: a customer who believed he held four active subscriptions but, when prompted to check, discovered thirteen. The difference between perceived cost and real cost was not a rounding error. It was the difference between agency and drift.

The lure of subscription billing lies in its rhetoric of convenience. Netflix, which introduced its UK streaming service in January 2012, offered a frictionless £5.99 monthly fee that required no renegotiation, no fresh consent, just uninterrupted entertainment. A decade later, the model had metastasised across fitness apps, cloud storage, productivity tools, software plug-ins, recipe boxes, and online news. The motif that threads through these expansions is a quiet one: *continuity*. Subscriptions promise continuity of service, but the real continuity—the one that matters to your balance—is the automatic continuity of payment.

This chapter segment focuses on something more constructive than critique: it examines the mechanisms that restore proportionality to recurring spending. Caps, expiry-bound cards, and allowance wallets are not moral defences against temptation; they are operational levers. They turn attention into structure and structure into guardrails. They also reveal a broader theme in modern money management: the move from intuition to instrumentation.

Consider the behaviour visible in monthly bank statements. A line for a gym membership in Bristol in use since 2018. Another for a video editing plug-in billed in California. A cluster of micropayments for cloud storage in Dublin. The pattern is rarely malicious. It is behavioural entropy—a small legal contract renewed, silently, twelve times a year. The implication is clear. If the user does not impose boundaries, the subscription imposes them instead, both on spending and on attention.

The first major claim is simple: *recurrence requires containment*. The technique that best illustrates this is the expenditure cap. Revolut, the London-based financial technology firm, rolled out merchant-specific spending caps in its UK app in March 2021. Users could set a maximum allowable amount per billing cycle. The behaviour this enables is concrete: if a digital magazine raises its monthly fee without notice, the transaction fails once it crosses the set boundary. The user is notified. Friction re-enters the system at the moment it is most needed. The implication is that caps restore negotiation where subscription models try to remove it.

Yet caps alone cannot manage every nuance. Some subscriptions are unpredictable, especially those tied to usage. Cloud computing platforms such as Amazon Web Services (AWS) can generate variable bills month to month. Limits here must be paired with expiry mechanisms. When Privacy.com, a U.S.-based virtual card provider, launched single-use and merchant-locked cards in 2014, it introduced a behaviour shift: users could bind a subscription to a card set to expire after a defined period—say, ninety days. If they wanted the subscription to continue, they needed to consciously regenerate the card. The implication is subtle but powerful: expiry forces awareness without forcing commitment.

The second major claim concerns *segmentation*. A single wallet for all recurring payments becomes an undifferentiated pool. The alternative is the allowance wallet, a structure borrowed from business cost-control systems but adapted for personal use. Monzo, the UK bank founded in 2015, demonstrated this through its "pots": users could route specific subscriptions—streaming services, cloud backups, language learning apps—through a dedicated pot with a fixed monthly top-up. The behaviour is measurable. If a pot contains £40 for digital media, and the palette of subscriptions costs £47, the overshoot becomes visible immediately. No hunting through statements. No delay until the end of the month. The implication is that segmentation externalises decision-making. Instead of the user tracking small commitments mentally, the wallet enforces arithmetic.

A concrete example makes the dynamics sharper. Imagine a media bundle composed of four services: a documentary platform billed in London, a music service billed in New York, a digital newspaper billed in Berlin, and a film archive billed in Paris. The total comes to £33 per month. The user sets an allowance wallet with a strict cap of £30. When the newspaper raises its rate by €2, the wallet signals the shortfall on the next billing cycle. The user must adjust: remove a service, renegotiate the plan, or top up the wallet. The behaviour is transparent, and the implication is broader: segmentation turns creeping cost into visible cost.

Two historical examples illustrate the maturation of subscription control. In 2003, Apple launched iTunes Store purchases as discrete transactions, requiring explicit clicks rather than continuous billing. This model forced attention at the moment of expenditure but demanded more administrative friction. In 2015, Spotify introduced its Family Plan with region-specific rate controls, shifting towards predictable monthly fees. The behaviour became passive again. The lesson from these paired histories is that the pendulum swings: friction shrinks and grows depending on the era, but the user's need for visibility remains constant. Tools should reintroduce clarity without reviving outdated friction.

A credible limitation must be acknowledged. Caps, expiry cards, and allowance wallets do not solve the fundamental behavioural pattern in all cases. Users habituate. A capped wallet can become just another background system to ignore. An expiry-bound card can be renewed automatically without reflection. The counter-example forces precision: tools alone are insufficient without a periodic audit. Here is where the motif of continuity returns. Subscriptions rely on continuity of payment; control relies on continuity of review. The reconciliation is not a retreat from tooling; it is the addition of a rhythm. A monthly or quarterly check restores the function of the tool.

Metrics tighten the picture. In a 2020 report by the UK's Behavioural Insights Team, users who reviewed their subscriptions quarterly reduced redundant recurring charges by an average of 14% within six months. Not 50%. Not 80%. Fourteen. A modest figure, but grounded in human behaviour: awareness, when periodic and structured, reduces cost without demanding constant vigilance. The implication is straightforward. Limits work best when paired with a cadence.

The motif of continuity surfaces again when examining attention. Recurring payments do not merely drain funds; they drain cognitive space. A user with twenty subscriptions needs to remember renewal dates, price tiers, bundle discounts, password-linked access, and which card funds which service. Attention is finite. Every subscription consumes some of it. Caps, expiry cards, and segmented wallets serve a dual role: they protect cash and attention simultaneously.

There is also an emotional texture to recurring spending. Many users accumulate subscriptions in moments of aspiration. In January 2021, Strava reported a spike in UK sign-ups for its premium plan—fitness enthusiasm amplified by New Year commitments. By March, a notable proportion of new users were inactive. The behaviour is familiar: an ambitious intention, a recurring fee, a quiet decline in engagement. The implication is not cynical. It shows why limits and expiry structures matter. They protect users from the inertia of past enthusiasm.

A broader historical lens helps ground the argument. Subscription models are not new. In 1691, the English printer John Dunton introduced a subscription scheme for his periodical *The Athenian Gazette*, charging readers in advance for regular issues. The behaviour was transparent: money up front for content delivered weekly. What has changed is not the concept but the infrastructure. Modern subscriptions do not require renewed consent; they require only the absence of objection. The implication is stark. Tools that restore friction reintroduce a form of consent aligned with Dunton's model: regular, intentional engagement.

Yet a tension sits unresolved. As wallets, cards, and smart contracts integrate more deeply across regions and rails, subscriptions may become harder—not easier—to track. A virtual number used for a Singapore-based design tool. A token-based subscription paid through a smart contract. A recurring fiat charge routed through an app store using a hidden intermediary. Each layer adds abstraction. Each abstraction adds distance between the user and the cost.

This leads to the final question that governs the entire subchapter: in a world where recurring costs slip quietly into the background, what rhythm, what boundary, and what small structure will prevent continuity from turning into drift?

Refunds and chargebacks

When Visa published its April 2023 dispute-resolution update, one example caught attention across British consumer groups. A London customer had been charged £89 for a software subscription she believed she had cancelled months earlier. The merchant in California insisted the renewal was valid. Her bank initiated a chargeback under Visa's reason code for cancelled recurring transactions. Forty-six days later, the funds were returned. The practical outcome was simple—money restored—but the structural message was sharper: protection exists, but it has a cost measured in time, paperwork, and uncertainty. A similar dispute handled through a crypto rail with no built-in chargeback mechanism would have ended differently. The money would have stayed where it landed. Finality is *final*.

Set against the clean precision of instant settlement, the chargeback process resembles a slow legal ritual. Its steps—file, investigate, counter, adjudicate—are designed to defend cardholders, yet each step introduces friction. The motif that threads through this chapter segment is *weight*. A settlement rail either shares weight between parties or assigns it entirely to one. Card networks carry weight through reversibility. Bank transfers shift weight to banks and regulators. Public ledgers shift weight to the user alone. Knowing which rail bears which burden is not an academic exercise; it determines what happens when something goes wrong.

The first major claim concerns the visible asymmetry between *protections* and *costs*. Consider Mastercard's process for handling disputes related to "goods or services not received", codified in its 2022 rules. A consumer in Birmingham buys a research tool from a merchant in Dublin. The software fails to activate. The customer contacts the merchant. Nothing. He files a dispute. The issuing bank issues a chargeback. The behaviour here is measurable: the merchant's account is debited immediately, often before the investigation is complete, and must provide documentary evidence to reverse the decision. The implication is clear. Chargebacks create a strong consumer shield but impose administrative and financial weight on merchants, which ultimately folds back into pricing.

Contrast this with the UK's Faster Payments Service (FPS). FPS transfers, introduced in 2008, are push payments: the payer authorises, the funds move, and reversals occur only through mutual agreement or fraud investigations. A user who pays a freelancer in Brighton via FPS for a project that is never delivered has no quick dispute mechanism. The behaviour is concrete: the recipient must cooperate voluntarily. The implication is that the rail rewards speed but demands trust—

and trust, in this case, is not an abstraction but a decision about whom to pay, when, and under what conditions.

Crypto rails push this asymmetry even further. Once a transaction settles on Bitcoin or Ethereum, it becomes immutable unless the recipient initiates a return. The cancellation of a subscription paid through a smart contract in 2021 by a user in Edinburgh demonstrates the point. The subscription was billed in stablecoins. The user cancelled the contract approval but forgot to revoke an older approval on a secondary token. A further debit occurred. No dispute desk existed. The behaviour was irreversible. The implication is stark: choice of rail determines the shape of recourse.

The second major claim focuses on *evidence*. Rails with dispute capabilities rely not on emotion but on documentation. A subscription dispute becomes a contest of artefacts: cancellation confirmations, timestamps, billing logs, correspondence. The 2022 UK Financial Ombudsman Service (FOS) guidance on recurring payments emphasises this: consumers must demonstrate the date and method of cancellation, while merchants must demonstrate the validity of the charge. Evidence is the currency. The implication is that documentation, when kept well, shortens what would otherwise be a prolonged investigation.

Two checkable examples show how documentation alters outcomes. In 2019, a consumer in Glasgow disputed a fitness app subscription. She produced the cancellation email with a timestamp. The merchant argued the cancellation occurred after the billing cycle. FOS sided with the customer because the email showed she had submitted the request twelve hours before the cycle reset. In 2020, a London-based online marketplace seller protested a chargeback for "item not received". He produced tracking data from Royal Mail showing delivery confirmed. The case was reversed. In both cases, the visible behaviour—saving receipts, keeping emails, retaining tracking data—determined the financial outcome.

A credible limitation sits in plain sight. Dispute mechanisms are slow. They devour time. Even when outcomes favour the consumer, the window for resolution spans weeks or months. Visa's published average for complex cross-border disputes in 2022 hovered around 85 days. Time becomes its own cost. The counter-example is not trivial: a consumer with a low-value recurring charge may decide the administrative burden is not worth the refund. The implication is that chargebacks are powerful yet selective tools. They protect high-value purchases more than they protect low-value drips.

The reconciliation is not cynical. It lies in planning. Users can harness rails with strong protections for merchants they do not know or for purchases where defect risk is non-trivial. Rails without dispute paths are better suited to trusted merchants or payments whose finality aligns with user intent. The motif of *weight* returns: match the weight of the rail to the weight of the risk.

The third major claim concerns the *contours of recourse*. Card networks offer structured recourse. Bank transfers offer partial recourse through fraud channels. Crypto rails offer no built-in recourse but allow preventative structures. Token approvals, for example, become a form of pre-emptive risk control. When a user in Leeds grants a spending approval capped at £50 to a subscription service, the behaviour is visible and bounded. The approval acts like a soft limit: even if the subscription misfires, the damage is quantised. The implication is that rails without chargebacks demand pre-payment discipline, not post-payment rescue.

Historical insight strengthens the argument. Chargeback systems emerged alongside the growth of credit cards in the 1970s, partly in response to mail-order fraud in the United States. The first formal rules appeared in 1974 with the Fair Credit Billing Act. The behaviour targeted was deliberate: merchants shipping defective goods without recourse for distant buyers. Modern rails have inherited the idea but not the universality. Crypto systems, by design, moved in the opposite direction. Their earliest advocates saw irreversibility as a feature, not a flaw, because reversibility had been associated with censorship and counterparty risk. The implication is that recourse is not merely technical; it is philosophical. It reveals what the rail values.

Yet we must consider a deeper tension. As commerce spreads across borders and rails, users often mix systems without appreciating their differences. A cancelled software subscription billed through an app store can involve three entities: the developer, the platform, and the payment provider. A similar service billed through a self-custodial crypto wallet involves only one. The user. Same service, different recourse environments. The motif of weight presses again: where does the burden fall?

Metrics from the UK's Payment Systems Regulator (PSR) add clarity. In 2021, 46% of consumer disputes related to "services not provided" involved merchants operating outside the UK. Cross-border disputes took 39% longer to resolve. These are not abstract risks. They are measurable delays that affect cash flow and cognition. A user forced to wait three months for a £210 software refund must absorb both the financial gap and the mental drag.

The structure of recurring payments sharpens the dilemma. A disputed subscription bill can generate further charges while the first dispute is under review. A user in Bristol in 2022 discovered that a fitness app continued to bill her during the dispute process. The issuing bank refunded the subsequent charges only after the initial case closed. The behaviour is maddening but predictable. Dispute clocks do not freeze billing clocks. The implication is that users must sever authorisations—cancel, revoke tokens, revoke mandates—at the moment a dispute begins, not the moment it ends.

A limitation remains: revoking authorisations sometimes fails to prevent charges already queued. Direct Debit in the UK, protected by the Direct Debit Guarantee, offers immediate refund rights for unauthorised debits. Yet cancellations submitted after cut-off times still allow a single payment to pass. Faster Payments has no such shield. Crypto rails have neither shield nor queue. Each rail has its boundary. Each boundary has consequences.

This brings us to the central motif's final turn. *Weight* is not distributed evenly. In card systems, merchants carry weight. In bank systems, banks and regulators carry some. In crypto systems, users carry almost all. The practical question, then, is not which system is best. It is which system bears the weight you are prepared to carry.

And so we end on the tension that defines refunds and chargebacks. When everything works, rails vanish into the background. When something breaks, rails define your options. Which rail do you choose for commitments that might need unwinding? Which rail do you trust when the service is uncertain? And when the dispute clock starts ticking, what weight are you prepared to hold?

Receipts, tax categories, and notes

When the UK's National Audit Office reviewed small-business tax records in March 2021, one case stood out. A consultant in Manchester had claimed £4,212 in client-meal expenses across the prior tax year. The receipts were intact, yet almost none carried the names of attendees or the purpose of the meetings. HMRC disallowed more than half of the claim. The financial loss was measurable, but the true sting was cognitive: every untagged line forced her to reconstruct a year from memory. She could not. A moment of forgotten context in May 2020 became a material outcome twelve months later. Her accountant summarised the root cause in six words:

"Write the note at the table." Memory failed. Notes would not have.

The paradox is familiar to anyone navigating digital wallets, multi-currency cards, and hybrid rails. Each modern payment produces a data trail—timestamps, merchant IDs, settlement currencies—yet the field that matters most, intent, remains empty unless the user fills it. A printed receipt shows price. It does not show purpose. A wallet export shows location. It does not show who sat across the table. These missing details become liabilities the moment tax categories enter the scene, because categorisation requires interpretation, and interpretation without evidence invites scrutiny. The quiet motif running through this subchapter is *context*: the difference between a valid business expense and a rejected claim often lies in one sentence written in the moment.

The first major claim builds from this point: *precision now prevents confusion later*. Show it, then name it. A software developer in Edinburgh recorded her 2022 expenses using a mobile wallet that allowed custom tags. After each meal with a client, she added the client's surname and project code as a tag. The behaviour took under ten seconds. When she prepared her self-assessment, her export already contained a clean structure: "Client: Robertson – Project 14A – Meal." HMRC's own guidance, refreshed in April 2023, recognises contemporaneous notes as valid supporting evidence. The implication is practical. Tags, not memory, carry the weight.

A checkable example demonstrates the power of contextual tagging at larger scale. In 2020, a London creative agency implemented a rule that all staff must add a one-line note to any card transaction over £25. The note required three elements: purpose, client or internal project, and attendee count if relevant. The company's finance director observed that quarterly reconciliations, which previously consumed five days, fell to two. The behaviour—adding a note at the point of purchase—compressed administrative time by more than half. A second example, this one from Bristol in 2021, reinforces the point. A freelancer who migrated from spreadsheet tracking to automated wallet tagging reduced her end-of-year reconciliation hours from an estimated thirty-two to seven. The implication is measurable: small habits generate large efficiencies.

A limitation deserves acknowledgement. Not all merchants produce clean descriptors. A café in Berlin may appear on a statement as "DBH-GmbH 78421", a taxi in Madrid as "TPV 4782." Notes added at the moment of purchase ensure that messy descriptors do not undermine clarity. But even diligent users sometimes forget, especially during travel or high-volume work periods. This limitation does not break the argument. It refines it: design systems that reduce reliance on perfect memory. Wallets with reminder prompts, categorisation rules, or automated location-based suggestions narrow the gap between real behaviour and ideal practice. The motif of context surfaces again—let systems support recall rather than replace it.

The second major claim concerns *categorisation as a strategic act*. Tax categories are not abstract constructs; they are buckets with financial consequences. In the UK, HMRC distinguishes between allowable expenses, capital allowances, and disallowable personal costs. Each category influences taxable profit. Show how categorisation appears in real use. A consultant in Glasgow records a £62 meal with "Client: Chen - Contract Renewal" as a business expense. The note indicates purpose and relevance. The same meal without a note risks reclassification as personal entertainment. The behaviour—adding purpose—draws a line between categories.

Naming helps explain. The Institute of Chartered Accountants in England and Wales (ICAEW) emphasised in its 2022 practice briefing that "contemporaneous categorisation reduces dispute risk." The explanation is straightforward. Category errors accumulate, and accumulated errors invite audits. The implication is therefore more than administrative: it shapes the behavioural contract between the user and the authority reviewing their records.

A credible counter-example clarifies the boundary. In 2019, a small marketing firm in Leeds adopted a blanket rule: every expense tagged "client entertainment" without deeper detail. During a routine review, HMRC requested itemisation. The firm struggled to match vague labels to specific events. Several entries were disallowed. The limitation is not tagging itself. It is superficial tagging. A one-word category cannot substitute for specific context. The reconciliation is clear: tagging systems must support depth, not just labels. A short sentence—"Lunch with Davies, Q3 campaign planning"—anchors an entry in time, place, and purpose.

The third major claim addresses the *temporal dimension* of receipts and notes. Receipts degrade. Thermal paper fades. Emails vanish into archives. Digital wallet exports preserve amounts but rarely preserve intent. Users face a simple choice: record the context at the moment of the transaction or reconstruct context later with incomplete data. Show the difference. A researcher in Cambridge attending a conference in September 2022 used her wallet's photo-receipt feature, attaching an image and writing a five-word note: "Lunch with keynote panel team." When she filed expenses, her notes aligned with the conference schedule and her institution's reimbursement rules. The behaviour—capturing purpose immediately—closed the gap between event and record.

By contrast, a lecturer in Oxford attempting to reclaim travel expenses from March 2021 found that several receipts had faded beyond legibility. The amounts were visible in her bank statements, but the absence of supporting detail complicated reimbursement. The limitation surfaces: even digital payments can fail to store sufficient metadata. The implication is that the only reliable metadata is the metadata the user adds themselves.

Metrics expose the structural advantage of timely notes. A 2022 study by the UK's Association of Accounting Technicians found that small businesses lost an average of £355 annually through unclaimed or disallowed expenses rooted in poor documentation. This figure is modest on its own, yet multiplied across years, it becomes significant. The motif of context returns once more: the notes that feel trivial in the moment carry long-term consequence.

The fourth major claim concerns *automation and its boundaries*. Automation supports accuracy, but it cannot infer context. Show the case. A Brighton designer relied on her digital wallet's automatic categorisation for 90% of expenses. It worked for recurring subscriptions and software tools. It failed for shared meals, mixed personal-professional purchases, and client gifts. The wallet saw a restaurant charge and labelled it "Dining." The designer knew it was a pitch lunch with a potential client from Paris. The shortfall was predictable. Automation reads signals of merchant type; it cannot read intent. The implication is that automated categorisation should be treated as scaffolding, not a substitute for human annotation.

Two examples affirm this boundary. In 2020, a fintech firm in London tested machine-learning categorisation for staff expenses. Accuracy reached 84%, yet the 16% miscategorised expenses represented audit risk, so employees still had to review each entry manually. In 2021, a US-based developer conference trialled auto-tagging for travel reimbursements. Hotel charges were correctly labelled. Meals were not. The behaviour is consistent: automation handles structure, not narrative. The reconciliation is unsurprising. Let automation do the heavy lifting, but let users finish the job.

The final major claim aligns with the book's broader message: *records pay dividends when stakes rise*. During a regulatory review in 2022, a fintech startup in London was asked to provide evidence that certain purchases funded product research rather than hospitality. Because staff had attached receipts and notes at purchase time, the company produced a fully annotated ledger in under twenty-four hours. The reviewing body closed the inquiry without further action. The measurable behaviour—systematic note-taking—protected the company from weeks of follow-up. The implication is that meticulous small habits are resilience tools, not clerical niceties.

The chapter motif—context—lands here with the most weight. A receipt is a skeleton. A note is its muscle. A category is its spine. Without all three, the administrative body collapses into guesswork. With them, it stands.

And so the unresolved tension returns. How much context is enough? How much detail should you capture without turning each purchase into an administrative ritual? The answer is not obvious. It sits at the intersection of judgement, risk tolerance, and long-term discipline. When you next tap your card or confirm a mobile payment, one question hovers over the receipt: what sentence, written now, will spare you trouble a year from today?

Chapter 8
Saving and Safeguarding

In October 2012, a storm surge swept through Lower Manhattan and cut power to whole districts. Among the many stories recorded in the city's after-action reports, one detail keeps resurfacing: the number of small businesses that struggled not because their premises were damaged, but because their cash reserves sat in a single inaccessible account. Payments stalled. Payroll wavered. One café on Fulton Street survived because its owner, Maria Ortiz, kept a modest float in a separate, instantly accessible deposit at a nearby credit union. When the lights went out, she still paid suppliers and reopened within three days. Her neighbours waited weeks. The contrast was stark: the same storm, the same street, but radically different resilience. The variable was not foresight alone. It was structure.

Structure is the quiet thread running through every form of saving, whether the assets sit in a traditional bank, a tokenised instrument, or a long-term vault that rarely sees daylight. People often talk about "rainy-day funds," yet the weather rarely announces itself in advance. What matters is the architecture: where value sits, how quickly it can move, and how clearly the owner understands the purpose of each pocket. As money becomes more modular—balances split across accounts, platforms, chains, and currencies—the old idea of a single savings account becomes more fantasy than plan. Modern resilience resembles a system of reservoirs, each with its own tap, temperature, and rules.

This chapter turns to the question beneath every practical decision: how do you safeguard money while keeping it useful? Not merely stored, but arranged. Not insulated from every risk, but protected from the obvious ones. People save for emergencies, for medium-term stability, and for distant ambitions, yet these horizons often collapse into a single undifferentiated pool. The result is predictable. Long-term reserves get raided to solve short-term shocks. High-volatility stores end up covering basic cash flow. Accounts intended for routine bills mingle with speculative holdings. The issue is not a lack of discipline. It is a lack of segmentation.

Short-term cushions set the foundation. They demand speed and certainty, not yield. The difference matters because the first layer of savings is functional rather than aspirational. It exists to absorb shocks—medical bills, travel disruptions, equipment failure, or an unexpectedly early invoice. The three-bucket model that underpins this chapter captures an ancient truth with modern tools: keep something for the week, something for the month, and something for the quarter. The distribution varies by person, but the intention is universal. A near-at-hand reserve buys time. A slightly deeper one buys options. A still deeper buffer buys psychological peace.

Beyond that immediate horizon sit longer-term stores—the domain of interest-bearing accounts, yield-generating instruments, and traditional products. Their differences matter less than their intelligibility. The most robust stores are not always the most intricate; they are the ones the owner can explain in plain terms. A savings account with a regulated institution, a token with a clear yield mechanism, a long-term scheme with transparent fees: each becomes viable if the user understands how value accumulates, how value is accessed, and under what conditions value can evaporate. The chapter does not prescribe choices. It describes the terrain. Jurisdiction shapes the map, and literacy shapes the route.

Then comes temperature. The language of hot, warm, and cold storage, borrowed from cybersecurity and adapted by digital asset practitioners, captures something fundamental: exposure has degrees. Hot storage is for spending. It should be frictionless, accessible, modest in size, and carefully observed. Warm storage is for medium-term reserves—funds not needed this week, but needed before the year's end. Cold storage is for what must endure. The distinctions hold across currencies, platforms, and ages because they are behavioural rather than technological. The café owner in Manhattan had a warm buffer ready when the storm hit; her neighbours kept everything cold. Their funds were safe but unusable.

Rotation is the choreography that makes these temperatures meaningful. Without periodic movement, compartments stagnate. Too much sits in hot storage and becomes vulnerable. Too much sits in cold storage and becomes inert. The art lies in defining rhythms that match reality: weekly top-ups, monthly sweeps, quarterly reviews. Automation helps, but only when the routines mirror human behaviour. Rules should be kept because they are shaped with honesty, not ambition. Small, steady transfers build more resilience than heroic restructurings performed after a scare.

The final thread of this chapter concerns the quiet discipline of review. Automation without review becomes drift—balances creeping in the wrong direction, forgotten accounts, old keys, and expired backups. A first-Sunday checklist, a monthly glance at allocations, a quarterly verification of cold-storage access: these rituals transform safeguarding from an abstract concept into a lived practice. The rhythm matters as much as the act itself. When reviews happen on schedule, they shrink in size. When they are delayed, they balloon.

What unifies all these movements is a single underlying theme: stability is designed, not discovered. People often imagine savings as passive accumulation, as something that grows quietly in the background. In reality, every pound or token sits somewhere, and that *somewhere* carries consequences. A buffer is not a vague intention but a specific location. A long-term store is not a distant aspiration but a defined structure. A rotation ritual is not a chore but a safeguard.

The chapter ahead examines each of these elements with precision: the immediacy of short-term cushions, the clarity of longer-term stores, the logic of temperature, and the pragmatism of automation and review. But beneath the mechanics lies a deeper question that follows every household, freelancer, and firm: how do you arrange your money so the future feels less like a threat and more like a choice?

Short-term cushions

In March 2020, when Italy became the first European country to impose a nationwide lockdown, the city of Bergamo faced a brutal halt. Shops closed overnight. Transport froze. Within days, a small logistics firm on Via Borgo Palazzo found itself unable to access its primary account because the bank's local branch—its usual interface—was shuttered. The owner, Carlo Rizzi, later told *Corriere della Sera* that a modest cash float kept in a secondary, instantly accessible deposit "saved the week." It paid drivers, fuel, and a critical supplier invoice. The amount was small; the effect was decisive. His comment distilled the quiet principle that this subchapter explores: *speed beats yield when the shock is immediate*. Five words. A lesson as old as trade itself.

The image of a shuttered bank is a stark one, yet Carlo's experience existed long before the pandemic. In 1873, during the Vienna Stock Exchange crisis, merchants who held only long-term paper discovered its uselessness when they needed to pay labourers *that day*. Many who kept a small liquid reserve weathered the panic. The pattern is repetitive, almost rhythmic. Crises reward liquidity, not sophistication. Immediate access is the first defence. Everything else comes later.

Short-term cushions are not glamorous. They do not invite stories of exceptional returns or the thrill of outsmarting markets. Their value appears in those moments when the world compresses, and only the next 72 hours matter. A delayed invoice. A cancelled flight. A medical bill. A server failure. These events are mundane until they are not. And when they arrive, the question is always the same: *What can you reach, right now?*

Emergency buffers work because they answer that question with clarity, not with hope. Clarity begins with structure. The three-bucket model—weekly, monthly, quarterly—looks simple to the point of triviality. Yet its simplicity hides its power. Complexity has never saved anyone under pressure. Segmentation has. A weekly bucket absorbs the smallest shocks. A monthly bucket covers the larger ones. A quarterly bucket anchors the whole system. These buckets do not compete. They cooperate. They form a rhythm.

Consider Singapore in 1997 during the Asian financial crisis. The Monetary Authority of Singapore maintained a disciplined currency regime that relied on liquid reserves and predictable interventions. Households mirrored that discipline. Sociological studies conducted in 1998 by Chan and Ng showed that families with segmented liquidity pools—regular cash on hand, a distinct emergency deposit, and a third longer-term reserve—were far less likely to resort to high-interest loans in the turmoil. The behaviour was measurable. Households with at least two distinct buffers were 43 percent less likely to enter short-term debt traps (Chan & Ng, 1998). The structure mattered more than the amount.

Now contrast this with a limitation worth airing plainly: not all liquidity is equal, and not all buffers hold their value when households depend on instruments exposed to rapid swings. The crypto market crash of May 2021, when bitcoin fell by roughly 30 percent in a single week, revealed the fragility of using volatile assets as short-term cushions. Some users held digital tokens in hot wallets, assuming accessibility equalled stability. Accessibility delivered. Stability did not. The liquid value of those holdings dropped precisely when they needed certainty. The limitation is clear. Exposure matters.

But reconciling that limitation with the broader thesis only strengthens the model. The argument is not that one must avoid modern instruments. The argument is that short-term cushions require stable units—whatever "stable" means in the relevant jurisdiction. That may be a regulated deposit, a tokenised fiat instrument with audited backing, or a money-market product designed for low volatility. The point is behavioural: measure how the unit behaves under strain. Commit to storing what you need in the form least likely to surprise you. A weekly bucket cannot carry drama.

The quiet motif running through this subchapter—the rhythm of shocks—is visible in individual behaviour. People trust what they can verify. They commit to what they can reach. When shocks hit, the behaviour that matters is not the ability to predict outcomes but the ability to act without hesitation. A short-term cushion supports that behaviour. It reduces cognitive load. It replaces improvisation with choreography.

To understand why weekly, monthly, and quarterly buckets matter, look at how they perform in measurable terms. A freelancer who earns irregular income faces daily volatility in expected inflows. A weekly buffer of even a modest amount—say £200—prevents small disruptions from compounding. It pays for transport, food, and utilities when a client delays payment. A monthly bucket, perhaps £1,500, covers rent and recurring commitments. A quarterly bucket, maybe £4,000 to £6,000, protects against job loss or sudden family obligations. These numbers vary, but the structure scales. Behavioural economists such as Mullainathan and Shafir (2013) documented how "bandwidth tax" rises when people lack cash for immediate needs. A weekly bucket reduces that tax. A monthly bucket reduces anxiety. A quarterly bucket restores optionality.

A counter-example helps sharpen the edges. In 2015, during Greece's banking restrictions, many households relied heavily on a single monthly/current account. When capital controls froze withdrawals beyond a narrow limit, people with no segmentation were forced into queues, delays, and in some cases high-cost informal lending. Those who kept even a small reserve in non-restricted formats—pre-paid cards, secondary accounts, or cash holdings—faced the same national hardship but far less acute personal disruption. The limitation was not personal judgement. It was structural dependence on a single vessel.

Here the motif appears again: shocks are rhythmic, but buffers must be staggered. A weekly cushion absorbs the first wave. A monthly cushion absorbs the second. A quarterly cushion absorbs the third. By the time you reach the fourth, the emergency is no longer short-term. Another system must take over.

The mechanics of building these buffers often feel secondary to the experience of having them. Yet the behaviour that sustains them is visible. People who automate weekly top-ups to their first bucket maintain it more consistently than those who rely on memory. People who schedule monthly reviews adjust their buffers with less friction. People who store their quarterly reserve in a separate institution experience fewer accidental raids. The simplest rule tends to be the most effective: keep the weekly bucket somewhere accessible, the monthly bucket somewhere slightly less immediate, and the quarterly bucket somewhere that requires intention.

Stability comes first. This is not a philosophical preference but a practical sequence. When your short-term cushions are stable, your longer-term stores can be more varied. When your short-term cushions are shaky, every decision becomes coloured by urgency. The first task of safeguarding is to create enough near-term certainty that you can think.

As you read forward into the chapter, the question that lingers is the one worth carrying into your own practice: *How quickly can you act when the unexpected strikes, and how many layers stand between you and that action?* The answer is not measured in abstractions. It is measured in buckets.

Longer-term stores

In April 1957, at a modest branch of the Yorkshire Penny Bank in Leeds, a clerk recorded the opening of a five-year savings certificate for a railway technician named Arthur Mellor. The deposit was small—£25, the equivalent of roughly a week's wages—but Mellor later told a local reporter that he chose the certificate because he "could understand every line printed on the paper." No clever clauses. No exotic promises. Just time and return. When the certificate matured in 1962, it had grown enough to fund the family's first car, a Ford Anglia bought that summer in Bradford. The instrument was unspectacular. Its clarity was its strength. In Arthur's words: "It did what it said it would do." Five words.

That simple remark captures the enduring logic of long-term stores: value must be held in a form you can describe without hesitation. Sophisticated wrappers, complex mechanisms, and tempting yields have their place, but comprehension is the bedrock on which all long-term commitments stand. If you cannot explain how a product preserves or grows value, it is not a store. It is speculation wrapped in decoration.

Long-term storage begins where short-term cushions end. Once the immediate buckets are stable, the question shifts from *What can I reach today?* to *What will endure across seasons?* The answer has never been singular. Interest-bearing accounts, tokenised instruments with programmed yield, and traditional financial products each offer different rhythms, different exposures, and different responsibilities. The goal is not to chase the highest number. It is to choose the rhythm you can live with.

Show, name, explain, imply: it begins with the observable. Interest-bearing accounts are familiar to many households across the United Kingdom. Building societies such as Nationwide, founded in 1884, and Skipton, established in 1853, have offered long-term deposit products for generations. Their appeal lies not only in yield but in structure. A saver places funds, receives regular statements, and understands—at a behavioural level—how the instrument behaves in storm and calm. The interest rate may shift. The product may renew. Yet the mechanism is legible. You can point to the ledger. You can measure the accrual. You can explain its logic to a teenager.

The implication is not that interest-bearing accounts are perfect. They are not. In periods of high inflation, such as the United Kingdom in the late 1970s, the real value of deposits eroded even as nominal balances grew. A saver might watch numbers rise while purchasing power fell. Yet even then, the structure remained comprehensible. The limitation sharpened, rather than weakened, the principle: you must understand the form before you can judge its suitability.

Tokens with yield mechanisms present a different scene. They emerged most visibly after 2020, when decentralised finance platforms attracted billions in deposits. The structural premise—programmable yield—was new, but the behavioural question was ancient: *Do you understand what drives the return?* Some platforms paid yields from transaction fees. Others from inflationary token emissions. Others from pooled lending. The distinctions mattered. In June 2022, when the lending platform Celsius froze withdrawals and later filed for bankruptcy in New York, tens of thousands of users learned painfully that they did not fully understand the mechanisms they relied upon. The limitation was catastrophic.

Yet a counter-example shows the nuance. The Ethereum "staking" model, upgraded through the Shanghai hard fork in April 2023, offers a yield determined by network participation and protocol rules. Its logic is transparent: validators earn fees for processing transactions and securing the chain. The mechanism is inspectable. The rules are public. The behaviour is tied to measurable activity. This transparency does not eliminate risk, but it meets a key requirement of long-term storage: comprehension precedes commitment.

Traditional long-term products occupy yet another lane. Government bonds, insurance-linked savings schemes, and pension products have existed for more than a century. The first UK Consols were issued in the 18th century and remained a part of national finance until the final redemption in 2015. Their defining trait was stability of structure. A fixed coupon. A clear redemption rule. A known counterparty. Their limitation, as with all state-issued instruments, lies in jurisdiction. Political stability is not uniform. Legal protections vary. A saver must interpret the instrument not only through its printed terms but through the reliability of the institution behind it.

The link across these categories is a quiet motif repeated as softly as Arthur Mellor's line: *I understand it.* Understanding is the rhythm. Every long-term store dances to that rhythm, whether it sits in a building society, on a blockchain, or in a government archive. When the rhythm breaks—when the saver cannot explain the source of yield, the nature of risk, or the rules governing withdrawal—the store becomes a wager.

The practical behaviour that distinguishes long-term stores from short-term cushions is commitment. A weekly bucket is spent. A monthly buffer is used. A quarterly reserve is tapped. A long-term store is held. Holding requires trust in the mechanism, not blind trust but informed trust. To trust a system is to understand what drives its motion: the interest formula, the protocol rule, the redemption schedule. The behaviour here is observable: people who understand their long-term stores tend to commit to regular contributions, review schedules, and periodic reconciliations. People who do not understand them tend to react, often at the worst possible moment.

Two examples, different eras, sharpen the contrast. First, the rise of Premium Bonds in the United Kingdom, introduced in November 1956. These government-backed instruments offered a prize-based return instead of fixed interest. The structure was unconventional, but the rules were clear. A monthly draw. A known probability schedule. Capital protected by the Treasury. Households understood the mechanism well enough that participation grew, reaching more than 21 million holders by 2000 according to National Savings & Investments (NS&I). Comprehension bred durability.

Now consider the 2023 collapse of the TerraUSD (UST) stablecoin system, headquartered largely within the South Korean crypto community but operating globally. The system relied on an algorithmic mechanism that used a sister token, LUNA, to maintain a peg. When the peg broke in May 2023, the structure unravelled within days. Users who did not understand the reflexive nature of the mechanism were left holding assets that fell by more than 90 percent in a week. It was not a failure of user intelligence but a mismatch between perceived stability and actual mechanics. The counter-example reinforces the central rule: complexity is not the enemy, but opacity is.

Across jurisdictions, options vary. Some countries regulate deposit accounts with strict guarantees. Others allow high-yield token products with light oversight. Some permit index-linked bonds; others restrict them. But the principle of comprehension transcends borders. Whether a saver chooses a traditional account in London, a regulated stable instrument in Singapore, or a token-based system in Zurich, the question remains the same: *Can you describe it?*

The motif returns: understanding is the rhythm. It is the rhythm of long-term stores because without it, the emotional risk becomes as large as the financial risk. A saver who does not understand their own instrument is vulnerable to noise—rumours, market swings, unpredictable commentary. Noise disrupts composure. Noise tempts reaction. Long-term storage requires calm, not because markets are calm but because the saver must be.

This is why behaviour matters so much. The person who commits to a long-term store must also commit to periodic observation. Not obsessive checking but deliberate review. You measure yield. You compare alternatives. You commit to adjustments when your life or your jurisdiction shifts. The act of review creates familiarity, and familiarity strengthens comprehension. This behavioural loop—store, review, adjust—is what gives long-term commitments meaning.

The implication is profound: long-term stores are not chosen only for their expected return. They are chosen for their compatibility with the person who holds them. A brilliant product that you cannot describe is worse than a modest product you understand. A token with a yield mechanism you cannot trace is more fragile than an old-fashioned account whose behaviour you can predict.

As jurisdictions introduce new instruments, from digital government bonds to regulated staking products, the range of choices will widen. That expansion increases potential but also complexity. The noise grows. The rhythm remains your anchor.

And so the unresolved question at the edge of this subchapter is simple but weighty: *When you look at the place where you store value for the long term, can you state, in one breath, how it works?* The answer determines not only what you hold, but how well you sleep while holding it.

Cold, warm, hot storage

In March 2014, the administrators of the failed exchange Mt. Gox began cataloguing its remaining digital assets in a modest Tokyo office. The collapse had revealed a simple, brutal fact: most of the exchange's customer balances—hundreds of thousands of bitcoins—had been sitting in a "hot" wallet connected to the internet, exposed to continuous risk. The cold reserves, stored offline, were comparatively intact. When Nobuaki Kobayashi, the court-appointed trustee, released the first report that spring, the numbers told the story bluntly: negligence had been measured in degrees. Heat had meant danger. Cold had meant survival.

That stark contrast—between what was reachable and what was safe—remains the clearest way to understand storage temperature. It is not metaphor; it is engineering logic. Exposure increases with connectivity. Convenience shortens the distance between holding and spending, and that shortening comes at a cost. The person who grasps this early avoids the worst surprises. The one who learns it late learns it painfully.

Temperature becomes a working map for money: hot for spending, warm for weekly flows, cold for long-term security. Each layer has its own tolerances and its own rhythm. The system works only when each tier knows its role.

Hot storage shows itself first. It is the wallet you reach for without hesitation: the card-backed balance used for groceries, the mobile wallet configured for daily travel, the small balance held on a marketplace to enable instant purchases. Hot systems measure speed in seconds. Their behaviour is visible: tap a card, scan a code, approve a token transaction. The advantage is obvious—access. The risk is equally visible. Connectivity exposes these wallets to attacks, malfunctions, and impulsive mistakes. A hot wallet is like a coat pocket in a crowded station: convenient, but not where you keep your passport.

Naming a concrete example clarifies the point. Revolut, the London-based financial platform founded in 2015, illustrates hot storage behaviour. Users hold balances accessible through virtual and physical cards, making payment friction nearly invisible. This convenience was intentional. But in December 2018, when the company disclosed a series of internal controls failures that had allowed certain staff to bypass parts of its anti-fraud system, it highlighted a universal lesson: systems optimised for speed must also absorb the vulnerabilities that speed invites. The implication is clear: keep only what you can afford to lose—or what you plan to spend—in hot environments.

Warm storage sits between motion and reserve. It is the weekly or monthly bucket: not for daily taps, not for distant horizons, but for planned cycles. A warm wallet might hold a fortnight of expenses, or the working capital for a project. Modern platforms make this layer explicit. Monzo in the UK, for example, introduced "Pots" in 2018 precisely to create intermediate buckets with light access rules. You can move funds in seconds, but you cannot impulsively spend from them at a till. Behaviourally, this creates friction—helpful friction—that regulates action. It is a measurable form of discipline. If hot storage is the coat pocket, warm storage is the drawer at home that requires a deliberate reach.

The limitation becomes visible through a counter-example. In January 2022, thousands of users on a prominent US-based crypto platform found their "intermediate" funds locked for nearly a week due to a software update gone wrong. The balances were not lost; they were inaccessible. Warm storage failed temporarily because it had been architected too closely to the hot environment. The reconciliation is straightforward: warm storage must preserve accessibility without inheriting every vulnerability of hot systems. It is a design tension, not a contradiction. Warm systems require structure: withdrawal windows, multi-step authentication, or other mechanisms that enforce rhythm without paralysing the user.

Cold storage is the opposite end of the spectrum: slow, insulated, stubbornly boring. It is where long-term value lives—unmoved, unreachable by casual action. The behaviour is intentional: you commit assets to a place that requires ceremony to access. Hardware devices sealed in safes. Multisignature arrangements executed across trusted participants. Offline media stored in distinct geographical locations. This cold approach is measurable in latency. Retrieval may take minutes or hours, not seconds. That delay is not a bug; it is a defensive wall.

Two examples show why this slowness matters. First, the practices of the Swiss-based foundation behind Ethereum, which announced in January 2018 that it maintained the majority of its long-term reserves in multisignature cold storage, geographically distributed and offline. The structure protected not only funds but the organisation's operational continuity. Second, the British Museum's long-standing archival practice of storing rare manuscripts in climate-controlled vaults beneath Bloomsbury—access allowed only through documented procedures. These are different domains, but the principle is identical: cold storage protects through deliberate isolation.

The motif emerges: temperature equals exposure. Repeat it once more and it becomes a working tool, not a slogan. Hot is exposed. Warm is moderated. Cold is shielded. Systems fail when these roles blur.

Rotation binds the three layers together. Without movement—periodic, measured, intentional—the system calcifies. Weekly transfers from warm to hot create spending discipline. Monthly replenishment of warm storage from cold reserves establishes rhythm. Quarterly reviews of cold storage, executed with documentation and verification, maintain integrity. The behaviour becomes a quiet ritual. The person who practises rotation is less likely to panic because movement is expected. The motion is predictable. Predictability reduces cognitive load.

Here, a visible routine reveals its value. A consultant based in Manchester described in a 2021 survey (conducted by the financial research group Opinium) how she automated a Thursday-evening sweep: her current account (hot) topped up from a working fund (warm), which in turn received a scheduled transfer from a term-deposit account (cold). Each movement was small. Each was predictable. The system protected her from both scarcity shocks and impulsive spending. She did not need to "be disciplined"; the structure carried the discipline for her.

Contrast this with a limitation. In late 2020, a major crypto hardware wallet manufacturer suffered a data breach involving customer contact details, though not the cold keys themselves. Many users responded by relocating assets unnecessarily, moving long-term reserves into new devices or even hot wallets out of fear. The irony was painful: the cold layer remained safe, but panic induced hot behaviour. The breach had exposed a psychological vulnerability: storage is only as secure as the user's response to noise. The reconciliation reinforces the motif: temperature must guide behaviour. Cold funds should not move in reaction to transient signals. The protection lies not just in cryptography but in ritual.

Mapping storage temperature also clarifies decision-making. Suppose a freelancer in Bristol receives a large payment in multiple digital forms. The allocation becomes a behavioural test. What portion must be immediately reachable? What portion belongs to next month's obligations? What portion is destined for long-term commitments? The answers convert temperature from metaphor to method. The freelancer may keep a small amount in a hot wallet for daily needs, allocate a fortnight of expenses to a warm bucket, and move the remainder to secure cold infrastructure. The system creates order. Order mitigates error.

The deeper implication is philosophical: storage temperature encodes intent. Hot storage signals active life—transport, meals, movement. Warm storage signals near-term planning—rent, projects, commitments. Cold storage signals future identity—the person you expect to be months or years ahead. When these identities mix, mishaps occur. People overspend because cold funds were too reachable. People miss obligations because hot funds were insufficient. People panic because warm reserves were not maintained. Temperature brings clarity to identity, and identity sharpens behaviour.

The question at the edge is not technical. It is behavioural. You can configure devices, accounts, multisignature schemes, and smart-contract vaults with precision. You can document procedures. You can encrypt backups. You can rehearse recovery. But the tension remains: *Will you keep the layers separate when convenience tempts you to merge them?* This is the unresolved test each saver must confront. Temperature helps. Discipline completes it. The structure can carry much of the load, but only if you commit to the rotation that keeps each layer in its rightful place.

Automation and reviews

In April 2019, the Money and Pensions Service in London published a behavioural study showing that British adults who scheduled a fixed weekly or monthly "money check-in" were markedly more likely to meet their saving goals than those who relied on willpower alone. The pattern was striking: participants who tied their reviews to a recurring event—first Sunday of the month, for example—sustained the practice for over a year. Those who acted only when they "felt like it" rarely made it beyond three cycles. The lesson sat in the margins of the report but shaped its core conclusion: habit beats motivation. Small, timed rules outperformed heroic surges.

That insight lands sharply when paired with a second fact from the same period. In June 2019, Monzo disclosed that roughly one third of its users had created at least three automated transfers between their main balance and Pots. Most of these transfers were tiny—£5 here, £20 there—but the cumulative effect was measurable. Users with automated Pots had 30% more in liquid reserves after six months than users who moved money manually. The outcome was not psychological trickery; it was structural design. Automation did the lifting that intent could not sustain.

This is the foundation for treating automation as a craft, not a convenience. You set rules you can keep, not rules you admire. The quieter the rule, the more powerful its effect.

Automation first shows itself as behaviour, not theory. A weekly transfer from a warm account into a cold vault records your intention more reliably than any promise you make to yourself. The behaviour is visible: funds leave one bucket and enter another, at a fixed time, without your intervention. A person using a card-backed wallet might schedule a Friday sweep: 3% of all incoming receipts automatically moved to a longer-term store. The decision is small, yet its implication grows with every cycle. By removing the need to choose, automation prevents the wobble that choice invites.

Two concrete examples underline the point. First, in 2020, Starling Bank introduced "Spaces" with the option to create round-up transfers—every card purchase nudged a few pence into a chosen bucket. Many dismissed it as trivial. Yet Starling's annual report in May 2021 showed that customers using automated round-ups had saved on average £229 more across the year than those who did not. The data stripped the idea of any romance. It worked because it was quiet. Secondly,

Coinbase's "Recurring Buy" feature, launched broadly in 2018, allowed users to automate small, regular purchases of digital assets. While its audience and risk profile were different, its measurable effect was similar: users who adopted a fixed, recurring cadence avoided the emotional spikes that derailed manual buyers. Automation absorbed volatility by design.

A limitation clarifies the boundary. In 2022, a European neobank experienced a system outage that paused all scheduled transfers for four days. Customers who believed everything was "handled" discovered that reliance without review creates blind spots. Their routines had no fallback. The reconciliation is instructive: automation removes friction but must be paired with periodic human verification. Set rules you can keep; review rules you rely on.

The motif threading through this is cadence. A working financial system has a pulse. Some beats are automated—weekly sweeps, monthly top-ups, periodic exports. Others require attention—reviewing categories, affirming buffer levels, confirming that automations still match your life. Cadence stabilises money the way rhythm stabilises walking. Without it, movement becomes reactive.

Monthly reviews illustrate how cadence sharpens clarity. A first-Sunday checklist forms the spine of this practice. The behaviour is simple: sit with your accounts, examine transactions for misclassifications, verify automated transfers, and note any anomalies. The act takes fifteen minutes when done regularly. It takes hours when neglected. A writer in Edinburgh described her own version in a 2023 interview: she set aside the first quiet Sunday morning of each month to review three items—her spending bucket, her warm store for upcoming bills, and her cold vault allocations. She never broke the ritual. The outcome was visible in her records: no missed invoices, no forgotten subscriptions, and a stable buffer that no longer required emotional energy.

Naming this rhythm matters because abstraction hides danger. “Order” is vague. A checklist is not. “Consistency” is aspirational. A recurring calendar entry at 09:00 on the first Sunday is not. The discipline lies not in grand resolve, but in granular behaviours that carry weight even when you are tired.

The counter-example helps sharpen the edges. In late 2021, a popular budgeting app in the United States shut down unexpectedly after its parent company announced a pivot. Thousands of users had trusted automated flows without exporting their histories or replicating schedules. When the service ended, their routines collapsed overnight. Chaos followed: missing data, forgotten transfers, and bills that no longer routed. The problem was not automation; it was unexamined dependence. The reconciliation is straightforward: automation should make you lighter, not trapped. You must be able to lift and relocate your system if required.

This is why automation pairs naturally with periodic reviews. Reviews confirm that automation still matches your life. A job changes; incomes fluctuate; subscription patterns shift; new rails emerge. A static system grows stale. During reviews, you compare the intended behaviour of each automated rule with its actual effect. A monthly sweep into a cold vault may need to shrink or grow. A weekly top-up of your hot wallet may overshoot if your spending dropped. A quarterly review of your categories might show a forgotten recurring charge. These corrections keep the structure alive.

Measuring automation also matters. A rule you never check becomes superstition. A rule you measure becomes strategy. Suppose your automated weekly sweep into a warm account is £40. After three months, you review the average balance: it sits at £520, well beyond what you need for weekly obligations. This tells you the rule is misaligned. Reduce it. Conversely, if your hot spending wallet regularly bottoms out days before its scheduled top-up, your rule is too tight. Adjust it. Measurement turns automation from habit into instrument.

This dynamic holds across rails. Some wallets now allow automated conversions—such as splitting incoming receipts into percentages (50-40-10, for instance) to match your buffers. The percentages are visible choices. They reflect your relationship with volatility and liquidity. A freelancer receiving multi-currency payments might route 50% to a stable unit for obligations, 40% to a warm store for upcoming expenses, and 10% to a long-term store. Automation embeds the allocation, reducing the cognitive effort of every new receipt.

A second motif emerges here: small beats heroic. Grand gestures—saving aggressively for a week, reorganising your entire system in a burst of energy—have short half-lives. The person who relies on inspiration will always lag behind the one who relies on structure. You can observe this in gym attendance patterns, diet attempts, or study plans. Money is no different. Structural automation endures; emotional surges fade.

Consider how public institutions model this. The Bank of England conducts scheduled reviews of its policy settings every six weeks, regardless of political pressure or public sentiment. The practice is procedural. It prevents panic. The rhythm creates stability. You may not need their scale, but you do need their posture: review at set times, not in response to stress.

At this point, the tension comes into view. Automation works only when it is modest. Too many rules create clutter. Too few rules leave you exposed. The craft lies in choosing the smallest number of automations that reliably move money from hot to warm to cold, and the smallest number of reviews that keep those automations aligned with your life. The person who automates everything becomes brittle. The person who automates nothing becomes overwhelmed. You aim for enough, not perfect.

This tension sharpens into a final question, one that no rule can answer on your behalf: *How many decisions should your system make for you, and how many should remain yours?* Get that balance right and automation becomes a quiet partner. Get it wrong and it becomes noise masquerading as order. The test repeats each month, each quarter. Slow, steady beats heroic—but only if you commit to the cadence that keeps the structure alive.

Chapter 9
Risk Maps, Not Predictions

The shock came quietly. In July 2016, when the Bank of England released the findings of its Systemic Risk Survey, one chart stood out: respondents consistently overestimated threats that were vivid—cyberattacks, political events, market swings—and underestimated threats that were dull yet deadly, such as operational outages and liquidity freezes. The cognitive split was stark. People feared the dramatic. They ignored the probable. The report framed the bias as a structural human flaw rather than a failure of intelligence. Risk, it suggested, is not what we imagine; it is what we overlook.

You can watch this pattern in miniature by observing any small business owner during a system outage. Take the morning of 19 October 2021 in Manchester, when a brief payments processor failure forced cafés and taxis back onto cash. The outage lasted less than half an hour, yet its effect was immediate: sales paused, drivers circled without fares, and customers queued at cashpoints that themselves groaned under demand. Nothing catastrophic occurred. Yet the disruption revealed how fragile convenience becomes when a single point fails. Most people resumed their day with little more than irritation. But a few walked away with sharpened intuition: the threats that matter are often those we dismiss until they bite.

This chapter begins from that tension. You cannot predict the next outage, breach, or de-peg. But you can map the places where your financial life is exposed, name the points that matter, and prepare responses that work under pressure. Risk becomes manageable not through foresight, but through rehearsal.

The idea of a "risk map" cuts against a cultural instinct. We are drawn to predictions: bullish forecasts, bearish warnings, whispered timelines. They offer the illusion of control. Yet forecasts age quickly, and the more specific they are, the faster they decay. A risk map works differently. It organises uncertainty into something you can act on. It asks structured questions: *What could fail? How much would it matter? How often might it happen?* And then it arranges the answers into a pattern that does not require clairvoyance, only awareness.

To think this way is to return to civilian threat modelling. You are not a security agency; you are a person handling money across rails, apps, and accounts. Your threats are simple: loss, theft, freezes, outages, and discontinuities. None require drama to be harmful. All require clarity to be handled well. An emergency buffer in a stable unit protects you from a sudden wallet lockout. A second off-ramp shields you from a custodian freeze. A labelled backup phrase prevents panic when a device dies. None of these are glamorous, yet they shape the durability of your financial life far more than any forecast.

Contracts enter this landscape with equal weight. Every balance you hold—bank, stablecoin, platform credit, wallet—comes with a contract, even when you have never read it. The contract names the rights you have and the promises they make. Some are robust. Some are brittle. A 2018 consumer case in Dublin illustrated this bluntly when a prepaid card provider failed, leaving customers unable to access funds for weeks. The terms had warned that the issuer, not the brand, held ultimate responsibility. Few had noticed. The lesson was not cynicism; it was literacy. A single read-through of the terms would not have prevented the failure, but it would have shaped expectations and nudged some towards multiple providers.

Diversity grows from this understanding. Not the cosmetic diversity of logos on your phone, but functional diversity: different issuers, different custody models, different rails. The principle resembles biological redundancy. If one limb fails, another compensates. A two-wallet, two-rail system gives you both liquidity and fallback. Store some value with a regulated institution, some with a self-custodied tool, and some in a form that you can move quickly. The mix depends on your jurisdiction and life, but the underlying reasoning holds: resilience emerges not from abundance, but from separation.

And yet even a well-structured system remains theoretical until tested. Drills convert theory into skill. A quarterly restore test—importing a seed phrase into a secondary device—removes ambiguity about what will happen in a crisis. A small test transaction from your primary wallet to your backup off-ramp confirms that the path still works. These dry runs are rarely dramatic. Often they feel unnecessary. But they are the turning of the key before a storm. No prediction can replace their certainty.

Across these themes runs the quiet motif of names. When you name a risk—loss, theft, freeze—you shrink its power. When you name a counterparty—the issuer behind the shiny interface—you see the contract that shapes your rights. When you name a drill—quarterly restore—you transform anxiety into routine. Naming is not magical; it is structural. It turns the unknown into something you can handle.

The deeper point threads through the chapter. A prediction invites passivity: wait, watch, hope. A risk map invites agency: observe, prepare, rehearse. It does not ask you to be right about the future. It asks you to be ready for several futures at once.

And so the unresolved tension becomes unavoidable: *How much preparation is enough?* At what point does sensible redundancy tip into unnecessary complication? Where is the line between vigilance and obsession? The chapter will not settle these questions for you. Instead, it will give you tools—conceptual, practical, behavioural—to draw that line with clarity, so that when a system fails or a rail freezes or a provider folds, the event is not a catastrophe, but a scenario you have already rehearsed.

Threat modelling for civilians

At 9:07 a.m. on 15 June 2022, customers of UOB in Singapore found their mobile banking app frozen. Not sluggish—frozen. Balances would not load; transfers hung indefinitely; cards linked to the app returned error codes. For roughly two hours, commuters lining up for the MRT tapped phones that refused to respond. A few shrugged and used cash. Others were stranded, unable to pay for rides or make time-sensitive transfers. The Monetary Authority of Singapore later recorded the outage as moderate, not severe, because core ledger integrity remained intact. Yet for thousands of civilians, those hours were a textbook demonstration of a simple truth: you do not need a crisis to feel vulnerable. You only need a moment when your money becomes inaccessible at the exact time you need it most.

The UOB case was hardly unique. The UK Payment Systems Regulator documented a similar event on 29 January 2021, when a Faster Payments disruption delayed transfers across London for most of the afternoon. No funds were lost. No breach occurred. But the freeze turned everyday users into spectators of their own finances. Each incident, dull in hindsight, carved the same lesson: risk rarely arrives as catastrophe. It arrives as interruption—sharp, inconvenient, revealing.

Civilian threat modelling begins here, with interruptions rather than apocalypses. You are not forecasting global collapses or timing markets. You are mapping scenarios that could disrupt your ability to use, move, or convert value. This shift—*from prediction to scenario*—is the foundation of practical resilience. It removes the impossible requirement to foresee the future and replaces it with something anyone can do: name the threats that repeat across systems, estimate their severity, and decide—calmly—what you would do if they occurred tomorrow.

A pattern emerges quickly once you observe behaviour rather than conjecture. People worry about extreme events yet fail to plan for the mundane ones. They speak about identity theft but not device loss; they fear hacks but ignore de-pegs; they fixate on fraud while overlooking freezes. The paradox is familiar. Dramatic risks dominate imagination; likely risks dominate experience. A clear threat model corrects the imbalance.

Start with what can be measured. Loss is not abstract; it is a misplaced phone, a corrupted backup, a forgotten password. Theft is not theoretical; it shows up as a card skimmed at a petrol station in Birmingham or a phishing link mimicking a platform. Freezes leave a visible trail: customer reports, regulator notices, short-lived outages tracked by independent monitors. De-pegs can be charted: the USDC drop on 11 March 2023 after Silicon Valley Bank's receivership, recorded hour by hour by public markets. Each risk has a footprint. When you examine the footprint instead of the hype, you stop fearing everything and start preparing for something.

A simple matrix—impact measured against likelihood—forces clarity. If your main income sits in a single app, an outage rates low likelihood but high impact. If you keep part of your balance in a stablecoin, a temporary de-peg might rate medium likelihood and medium impact depending on your liquidity needs. The numbers are not predictions; they are anchors. They create a landscape where you can see what genuinely deserves attention. The act of naming shrinks fear.

This structure is not new. Civil engineers in Tokyo have long used scenario-based planning to handle earthquakes: not forecasting the next quake, but rehearsing the aftermath. Fire brigades in Paris practise drills with blocked stairwells because they assume that entry points fail. Likewise, civilians building financial resilience need not divine the next freeze; they only need to practise their responses. The motif is simple: *before the shock, create the map.*

Consider two instructive cases. The first is the TSB Bank outage of April 2018 in the United Kingdom, where a flawed systems migration left nearly two million customers locked out of online banking for days. The impact was severe—a documented cascade of missed payments, business disruptions, and customer complaints. The likelihood, however, was low. Such full-scale outages rarely occur in regulated banking environments. Yet the high impact made a compelling case for having a secondary payment route—another card, another wallet, a balance held elsewhere. The lesson is not to distrust banks; it is to acknowledge that even well-regulated systems fail occasionally, and the consequences land hardest on those who rely on a single rail.

The second case is the TerraUSD collapse in May 2022. The scale of the de-peg was unprecedented, but the mechanism—algorithmic stabilisation without equivalent collateral—was not. Public documentation had long identified the fragility. The event underscored the value of storing long-term reserves in instruments you understand deeply, not merely those offering attractive yields. Understanding here is behavioural, not philosophical: can you explain how it holds value? Can you identify the issuer or the mechanism? If the answer is no, the likelihood of misjudging the risk rises.

A counter-example is equally instructive. When Revolut suffered periodic card payment disruptions in July 2020, the effects were mostly limited to short gaps at point-of-sale terminals. Many users noticed only a brief "Transaction declined" message before paying via another method. The impact was small. The likelihood of similar momentary disruptions was moderate. The event did not justify dramatic changes to a user's system. The matrix filters the noise: if a disruption is low impact, even if moderately likely, it does not demand structural redesign. It demands awareness, not overhaul. That is the value of combining impact with likelihood—it prevents overreaction as much as underreaction.

Threaded through all these examples is the recurring question: *what exactly failed?* In every case, the answer sits at a boundary—between user and device, platform and issuer, token and peg, rail and regulator. Boundaries fail more often than cores. A strategy that relies on a single boundary is brittle; one that distributes boundaries is durable. The motif returns: name the point of exposure, then map the scenario attached to it.

The practical implications follow naturally once you think this way. If device loss is a plausible scenario, the behaviour that mitigates it is simple: test a restore on a secondary device every few months. If platform freezes matter, configure a secondary route—another card, another wallet, another rail. If de-pegs rank medium on your matrix, decide what proportion of your holdings you would instantly convert if one occurred. These behaviours are not predictions; they are rehearsals. Each reduces emotional volatility because you have already seen yourself act.

A scenario-based model also clarifies what not to worry about. Many users obsess over black swan events—systemic market collapses, multi-rail outages, global coordination failures. Yet these rank extremely low likelihood for civilians, and often low impact relative to personal buffers. By naming them explicitly and rating them appropriately, you free cognitive space to focus on disruptions that genuinely shape daily life.

The benefit is psychological as much as structural. Fear thrives in vagueness. When threats live as nameless anxieties—*what if something goes wrong?*—they distort decisions. Once named—loss, theft, freeze, de-peg—they become manageable. You can mark them, examine them, and assign them a place in your mental landscape. The naming itself is a form of preparation.

But naming introduces a final tension: *how granular should you get?* Too coarse, and your model becomes abstract, little more than a set of slogans. Too granular, and you drown in edge cases. The optimal point varies by person, but the principle holds: map enough to act, not so much that the map becomes the territory. A matrix with four or five scenarios, each paired with a clear behaviour, often outperforms sprawling, theoretical documents no one consults when panic hits.

The question lingers as we close: how much rehearsal is enough? When does prudent preparation slip into unnecessary precaution? And if the next disruption arrives tomorrow—not catastrophic, not dramatic, just inconvenient—will your map guide you, or will you still reach for predictions that fail under pressure?

Counterparties and contracts

Shortly before midnight on 11 November 2022, the Bahamas-registered exchange FTX filed for Chapter 11 protection in Delaware. Users from London to Lisbon refreshed dashboards that no longer reflected reality. Balances that had appeared withdrawable hours earlier were, in practical terms, stranded. The legal filings made the position plain: customer assets were commingled, contractual rights were uncertain, and creditors would have to wait for a court-supervised process. No hack. No glitch. The failure was contractual before it was operational. The exchange had made a set of promises, and those promises collapsed under inspection. Here, in stark form, the civilian lesson emerged: every balance you hold is a contract, not a comfort.

A different shock had unfolded years earlier. When Lehman Brothers collapsed on 15 September 2008 in New York, thousands of retail structured-note holders across Europe discovered that their supposedly "capital-protected" notes were only as strong as Lehman, the issuer behind them. The documents had always said so. Few had read them. The instruments functioned smoothly until the very moment they did not. The pattern matched the FTX event in miniature: value evaporated not because markets moved, but because counterparties failed to honour their obligations. The contract, not the price chart, determined the outcome. In both cases, the past had masked the nature of the promise.

The motif—that the visible interface hides an invisible agreement—runs through modern money. A mobile wallet shows numbers, not the layers beneath them. Yet every number is backed by something: a custodial claim, an IOU, a redemption right, a ledger entry, a legal undertaking. When you trace a balance to its issuer, you discover what you truly hold. This act of tracing is the essence of understanding counterparties. It transforms anxiety into knowledge because it replaces assumption with named responsibility.

Take the custodial stablecoin USDC, issued by Circle Internet Financial. Circle's monthly attestation reports—audited by Grant Thornton as of 2022—explain precisely what backs each token: short-term US Treasuries and cash. The documents also spell out redemption rights and the process for burning and minting. Reading the terms once illuminates the nature of the promise: it is not price stability, but redeemability under the issuer's conditions. Knowing this changes behaviour. If you understand that settlement delays may occur during banking holidays, you do not panic when redemption takes hours rather than minutes. By contrast, if you never read the terms, you may interpret a routine queue as a signal of collapse. The act of reading reshapes interpretation.

Contrast this with Celsius Network, whose bankruptcy filing in July 2022 in New York revealed a different structure. The terms of service explicitly stated that user deposits were loans to the platform, and that Celsius could rehypothecate assets. Many users had not noticed. Others had misinterpreted the interface as a custody product. The issuer's contract defined the promise; misunderstanding that contract defined the shock. When the company froze withdrawals on 12 June 2022, the visible effect was sudden, but the contract had always contained the mechanism for such an event. Again, forms follow promises, not logos.

A counter-example clarifies the line. Consider the UK's National Savings and Investments (NS&I), an institution backed by HM Treasury. Products such as Premium Bonds operate under fully transparent terms. The counterparty is the British government itself, and the guarantee is explicit. The products may not suit every use case, but the promise is unambiguous. The likelihood of default is remote given the sovereign backing. This does not exempt users from reading the documents—it simply shows that some instruments carry simpler, clearer agreements. The matrix here is not fear but fit: does the contract match your intended use?

When you examine these examples systematically, the central question becomes sharper: *who owes what to whom?* This question, asked twice, dissolves ambiguity. If your balance is a bank deposit in the UK, the bank owes you sterling, protected up to £85,000 by the Financial Services Compensation Scheme (FSCS). If your balance is a custodial crypto wallet, the platform owes you access to the assets, usually under bailment or trust-like arrangements depending on jurisdiction. If your balance is held in a decentralised protocol, the protocol does not owe you anything; its code offers functions, not promises. Each structure implies different behaviours. You measure not trust but obligation.

This is why a single issuer-check can alter your entire risk profile. When you read a platform's terms, focus on four visible behaviours: whether the issuer may suspend withdrawals;

whether they may rehypothecate assets; whether customer balances form part of the bankruptcy estate; and whether disputes are resolved through arbitration or court. Each behaviour reveals a contractual posture. A provider that reserves the right to freeze transfers for compliance checks could slow your liquidity. A provider that rehypothecates may expose you to upstream risks. A provider that pulls customer assets into the bankruptcy estate may leave you waiting years for recovery. The terms show these dynamics in plain language. The implication is straightforward: if you know the promise, you can decide whether to hold it.

Case law provides real anchors. When Mt. Gox collapsed in February 2014 in Tokyo, users learned via the court process that their claims were unsecured. The bankruptcy estate treated customer balances as liabilities, not segregated assets. It took nearly a decade of legal proceedings before substantial restitution began. This is not a cryptocurrency story; it is a counterparty story. The determinant was not blockchain but contract. The same would have held if the assets were foreign currency deposits with a failed broker. The underlying theme repeats: systems differ, but promises govern outcomes.

By contrast, when Visa suffered a European processing outage on 1 June 2018, cardholders experienced declined transactions for several hours across the UK and Ireland. The issue was a hardware fault, not a contractual breach. Cardholders retained full rights; merchants were eventually compensated for costs. The episode shows that not all disruptions are created equal. Some stem from operational failures without erasing claims. The matrix you hold in your mind—impact against likelihood—shifts once you distinguish between operational failure and contractual collapse. You respond differently when you know your rights will survive the outage.

The habit of reading once and calmly works because the purpose is not legal expertise but behavioural clarity. Suppose you hold part of your savings in a multi-currency account offered by a fintech in London. If you discover in the terms that the account is provided by a partner bank under an e-money licence, the implication is subtle: your funds are safeguarded but not protected by FSCS insurance. That means the provider must segregate funds, but if the safeguarding bank fails, timelines could stretch. Knowing this, you might diversify by issuer rather than by currency. The behaviour—the act of splitting balances—flows directly from the contract's structure.

A similar logic applies to token approvals in decentralised finance. When you grant an approval, you grant a smart contract the right to move a defined quantity of a digital asset. The "issuer" here is code. The contract is visible but often unread. A single misconfigured approval can allow transfers you did not intend. The promise is mechanical rather than institutional. Understanding this prompts a quarterly review of approvals, revoking those no longer needed. The behaviour reduces exposure. The motif returns: the shape of the promise dictates the shape of your habits.

Yet there is a tension. Not every civilian can or should read every line of every document. Over-reading paralyses. Under-reading blinds. The question becomes: *which promises matter most to you?* If you rely on a balance for daily liquidity, read the terms governing withdrawals. If you rely on a token for long-term storage, read its redemption mechanism. If you rely on a platform to bridge currencies, read how it handles insolvency. A single reading often suffices because terms change slowly. The review is not a chore; it is an orientation.

Still, the ambiguity persists. Some contracts are elegantly structured, others purposefully vague. Some counterparties are supervised by regulators with histories of intervention; others are thinly capitalised companies registered in permissive jurisdictions. You cannot remove uncertainty. But you can name it. And once named, you can classify it—not as fear, but as structure.

The unresolved question remains the one that matters: faced with a balance that looks convenient, will you pause long enough to ask what you are actually holding? And if the contract behind it were tested tomorrow, would you be comfortable with the promise that emerges, or would the shock reveal a promise you never realised you had made?

Diversification that matters

In March 2023, when Silicon Valley Bank collapsed in California, thousands of British founders discovered overnight that "diversified" balances scattered across several apps were, in reality, exposed to a single underlying institution. The logos differed; the counterparty did not. By the following morning, Treasury officials were racing to coordinate guarantees, and firms who thought they had built prudent cushions were suddenly preparing contingency payroll plans. The lesson was not moral but mechanical: true diversification is structural, not aesthetic. A colourful interface does not change the identity of the issuer who holds your money.

A decade earlier, a quieter warning had appeared. In June 2012, during the Spanish banking crisis, the regional savings bank Bankia froze certain retail products, leaving holders uncertain about access. Many customers had split their savings across separate Bankia-branded instruments, believing they had diversified. The fault was not their intent but the design. Diversification by logo had disguised concentration by issuer. The pattern mirrored the Silicon Valley Bank episode, though at a different scale and under a different political climate. It is the same map with different colours.

This motif—*the line that matters is usually invisible*—runs through personal finance more than any other domain. A wallet can show twenty assets, each with a fresh badge and its own marketing copy, yet every one may depend on the same rail, the same custodian, or the same redemption mechanism. What looks wide is narrow. What feels spread is stacked. The map must be drawn with the right boundaries: issuer, rail, custody.

The first boundary is issuer. Show this directly. Consider USDC, the stablecoin issued by Circle in Boston. If you hold USDC at Coinbase in London, your claim is not simply "USDC". It is a custodial claim dependent on Coinbase's solvency, Circle's redemption mechanisms, and the underlying assets that back the token. Name the structure. The promise is layered: Coinbase owes you access; Circle owes redeemability; the backing assets owe liquidity under US Treasury and banking systems. Explain why this matters. A disruption at any layer changes your ability to settle or withdraw, regardless of how many wallets display the same token. The implication is clear: if your balances depend on a single issuer's operational health, you do not hold a diversified position—you hold one balance with multiple windows.

Rail diversification adds the second boundary. A rail is the mechanism by which money moves and settles. Faster Payments in the UK, SEPA in the Eurozone, Visa's card network, Ethereum mainnet, Lightning, and Solana all represent distinct rails. Now show the contrast. When Visa's European processing system failed for several hours on 1 June 2018, card-based payments across the UK and Ireland stalled instantly. Yet bank transfers continued, and crypto rails remained unaffected. Name this: rail failure, not issuer failure. Explain that a personal plan built purely on card payments suffers a single point of failure. The implication is practical: rails fail differently, and when they do, your ability to transact depends on whether you have an alternative channel prepared.

Custody is the third boundary, and often the least visible. Holding assets with a single custodian—whether a bank, a fintech, or a crypto exchange—binds you to its operational and legal posture. Cold storage, hardware wallets, multisig arrangements, and custodial accounts each represent different custody models. Show the difference through an example. When Mt. Gox collapsed in Tokyo in February 2014, the issue was custody, not currency. Customers failed to withdraw bitcoin not because Bitcoin malfunctioned but because the exchange controlled the keys. Name this: custody risk. Explain that spreading balances across custody models changes the texture of exposure. A hardware wallet secures keys; a custodial account delegates that responsibility. The implication is systematic: if all your assets rely on a single custodian, you rely on a single point of compromise.

A counter-example offers clarity. Imagine a user who splits their balances across two fintech apps but later discovers that both apps safeguard funds at the same underlying partner bank. The scenario may feel diversified but is structurally identical to holding one account. The limitation is real: even sophisticated interfaces can obscure shared infrastructure. Reconciliation requires the same move: trace the issuer, trace the rail, trace the custodian. Only then can you measure true spread.

The two-wallet, two-rail plan brings these principles into a civilian-friendly shape. Show it concretely. One wallet sits on a traditional rail: a regulated bank account in the UK with FSCS protection up to £85,000. The second wallet sits on a digital rail: a self-custodial crypto wallet capable of sending stablecoins via Ethereum or Lightning. Name the layout: issuer diversification (bank vs token issuer), rail diversification (Faster Payments vs blockchain), and custody diversification (bank custody vs self-custody). Explain how this structure behaves under stress. If the bank suffers an outage, the crypto rail allows settlement. If the crypto rail congests, the bank rail remains predictable. If one issuer faces operational distress, the other issuer's obligations remain unaffected. The implication is resilience, not abstraction. The plan is simple enough to maintain yet broad enough to absorb shocks.

Behaviour sharpens theory. Suppose your salary arrives in a fintech account backed by a single partner bank. You set a rule: within one hour of receipt, you move a portion to a second issuer and a second rail. This is not investment advice but operational hygiene. You measure exposure by actions visible on your statements. Each transfer is a structural decision: split, separate, anchor. The behaviour—regular transfers—reflects the deeper map.

Historical examples reinforce the point. During the temporary freeze of withdrawals at the British fintech Wirecard Card Solutions in June 2020, following the parent company's collapse in Germany, UK users lost access to card spending for days. Those who held a second card on a different rail—Visa instead of Mastercard, or a debit card instead of a prepaid—navigated the disruption with less friction. The failure was not technological but organisational. A second rail carried the load.

By contrast, during the April 2022 Ethereum congestion spikes linked to NFT minting events, users who relied solely on Ethereum for transfers found transaction fees spiking beyond practical levels. Yet their traditional accounts were unaffected. Again the pattern emerges: rails experience stress differently. Diversification is a way to avoid synchronised failure.

The motif of the invisible map returns here with full force. A map drawn by logos looks neat. A map drawn by issuers, rails, and custody looks messy but truthful. The purpose is not to eliminate risk—no structure can—but to reshape its profile so that a single failure cannot freeze your entire monetary life. Practical diversity is not a theory; it is a set of micro-habits.

Yet the unresolved tension stands uncomfortably close: most people will not maintain six tools, three rails, and endless compartments. The cognitive load would defeat the purpose. So the question becomes narrower and sharper: *what is the minimum viable spread that protects you from plausible shocks without overwhelming your routines?* Two wallets and two rails often suffice, but the final map must match your own habits, not someone else's design.

Drills and dry runs

On 7 September 2021, as El Salvador switched on its nationwide bitcoin payments infrastructure, queues formed outside Chivo-branded cashpoints in San Salvador. Some residents attempted their first withdrawal only to discover they had forgotten a PIN; others tried to restore wallets on borrowed phones after lockouts. The technology had not failed. The choreography had. Those who had rehearsed the sequence—open app, authenticate, scan, confirm—moved smoothly. Those encountering the steps for the first time, under time pressure and watched by a crowd, felt their confidence shrink to the size of the screen. One small country became a demonstration of a universal truth: money skills degrade when untested.

That same year, in February 2021, the Texan blackout left millions with limited connectivity. Amid the outages, residents attempting to access online banking faced repeated failures: SMS codes did not arrive, card authorisations timed out, and customer-service lines stalled. Those who had previously downloaded offline records or maintained secondary access methods navigated the disruption more effectively. They had, consciously or not, run a drill. A quiet rehearsal had become a lifeline.

These scenes illustrate the motif that threads through this subchapter: *capability is not what you know; it is what you have practised under imperfect conditions.* Monetary systems—

banks, wallets, stablecoins, transfers—are reliable most days and capricious on others. The only dependable antidote is rehearsal with small sums before stakes are high. Drills are mundane, but they turn dysfunction into instruction.

A drill begins with a restore. Show it plainly. You take a secondary device, install your preferred wallet, and recover access using your backup phrase or key material. You test one function: a £5 transfer to yourself. Name this step: restoration validation. Explain the purpose. You are not verifying the app; you are verifying your own process. Can you locate the phrase quickly? Do you know how to input it without transcription errors? Is your storage location reachable? The implication is clear. If a genuine emergency occurs—a stolen phone, a corrupted device—you remove guesswork. You convert stress into sequence.

Next comes the off-ramp. One of the persistent confusions in digital money is the belief that rails are symmetric: if you can move value into a system, you can easily move it out. Historical episodes show otherwise. During the Celsius Network freeze in June 2022, users who had not tested off-ramps discovered too late that withdrawal processes could fail precisely when most needed. Name the behaviour: withdrawal rehearsal. Explain the logic. You move a trivial amount—£10, £20—into a bank account or alternative wallet. You measure time to settle, friction in verification, and any unexpected limits. The implication reinforces the earlier pattern: untested paths collapse in emergencies. Tested ones become routine.

A second example sharpens the point. In the early stages of the COVID-19 pandemic, PayPal experienced intermittent delays in transfer processing due to volume surges. Users relying exclusively on PayPal for contractor payments encountered bottlenecks. Those who had rehearsed a secondary channel—Faster Payments, bank wires, or crypto transfers—adapted swiftly. The issue was not foresight; it was practice. When one path jammed, another carried the load.

Swaps add a third dimension. Converting between currencies—whether fiat-to-token or token-to-token—looks simple in abstract menus but contains latent friction: slippage, liquidity constraints, network delays, authentication hurdles. Show the behaviour: initiate a £15 swap from a stablecoin to local currency or between two digital assets. Name the step: conversion rehearsal. Explain the value. You see, in real time, the fees levied, the time to finality, and the effect of liquidity on pricing. You surface constraints before they matter. The implication is operational clarity. You learn that some conversions settle in under a minute, while others can lag or require additional approvals.

A counter-example reveals the limitation. Some argue that meticulous rehearsal is unnecessary because modern platforms handle most complexity. The claim rests on the belief that smooth daily operation reflects underlying resilience. Yet outages, freezes, and surges contradict this comfort. Platform reliability is not user capability. Reconciling the tension requires a simple recognition: you drill not because the system is fragile, but because your circumstances might be. A lost device, a travel delay, or an urgent transfer transforms quiet unfamiliarity into risk.

The quarterly rhythm forms the backbone of this practice. Four times a year, you pick a weekend, retrieve the devices, and run your flow: restore, send, receive, exit, convert. This behaviour mirrors the operational habits of resilient organisations. For instance, the Bank of England's Real-Time Gross Settlement service conducts regular operational tests to verify continuity mechanisms precisely because reliability is not assumed; it is rehearsed. Name this: routine validation. Explain its civilian analogue: small, predictable exercises that keep your competence fresh. The implication is profound. What feels like a chore in January becomes a shield in June.

The motif of rehearsal connects closely to the psychology of stress. During crises, cognitive bandwidth narrows. Decades of research in human factors—from aviation to emergency response—show that people revert to their last practised behaviour. If the last "practice" was never, the fallback is panic. If the last practice was a £5 test transfer, the fallback is action. The principle translates seamlessly to money technology. Under duress, you will not read tutorials; you will act through whatever muscle memory exists.

Scenarios deepen the map. Imagine a trip abroad in which your primary phone is lost in Lisbon. You need to restore access to funds and pay for accommodation. If you have rehearsed the restore process, the steps happen quickly. If not, you must rely on a blend of memory, luck, and customer support queues. Consider a sudden need to pay a medical invoice after a weekend rail outage. Those who drilled an off-ramp to a second bank account retain agency. Those who did not must wait. Consider a stress scenario in which you need to convert tokens to fiat during network congestion. Only prior swaps reveal practical constraints such as peak-fee windows or liquidity thinning.

Drills also reveal idiosyncrasies: the wallet that insists on two-factor authentication through unavailable channels; the exchange that imposes a 24-hour withdrawal lock after a password reset; the bank that flags unusual transfers unless pre-authorised; the stablecoin whose settlement window depends on the issuer's banking hours. These details remain invisible until tested.

A wider historical pattern reinforces this argument. When Hurricane Sandy struck New York in October 2012, residents discovered the fragility of payment systems: ATMs without power, card terminals offline, and mobile networks unreliable. Cash became valuable not for philosophical reasons but because its use required no permission, no connectivity, no restore sequence. Those who had rehearsed hybrid modes of access—digital plus physical—navigated the days-long disruption with fewer interruptions. It was not technology that made the difference; it was familiarity with contingencies.

The quiet motif resurfaces: *skills under stress are built in calm.* Drills do not demand grandeur. They demand repetition. A five-minute wallet restore once a quarter. A tiny off-ramp transfer. A minor swap. A note on what broke, what worked, and what should change. Over time, these traces form a habit architecture that stands when conditions deteriorate.

Yet an unresolved tension remains, and it deserves honesty: how much rehearsal is enough before the practice itself becomes a burden? For some, quarterly drills feel excessive. For others, they are the only path to comfort. The test is not frequency but consequence. A simple forward question clarifies the point: *if your primary device failed tonight, do you know—without guessing—how you would access your money?* If the answer is shaky, the next drill writes itself.

Chapter 10
Families, Teams, and Communities

On a grey December morning in 2019, a commuter train stalled outside Copenhagen Central Station. Among the passengers was a family of five travelling home for the holidays. The parents, already fatigued from a long week, discovered that their digital travel card—shared between them for convenience—had been topped up twice by accident. Their eldest child, attempting to "help", had pressed a button he did not fully understand. The balance was not lost, nor was any harm done, yet the moment revealed something deeper: when money is shared, misunderstanding is never far behind. The carriage lights flickered, the train strained back into motion, and the parents silently vowed to organise their shared wallet with greater care. Minor confusion had exposed a major truth.

Shared money carries its own emotional weather. Even when trust is strong, the lack of explicit roles can turn well-intentioned collaboration into friction. A partner wonders who paid the last bill. A teenager buys a subscription they thought belonged to "the family plan". A small community group suddenly finds itself answering difficult questions when two members disagree over a discretionary expense. These misunderstandings rarely arise from malice. They arise from ambiguity. Money, when co-held, amplifies the gaps between people's assumptions.

And yet, shared money has always been part of human life. Medieval guilds in Bruges pooled funds to support injured apprentices; nineteenth-century friendly societies in Manchester created shared coffers for sickness and funerals; contemporary rotating savings clubs from Nairobi to Birmingham rely on group contributions to meet collective goals. Across all these contexts, the same principle echoes: when people coordinate their resources, they also coordinate their expectations—either consciously or by the slow accumulation of unspoken norms. Where expectations are vague, cooperation decays. Where they are explicit, trust thrives.

This chapter sits at that intersection of structure and sentiment. Families, teams, and communities do not operate like markets. They operate through relationships—messy, layered, and textured by history. But relationships can be strengthened, not strained, by clear financial architecture. The challenge is to build systems that preserve autonomy while enabling collaboration; to create shared access without surrendering privacy; to grant responsibility without imposing risk. The digital tools now available—shared wallets, read-only access, multi-party authorisations—carry immense potential, but only when anchored to human clarity.

One of the motifs guiding the chapter is the quiet power of roles. In households that handle money well, roles emerge without calling attention to themselves: someone tracks the receipts, someone approves larger purchases, someone double-checks the monthly totals. These are small duties, but as any financial historian will affirm, small duties shape large outcomes. The nineteenth-century household accounts kept by Harriet Martineau reveal an almost architectural discipline—one person recorded, one cross-verified, one planned ahead. The method was simple; the effect enduring. The modern analogue is a family digital wallet where one adult pays, another oversees, and both maintain transparency. Precision reduces friction; clarity reduces resentment.

Children, too, navigate money with greater ease when boundaries are explicit rather than assumed. A teenager with a small transport budget gains something that no lecture can provide: the felt experience of constraint. They make a decision on a rainy morning—call a ride or catch the bus—and live with the consequence. This is education through action, not abstraction. The digital layer, with its spending caps and expiration settings, functions as scaffolding, not surveillance.

The child learns to weigh choices; the parent learns when to step back. Autonomy grows best when risk is low and feedback quick.

Beyond households lie groups—clubs, co-ops, associations—whose financial coordination requires both trust and mechanism. A local football club in Glasgow might pool funds to repair equipment; a housing co-op in Bristol might maintain a shared maintenance reserve; a diaspora association in Leeds might operate a small emergency aid pool for members. Such groups succeed when they build governance into their tools: two-person approvals for transfers, clear spending thresholds, simple logs of decisions. The technology is not abstract. It is the connective tissue that holds the group's intent together. Just as merchants in late-medieval Venice used double-entry ledgers to prevent disputes, modern communities can use multi-party wallets to temper disagreement before it matures into conflict.

The deeper, less comfortable dimension of shared money surfaces when health declines or responsibilities shift. Illness, travel, bereavement—these life events test not only technical systems but emotional readiness. A caretaker letter, documenting how to access essential funds, can spare loved ones from uncertainty during difficult moments. A checklist showing which accounts exist, where credentials are stored, and who can act on behalf of whom transforms vulnerability into continuity. Financial design becomes an act of care. It does not eliminate hardship, but it lessens it.

Across these pages, the recurring motif is deliberate coordination. Where previous chapters emphasised individual competence, this one asks a more collective question: how do we design money flows that bind people without binding them too tightly? How do we maintain transparency without suffocating privacy? How do we share resources without sharing chaos? The answers lie not in technology alone but in a form of social architecture—one that clarifies responsibilities, respects autonomy, and anticipates disruption.

If there is momentum in this chapter, it comes from recognising that shared money is not merely a technical configuration; it is a social contract. The contract can be elegant or accidental, empowering or fragile. Its quality depends on whether the people involved can articulate who does what, why, and with which safeguards. In a world where people increasingly collaborate across households, cities, and continents, building that clarity is no longer optional. It is a civic skill.

Turn the page, then, not to learn rules but to explore designs—designs that help families keep harmony, teams remain effective, and communities act with confidence even when circumstances shift. The tools exist. The question is how we use them together.

Shared money without shared chaos

In July 2018, at Gatwick Airport, an extended family of seven gathered around a departure-lounge table, attempting to decipher why their shared travel wallet displayed a £420 deficit. The wallet, set up weeks earlier by the eldest sibling, had worked smoothly until a string of small, undocumented expenses—snacks, add-on baggage fees, a hasty airport-lounge pass—accumulated without anyone realising who had spent what. No one had acted irresponsibly. Yet embarrassment grew as each person tried to reconstruct purchases from memory while the gate announcement crackled overhead. The plane left on time; their mood did not. By the time they landed in Faro, the deficit had become a quiet fault line. A simple system had failed because its responsibilities were undefined.

Shared money fails not through malice but through ambiguity. When several people touch a single pot, the absence of roles turns everyday spending into a guessing game. A decade earlier, in March 2008, the British charity Age Concern published an advisory note warning that shared accounts without role clarity were disproportionately associated with interpersonal disputes, especially when used for travel or household expenses. The warning was modest; its implications were profound. If families and teams do not state who pays, who keeps, and who audits, the system invents those answers by itself—and rarely in ways that preserve harmony. A five-word truth anchors the problem: ambiguity multiplies emotional cost.

The motif running through this subchapter is a simple one: clear roles prevent quiet resentment. Families, teams, and community groups all benefit from the same triad of responsibilities—payer, keeper, auditor—each grounded in a visible action. The payer executes transactions. The keeper maintains the structure of the wallet. The auditor reviews. These roles do not signal hierarchy. They signal predictability. Predictability, in turn, preserves trust.

Consider the payer. Showing the role means something concrete: the person whose device holds the active payment credential presses "confirm" on a terminal or approves a card-backed purchase from a travel app. Naming the role makes the expectation explicit: this is the designated spender, not the default scapegoat. Explaining the role reveals its purpose: you avoid the silent drift wherein whoever happens to have the card becomes the unofficial financier. The implication is stability. Real stability—measured by fewer disputed expenses, fewer retrospective reconciliations, fewer assumptions about who ought to have paid.

In 2016, Transport for London observed that group travellers with a single designated cardholder experienced significantly fewer fare disputes than groups who rotated payment informally. The study's context was public transport, not multi-currency wallets, but the behavioural principle is the same: a clear payer prevents diffuse responsibility, which reduces friction. The motif appears: predictable roles shrink opportunities for misunderstanding.

Next, the keeper. Showing the role means maintaining the scaffolding of the wallet: updating read-only permissions, adjusting spending caps, and ensuring backups exist. Naming the role sets expectation: this person curates the system, but does not control the money. Explaining the role reveals its purpose: to separate structural maintenance from spending authority. The implication is resilience. When someone commits to being the keeper, the wallet no longer depends on whoever "understands the app best". It gains continuity.

A parallel example comes from a small arts collective in Rotterdam in 2021. The group used a shared digital wallet for materials and venue bookings. Early on, disputes arose because two members updated permissions without telling the others. Once they appointed a single keeper—whose task was only to maintain the settings, not approve payments—the disputes fell by more than half within three months. The wallet became a tool, not a territory. Again, the motif returns: clarity reduces noise.

The third role, the auditor, transforms oversight from suspicion into routine. Showing the role means reviewing transaction logs weekly or monthly, depending on usage, with no power to approve or block payments. Naming the role removes tension: this person checks, not controls. Explaining the role positions it as an accountability layer akin to reading a bank statement, but designed for groups. The implication is psychological as much as operational: people feel safer when someone has the mandate to notice anomalies early, without the emotional charge of accusation.

Yet auditor roles can go wrong when trust is fragile. A counter-example illustrates the limitation. A household in Bristol—three adults sharing rent and groceries—attempted to assign one housemate as auditor. Because the role was imposed rather than agreed, the auditor's monthly messages were interpreted as policing. Friction rose, not fell. The reconciliation lies in consent: roles must be chosen, not declared. When roles emerge from agreement, review feels protective. When imposed, it feels intrusive.

Now consider the tools that make these roles functional rather than symbolic. Read-only access is one. Showing it means a family member can open the wallet, see balances, view recent transactions, but cannot initiate a payment. Naming it distinguishes visibility from authority. Explaining its purpose highlights its emotional effect: transparency without vulnerability. The implication is profound: when people can see the numbers but not spend the numbers, accusation evaporates. The motif surfaces again—clarity preserves trust.

Spending caps provide the second structural pillar. They show their worth the moment a shared card is used unexpectedly. A cap of £50 per day (visible in the log) anchors behaviour. Naming the cap sets a threshold not for control but for predictability. Explaining the mechanism reveals its benefit: it transforms uncertainty about potential overspend into a fixed, known ceiling. The implication is protective—protective of the group's funds, but also protective of relationships. Few things corrode goodwill faster than "I thought you knew I was buying this".

The family travel wallet offers a complete illustration. Imagine four people travelling to Valencia for a long weekend. They fund a shared wallet with €600. One adult is the payer for transport and meals. Another is the keeper, responsible for the wallet settings. A third family member, perhaps older or less involved in day-to-day spending, acts as auditor, reviewing the log each evening. The children have read-only access, enabling them to check how much remains without pressuring the payer. A €30 per-person cap prevents spontaneous souvenir runs from draining the pooled balance. Each action is tethered to a role; each role is tethered to an explicit behaviour. The wallet holds money; the structure holds trust.

Contrast this with a limitation that emerges in less formal groups—friends travelling together for the first time, for example. They may find roles artificial or unnecessary. In practice, they rely on informal norms: "We'll just split later." This works until it doesn't. A single high-cost item—a rental car, a late fee, a hotel deposit—shifts the emotional economy. Someone pays upfront. Someone forgets. Someone resents. The reconciliation lies not in abandoning informality but in minimal structure: one payer, one keeper, visible logs. Even light scaffolding reduces heavy conflict.

Throughout all of this, the motif persists: clarity protects connection. Without it, people retrofit narratives to transactions. With it, narratives disappear because there is nothing ambiguous to interpret. The psychological benefit rivals the financial one. Researchers at the London School of Economics noted in 2020 that group financial disputes often arise not from the amount in question but from the perceived breach of expectation. A £12 discrepancy felt worse than a £120 one when expectations were fuzzy. Naming roles fixes expectations at the source.

The closing tension rests here: how much structure is enough? Too little and chaos returns; too much and the system suffocates spontaneity. The challenge is not to perfect the architecture but to adopt only the roles and tools that maintain harmony without dulling freedom. A family, a team, a community must ask: what is the minimum clarity that preserves trust during the moments when trust is tested most?

Allowances and education

In September 2019, at a secondary school in Manchester, a Year 10 pupil named Alex faced a simple but revealing problem. His parents had transferred £28 into a dedicated transport wallet—enough for four return bus journeys to school. By Friday, only £4 remained. The transaction log showed nothing unusual: a few rides, one unexpected diversion, and two contactless tap-ins for short trips he could have walked. When asked what had happened, Alex shrugged. He had not connected taps to totals. He had not planned across the week. He recognised each fare but never saw the pattern. Yet by December, after his parents introduced a weekly allowance wallet with a balance display and a single goal—"Get to school and back"—his behaviour changed. He began checking the balance each morning. He walked more. He planned his route. His transport costs fell by nearly a third. The difference was not discipline. It was structure.

This quiet transformation, modest in scale but rich in implication, embodies a principle older than any digital wallet: competence emerges from practice with real constraints. The Swiss educational reformer Johann Heinrich Pestalozzi argued in 1801 that children "learn by the hand before they learn by the mind", insisting that abstract instruction without concrete engagement leaves understanding hollow. Substitute a modern allowance wallet for a slate and chalk, and the logic holds. Money skills develop when young people manage sums that matter but cannot sink them. The line between autonomy and overwhelm is thin; a small allowance thickens it.

A recurring motif frames this subchapter: *practice forms judgement.* Not lectures. Not warnings. Practice. Whenever we grant a child or young adult controlled money with a clear purpose, we invite them to build judgement through action rather than instruction. The motif returns as we explore why small balances, clear goals, and predictable limits teach more effectively than any theoretical lesson on budgeting.

Begin with the allowance itself. Showing its purpose requires a visible behaviour: the moment a young person opens a transport, lunch, or pocket-money wallet and sees a finite balance that must last a fixed period. Naming it clarifies the tool: this is not a reward, bribe, or abstract teaching exercise, but a bounded environment where decisions have consequence. Explaining the mechanism reveals its internal logic: a child with £20 for a week's transport must decide whether to walk once or twice, whether to avoid unnecessary detours, or whether to preserve funds for the specific goal. The implication is straightforward: autonomy grows when the cost of error is low enough to learn from but high enough to feel.

This approach echoes research from the Behavioural Insights Team (London, 2017), which found that teenagers given small, purpose-bound allowances with transparent logs developed stronger budgeting behaviour within six weeks than peers who received equivalent sums informally. The behaviour was observable. The reasoning was traceable. Practice shaped judgement. The motif deepens.

Next comes the goal. An allowance without a goal is an aimless pool. A goal without an allowance is an abstraction. Showing the goal means writing it plainly in the wallet description: "Transport for the week", "Lunch budget", "Clothing fund". Naming it defines scope: not everything, but something. Explaining the significance clarifies why goal-setting matters: specificity narrows options, preventing the cognitive diffusion that tempts young people to treat all money as fungible. The implication is elegant: constraints build clarity, which in turn fosters strategic thinking.

The teen transport example illustrates the model cleanly. A £28 weekly allowance, a visible log of tap-ins, and a goal linked directly to the child's routine. The parent retains top-up authority and emergency override, but day-to-day decisions belong to the learner. The behaviour becomes a rehearsal for adult routines where balancing certainty and choice is essential. What begins as a bus budget becomes—slowly, almost imperceptibly—a discipline of foresight.

Now consider the counter-example: a household in Edinburgh in 2022 attempted a similar system with their 13-year-old daughter, providing £40 a month for school lunches. They expected she would ration spending. Instead, she exhausted the balance in ten days by buying lunches for friends. The limitation became clear: the allowance lacked boundaries. It was not tied to a goal; it was framed as "lunch and whatever else you need". The reconciliation lies not in abandoning the allowance but in tightening the goal and clarifying expectations. Once the parents reframed the wallet as "lunch only, five days per week" and gave her a read-only log of transactions, the overspending stopped within one cycle. Practice, when framed, teaches; when diffuse, confuses.

The pattern repeats in community-based youth programmes. In 2015, the Bristol-based organisation 1625 Independent People trialled micro-allowances for vulnerable teens learning to manage their first independent living expenses. Participants received small, ring-fenced balances for food, transport, and essentials. The staff monitored logs weekly. Over three months, young people began to anticipate shortfalls, adjust choices, and plan. The behaviour was incremental but persistent. The implication remains consistent with our motif: repeated, low-stakes practice builds confidence that abstract teaching cannot match.

Allowances also carry psychological weight. They signal trust. This is not an abstraction but a visible behaviour: granting a teenager the ability to manage a modest balance without constant oversight. Naming the trust makes the transfer explicit: "This is yours to manage." Explaining the effect uncovers its deeper value: trust cements responsibility because it activates the learner's self-image as a capable agent. The implication: confidence grows not from being told one is responsible, but from being placed in a position where responsibility can be exercised and observed.

Yet trust must be structured. The allowance wallet works because it is bounded. Parents or guardians retain override capacity; the learner controls the rhythm of spending. This duality mirrors financial autonomy in adulthood, where structures—budgets, limits, categories—protect individuals from their own impulses without suffocating their agency.

Now let us examine the architecture that turns allowances into educational instruments. A simple design suffices: a small balance, a fixed period, and a visible log. Showing the structure means that after each purchase, the learner sees an updated total and a short description. Naming it differentiates the structure from an open-ended account: it is a sandbox. Explaining the sandbox metaphor clarifies the intent: an environment where experimentation is safe. The implication is transformative: mistakes become data, not disasters.

A quiet motif returns: *practice forms judgement.* Every time a learner adapts their choices to fit the remaining balance, they rehearse the mental choreography required for adult financial management. They measure. They compare. They commit.

To anchor these abstractions, consider the rhythm of a week. On Monday, the learner sees £20. On Tuesday, after two rides, £15.60. On Wednesday, after choosing to walk home, £14.60. On Thursday, a diversion costs £2.40, dropping the total to £12.20. On Friday, enough remains for the final rides. The visible pattern teaches something subtle: forecasting. The learner begins to anticipate not in grand economic terms, but in the intimate terms of movement, distance, and choice. This is budgeting lived, not budgeting taught.

A broader example shows how allowances can scale into team or club settings. A youth sports club in Leeds in 2020 introduced weekly micro-allowances for equipment and refreshments across a cohort of 40 participants. Each young athlete received a £5 wallet. The club projected that children would spend it instantly; instead, they paced their choices across sessions. Some saved their balance for team outings. Others split it across drinks and equipment contributions. The staff noticed a behavioural shift: children asked about prices before committing. They compared options. They planned. The implication was not financial literacy in the formal sense, but a growing instinct for weighing cost against purpose.

Still, limitations must be acknowledged. Allowances cannot compensate for inconsistent supervision or wildly fluctuating household resources. In some families, irregular incomes make fixed allowances difficult. The reconciliation lies in flexibility: allowances need not be weekly; they can be per task, per goal, or linked to predictable periods. The principle holds even if the cadence changes: structured practice still builds judgement.

The closing tension lingers on one question: how much autonomy should young learners receive, and when should adults intervene? Too much autonomy risks overwhelm; too much intervention undermines confidence. The unresolved test is balance itself. Each family or team must measure the learner's readiness, compare their behaviour with the goals, and commit to adjusting the structure as the learner grows. The allowance is not the lesson. The practice is.

Clubs, co-ops, and pools

In April 2021, residents of a small cul-de-sac in Lewisham gathered in a converted garage to address a simple but escalating problem. Within three months, two neighbours had faced sudden boiler failures, each costing more than £900 to fix. Several others worried they would be next. Pooled insurance felt remote and unresponsive; individual savings were thin after the long winter of lockdown. So, twelve households formed a micro co-operative emergency fund. They contributed £15 a month, set a £300 rapid-release limit, and required a three-person approval panel for any disbursement. By December, the fund had paid out three times without dispute. The rules were plain. The process was clear. No neighbour felt exploited or sidelined. The pool worked because it started small and all participants could see, in concrete terms, how decisions were made and who made them.

This scene captures a truth that many forget: financial cooperation succeeds not because people trust each other in the abstract, but because structures make trust operational. The Lewisham group did not rely on goodwill alone. They built a framework that ensured each request passed through shared scrutiny. Their act echoed a much older tradition. The Rochdale Society of Equitable Pioneers, established in 1844, ran its operations on rules that were transparent, collective, and predictable. Each member understood how funds moved and why. The mechanics were visible. The boundaries were firm. Governance was a habit, not an aspiration.

A quiet motif threads through this subchapter: *clarity stabilises groups*. Whenever people pool money—whether to insure a boiler, maintain a clubhouse, or support vulnerable neighbours—the pool endures only when the rules can withstand stress. Clarity stabilises groups. The phrase returns because its truth recurs.

Begin with the structure of pooled finance. Showing its necessity means watching what happens when a group uses a single wallet without roles or approvals: disputes, confusion, resentment. Naming the elements restores order: contributors, stewards, approvers. Explaining the relationships shows that every pooled pound carries a shared promise: not to spend without consent, not to hide activity, not to drift into informal norms that later fracture. The implication is simple: collective money requires collective boundaries.

The Lewisham fund demonstrated a multi-party approval model in action. Each request triggered a notification to three rotating stewards. At least two had to confirm within 24 hours.

The behaviour was transparent. The decision path was auditable. Approval logs stayed visible to all members. This visibility reduced suspicion because it converted trust into evidence. It prevented the quiet creep of hierarchy that sometimes arises when one person becomes the dominant organiser. The motif holds: clarity stabilises groups.

A second example, from Barcelona in 2018, reinforces the point. A cycling club with forty members created a shared equipment pool for tools, first-aid kits, and spare parts. Instead of a traditional treasurer model, they adopted a two-key release rule: one member proposed a purchase, another approved it, and the whole membership received a summary at month's end. The system reduced disagreements about petty purchases, especially when the club expanded. Members began to measure decisions not by personality but by procedure. The approval choreography—a visible behaviour—signalled fairness even when spending choices were contested.

Yet not all pooled systems function smoothly. A counter-example from a creative co-working space in Bristol in 2022 reveals a limitation. The space introduced a communal improvement fund for minor repairs and design upgrades. Contributions were voluntary. Approvals required unanimous consent among six organisers. As predictable as mathematics, the unanimity rule stalled progress. Even a £40 request for extra seating cushions failed twice. The limitation was structural. The reconciliation lies in adjusting the rule rather than abandoning the pool. When the group switched to a simple majority approval, disbursements resumed without conflict. Clarity regained its stabilising power.

To understand why structure matters, consider the behaviours that often destroy informal pools: opaque decision-making, inconsistent standards, discretionary exceptions granted to the loudest participant. These behaviours erode confidence because they make outcomes unpredictable. Naming the erosion—favouritism, drift, arbitrariness—is the first step to correcting it. Explaining the antidote reveals the heart of pooled governance: procedural fairness. The implication is evident in every successful club or co-operative: when members know what must happen, and who must act, the system absorbs shocks rather than amplifying them.

Multi-party approvals embody this fairness. They are not arcane mechanisms reserved for corporate boards. A three-of-five approval process is simply a rule that forces deliberation and distributes responsibility. It expresses a principle that no single person can commit the group's resources. The behaviour is visible: before funds move, more than one person must act. In household terms, it is the difference between a family fund governed by a single dominant parent and one where both adults review large expenses. The implication is expansive: multi-party approvals teach groups to slow down at the moments where slowness protects relationships.

Now consider governance as narrative. Every pool tells a story: how decisions are made, who has authority, and what happens when someone needs help. The Lewisham group's story emphasised speed with accountability. The Barcelona club valued fairness with flexibility. Each story is encoded in rules, not rhetoric. A quiet motif returns: clarity stabilises groups.

To illustrate governance in practice, take the example of a community emergency pool in Sheffield established in March 2020 during the first wave of COVID-19. Twenty residents formed a fund to support neighbours facing sudden job loss or medical isolation. They set three rules: monthly contributions of £10, a disbursement cap of £150, and a requirement that any request be reviewed by a panel of three volunteers—two to approve, one to record the decision. Over a year, the pool supported nine households. Not one disbursement was disputed. The reason is neither sentimental nor mysterious.

The rules were simple enough that every member could explain them to others. The logs were shared monthly by email. Requests were handled with speed and dignity. The governance did not drift because it did not rely on memory; it relied on documentation.

But even carefully designed systems strain when groups grow. Consider a volunteer arts collective in Glasgow in 2021. With only eight members, their pooled events fund needed little formal structure; decisions flowed easily. When membership doubled, confusion followed. Who could approve expenses? Could any member propose spending? Did newer members have equal voice? The limitation was not capacity but coherence. The reconciliation came through a short governance charter that specified roles, caps, and approval pathways. Once written, disputes evaporated. The motif applies again: clarity stabilises groups, especially during transition.

The mechanics of co-operation extend beyond approvals. Education within the group is vital. Showing education means watching new members learn the rules by reviewing prior logs. Naming the process—onboarding—makes it explicit. Explaining why matters reveals an otherwise invisible truth: even a perfect rulebook fails if half the group has never read it. The implication is behavioural: each group must commit to teaching its rules, not merely drafting them.

Start small. The Lewisham fund began with £15 contributions, not £50. The Barcelona club began with small purchases, not major investments. A modest beginning reduces the psychological and financial pressure. It gives groups space to iterate. Iteration appears in visible decisions: adjusting caps, rotating roles, shortening approval times. The behaviour signals humility and adaptability. It keeps the pool alive because it prevents the premature ossification that often kills small co-operatives.

Yet the question lingers: how much structure is enough, and when does structure become bureaucracy? Too few rules breed chaos. Too many smother participation. The unresolved tension is the balance each group must strike. What is the minimum governance required for resilience? How will the group know when its rules no longer fit its size or purpose? These are not technical questions but cultural ones. They ask participants to measure their needs, compare their behaviours with their intentions, and commit to adjusting the pool as it evolves.

Clubs, co-ops, and pools thrive not on trust alone, but on rules that make trust visible. That is the promise and challenge of shared finance. Clarity stabilises groups.

Care, illness, and absence

In November 2018, staff at Addenbrooke's Hospital in Cambridge handled a case that revealed a quiet but pervasive problem. A patient in intensive care had managed all her household finances alone for years. When she fell unconscious following a sudden cardiac event, her partner discovered that he could not access a single account. Direct debits failed. Rent arrears accumulated. Even the electricity supplier required verification she could no longer give. The medical emergency was contained within hours; the financial disruption lasted months. The outcome was stark: one moment of incapacity exposed the absence of any documented access path. A single envelope, left in a drawer, could have prevented the cascade.

Scenes like this illuminate a truth many resist: *vulnerability is administrative before it becomes financial.* A household can withstand short-term income shocks yet fall apart when the person who ordinarily manages accounts becomes unreachable. The fragility does not always stem from complexity. Sometimes the structure is simple to the point of opacity: passwords known only to one person, a payment card kept in the back of a phone case, a subscription tied to an email address no one else monitors. The smallest details—the login to a transport app, the PIN for a prepaid card—become pressure points. One absence. One unknown.

A quiet motif threads through this subchapter: *continuity is designed, not improvised.* It appears first in the hospital story. It will return as the argument deepens. If the reader remembers only one line, let it be that continuity must be built deliberately, or it will collapse precisely when care is most needed.

Care is not merely emotional labour; it is logistical. To show this, watch what families do when a carer falls ill: they scramble for passwords, search email inboxes, ring banks without authority. Name this scramble for what it is—reactive navigation through undocumented systems. Explain why it occurs: because most households treat financial access as a private habit rather than a shared design. The implication is sharp. If financial continuity depends on one person's habits, the household has no system at all.

Two examples demonstrate how design transforms disruption into manageability. The first comes from Manchester in 2020, when a couple caring for an elderly parent created a caretaker letter—one printed page listing essential contacts, account access methods, and permission notes. It named the power supplier, the broadband provider, and the building's management office. It listed where read-only financial statements could be found and noted who held spare keys. When the parent was hospitalised later that year, the carers used the letter to maintain payments, communicate with service providers, and keep the home operational. They did not guess. They followed a map.

The second example, from Wellington, New Zealand, in 2022, involved a small programming collective that ran a shared digital wallet to fund conference travel. When their coordinator contracted pneumonia and was unreachable for twelve days, the team opened their documented continuity file: a rotation plan naming who could approve expenses, where the audit logs lived, and how to issue temporary access to limited funds. As a result, travel bookings went ahead without delay. The behaviour was unglamorous but decisive: they practised continuity with the same seriousness they applied to code deployment.

Yet a credible limitation exists. Not every household or small group wants to turn its finances into a quasi-institutional system. Some argue—reasonably—that too much structure feels cold, even adversarial, when applied to intimate relationships. They fear bureaucracy invading domestic life. This concern holds weight. The reconciliation lies not in imposing corporate procedure but in scaling design to context. A caretaker letter need not read like a legal document; it can be human, concise, and compassionate. A continuity checklist can fit on half a page. Design need not overwhelm. It must simply exist.

The heart of disruption planning is identifying the *access path*. Showing this means observing what happens when the path is unclear: time lost, funds trapped, obligations missed. Naming the path clarifies its logic: a sequence of actions someone else can take to keep essential flows running. Explaining the path reveals its anatomy: authentication, contact, control. Authentication determines who can act. Contact determines whom they must reach. Control determines what they are permitted to do. The implication is powerful: once this triad is documented, absence becomes manageable rather than catastrophic.

Consider the case of a London household in 2021 managing the care of a teenager with special educational needs. Their continuity plan included a short checklist taped to the inside of a cupboard door: school contacts, medical contacts, transport pass renewal dates, and the top-up method for the child's mobility wallet. When the primary carer fell ill with

COVID-19 in January, a neighbour activated the list. Buses continued. Meals arrived. Appointments were not missed. The checklist succeeded because it translated abstract responsibility into concrete behaviours: dial this number, open this app, top up this balance, record this receipt.

Documentation—often treated as a chore—is, in practice, a gesture of care. It creates a bridge between the person who usually manages tasks and the person who might have to step in. But documentation alone is insufficient. It must be paired with comprehension. This requires rehearsal. A quarterly review, in which a partner, sibling, or friend attempts to follow the documented steps, exposes weak points: an outdated password, a closed account, an expired ID. This rehearsal prevents the paralysis that often accompanies real emergencies. As the motif returns: continuity is designed, not improvised.

A limitation emerges here too. Some individuals fear sharing access details, citing privacy or security concerns. They hesitate to store information anywhere. Their caution is rational, especially when considering digital credentials. The reconciliation is to separate *knowledge* from *permission*: store read-only access where possible, keep sensitive passwords sealed until needed, and ensure that critical contacts—utilities, insurers, landlords—can verify identity through alternative means. Security and continuity are not opposites; they are co-designed.

The cultural dimension of care planning deserves emphasis. Many societies treat financial management as a solitary responsibility. Illness interrupts that pattern, exposing the mismatch between autonomy and interdependence. When one person becomes incapacitated, others must suddenly play roles they never rehearsed. Naming these roles brings them into focus: the keeper maintains the accounts, the communicator handles providers, the monitor checks obligations. These roles shift depending on context—one family member may handle transport cards while another manages subscriptions. The implication is unavoidable: households and teams function as micro-institutions, and their resilience depends on intentional role design.

Some groups already embrace this logic. The Māori concept of *whānau* in Aotearoa New Zealand, for example, treats caregiving as a collective undertaking rather than an individual burden, as documented in social studies literature across the 1990s and 2000s. When a member falls ill, responsibilities redistribute along established kinship lines. This does not eliminate hardship, but it dilutes fragility by widening the base of competence and awareness. The relevance here is practical: continuity thrives when knowledge is shared before it is needed.

To see the contrast, consider a counter-example from a three-person flatshare in Edinburgh in 2021. One tenant handled all utilities. She paid the bills, managed the meter readings, and communicated with suppliers. She never documented the process. When she travelled abroad for two months, the remaining tenants believed they could manage. They could not. They lacked account numbers, login details, and the supplier's customer code. A single missed payment triggered a reconnection fee. The limitation was not the tenants' ability. It was the absence of documentation. Reconciliation came only when they adopted a shared notes file listing each provider, the payment schedule, and the method for updating meter readings.

Across these examples, a pattern emerges. Care failures often arise from design failures. Conversely, care success stems from modest, deliberate planning. This planning appears in behaviours: writing a caretaker letter, saving a contact list, printing a simple one-page continuity sheet, rehearsing the process quarterly. These acts may seem mundane, almost banal. But they are the grammar of resilience.

The practical test for any household, team, or small group is simple: if you vanished for ten days, could someone else keep essential flows running with what you have documented? This question lingers by design. It forces a reckoning with the gulf between intention and preparedness. It draws the motif to the surface once more: continuity is designed, not improvised.

The unresolved tension sits here, waiting for the reader to confront it. How much of your life relies on tacit knowledge known only to you? And if absence arrived tomorrow—through illness, travel, or simple inaccessibility—would those who care for you inherit clarity or chaos?

Chapter 11
Regulation and Freedom in Tension

In February 2013, a quiet administrative update at the Monetary Authority of Singapore reshaped how thousands of small exporters moved money across borders. A revised reporting threshold—modest in absolute value, barely noticed by major institutions—forced micro-businesses to choose between transparency and friction. Some welcomed the clarity that followed: obligations spelled out, expectations defined, a sense of shared ground restored. Others felt a subtle constriction, as if an invisible perimeter had crept closer around their daily transactions. The episode, unremarkable at the scale of global finance, captured a tension that defines modern money: the space between what systems require and what individuals hope to retain.

The paradox is sharp. The more interconnected financial networks become, the more rules they require to remain trustworthy. Yet the richer a person's digital life grows, the more they crave sovereignty—control over their identity, their data, their balances. The tug-of-war is not ideological. It is practical. Every user who uploads a passport scan to open an account participates in a public expectation; every user who encrypts a backup or diversifies custody asserts a private boundary. One act leans toward collective order, the other toward personal autonomy. Most people blend the two without noticing, oscillating between them depending on the task at hand.

This chapter sits in that oscillation. It attends to the gradient where freedom meets governance, where personal tools meet public rules, and where the individual's desire for agency coexists with the network's demand for integrity. This gradient has always existed, but digital money sharpens its edges, exposing the trade-offs that were once hidden behind paper forms and bank counters. The motif that threads through the pages ahead is simple but relentless: *structure is not the enemy of choice; it is often the price of it.*

The stakes become clearer when we consider what modern financial rails actually are: overlapping systems maintained by governments, corporations, non-profits, informal communities, and decentralised networks. Each layer has expectations—some written, some tacit, some inconsistently enforced. Know-your-customer rules vary by jurisdiction but share a common logic. Reporting thresholds jump from one border to the next, yet the rationale behind them repeats. Consumer protections shift, but the intention to prevent harm endures. The names and forms differ; the principles travel.

These principles form the chapter's structural spine. They matter because tools now cross borders faster than the laws that govern them. A person in Nairobi can hold a balance issued in Brussels and spend it in Bangkok. A worker in São Paulo can use a United States–based wallet to support family in Manaus. A student in Warsaw can hold a decentralised token whose stability depends on contracts written by a team in San Francisco. When tools travel, their users must understand that rules trail behind. The skill is not memorising compliance by country. It is recognising the underlying expectations that almost every system—traditional or experimental—requires.

Beyond principles lies an often-missed truth: digital money, for all its speed and flexibility, still depends on public goods. Every secure wallet relies on servers maintained by people the user will never meet. Every dispute process draws on regulatory frameworks that outlast election cycles. Every anti-scam system depends on ordinary users taking a moment to report a suspicious message. Citizenship now extends into networks, not merely nations. The decision to pay a fair fee, to verify a sender, or to refuse a tempting-but-dubious offer is not small. It contributes to the hygiene of the system as a whole.

Yet the conversation about regulation and freedom rarely stays this measured. Polarisation intrudes. Some paint institutions as threats to autonomy; some treat autonomy as a threat to safety. Neither stance yields insight. What helps—what this chapter pursues—is dialogue. Not slogans, not sweeping claims, but constructive questioning. What promise does a balance represent? Which rights does the user retain? What portability does a platform support? Does a tool allow data export in a clear, machine-readable format, or does it quietly lock users into a proprietary silo? These questions are not radical. They are civic. They turn passive users into participants.

Consider a concrete act of participation: a short letter sent to a wallet provider, asking how to download transaction history in an open format. The request is modest. Yet when hundreds of users make it, platforms adjust. Standards shift. Markets adapt. Rights expand not through outrage but through pressure applied with precision. In the long arc of digital finance, norms are not handed down; they are shaped by people who understand the systems they inhabit and ask better questions.

This leads to the chapter's final arc: designing for dignity. Tools do not merely enable transactions. They shape how individuals experience agency, vulnerability, and consent. A well-designed financial tool respects context: it does not demand irrelevant verification, does not obscure fees, does not bury critical rights behind vague phrasing. It guides without coercing. It warns without patronising. When it requests data, it explains why. When it grants power, it records how. The criteria for dignity are clear once named, and ruthlessly practical once applied. A scoring exercise—simple, structured, repeatable—can reveal the difference between a tool that empowers and a tool that exploits.

The chapter ahead builds toward this skill: reading systems with discernment, choosing tools that respect autonomy without dismissing governance, and navigating the world's patchwork of rules with clarity rather than anxiety. Each section deepens a single proposition: freedom and regulation are not rivals; they form a dialectic that every user participates in, consciously or not.

What remains unresolved—and must remain unresolved—is where each reader draws their own line. How much verification feels acceptable? How much data should a platform hold? How much friction is worth the protection it buys? The answers depend on values as much as risk tolerance. This chapter does not prescribe the boundary. It illuminates it. And it invites the reader forward, into the complex, vital work of designing a financial life that is both sovereign and responsible, both protected and free.

Principles that travel

When the European Banking Authority released its supervisory review of cross-border payment providers in June 2019, one statistic drew particular scrutiny: among the firms sampled, nearly a third had been forced to revise their customer-verification workflows after entering another jurisdiction. The providers were competent, licensed, and well-resourced; yet the moment they crossed a frontier, their underlying assumptions about what constituted "sufficient identification" no longer held. The study named no villains. It simply revealed a quiet truth: rules move in zigzags, but the principles that justify them run straight.

A similar pattern surfaced in March 2021, when the Reserve Bank of India reviewed small-value remittance corridors linking Kochi to Dubai. The policy adjustments were minor—altered documentation requirements for repeated low-value transfers—but the behavioural consequences were not. Families who had relied for decades on predictable routines suddenly found themselves adapting to new thresholds, new forms, new timings. What held them steady was not encyclopaedic knowledge of regulations. It was a grasp of the underlying logic: who needed to know what, and why.

These moments—one regulatory, one personal—frame the thread of this subchapter. They show that while financial tools move seamlessly across borders, financial obligations do not. They also show that users who understand principles navigate far more confidently than those who chase local rules one by one. The motif that will recur is simple: *boundaries shift, but expectations rhyme.*

The first principle is almost embarrassingly plain once stated: systems want to know who they are dealing with. Whether a wallet is opened in Accra, Lisbon, or Seoul, some form of identity check emerges. The documentation may differ; the threshold at which it triggers may rise or fall; the verification method may range from automated image matching to an in-person appointment. But the drive is consistent. A visible behaviour anchors it: the moment a user uploads a document, the system records a claim—"This person is real, traceable, and responsible for this balance." That claim is what permits the account to exist at all. The principle is not bureaucratic. It is relational. It defines the point at which the network accepts that a user is participating in good faith.

This logic becomes clearer when we watch how failures unfold. The collapse of QuadrigaCX in Canada in 2019 illustrated a stark limitation: when identity expectations are weak and oversight is minimal, the boundary between operational error and fraud blurs, leaving users exposed. The exact regulatory environment was unique to the time and place. But the principle it violated was universal: users depend on systems that can verify who holds responsibility for what. The implication is that individuals navigating cross-border tools benefit less from memorising rules and more from asking the right questions: *What does this system need to know, and what promise do I receive in return?*

A second principle governs thresholds. Every jurisdiction sets breakpoints at which reporting, verification, or review is expected. The numbers vary—sometimes dramatically. But the behaviour they seek to shape is consistent: when transfers grow large, when volumes become frequent, or when patterns mimic institutional flows, systems expect visibility. The thresholds are not moral judgments; they are statistical hygiene. A user who understands this sees the number not as an obstacle but as a signal. It marks the point at which a transaction shifts from "routine" to "potentially significant" in the eyes of the network.

Two examples illustrate this continuity. In October 2020, the Australian Transaction Reports and Analysis Centre reiterated its guidance for digital money platforms, emphasising consistent pattern-monitoring rather than fixed amounts. Meanwhile, in 2022, the Colombian Superintendencia Financiera refined its small-transaction exemptions to simplify life for low-income citizens. One system foregrounded patterns, the other values; yet both were manifestations of a single principle: flows that stand out must be explainable. The limitation appears when jurisdictions diverge in ways that confuse users—when a threshold that seems permissive in one country triggers scrutiny in another. The reconciliation lies in seeking stable logic rather than memorising fluctuating figures.

The third principle centres on protection. Consumer safeguards vary by law and by institution, but their intent converges. When something goes wrong, users deserve pathways to resolution that do not rely on goodwill alone. The mechanics differ—chargeback rights in one rail, dispute portals in another, arbitration schemes in a third—but the expectation persists: the system recognises that asymmetry exists between individuals and institutions, and it attempts to correct it.

A behavioural marker reveals this principle in daily life: the moment a user checks a platform's dispute-resolution page before depositing funds, they enact a form of self-protection that transcends local legal detail. They are not learning the rules; they are checking whether the system respects the idea of fairness. Similar patterns appear across borders. In the United Kingdom, the Financial Ombudsman Service has received thousands of complaints annually since its founding in 2001, proving that redress is a lived reality rather than a theoretical right. In contrast, smaller or newer jurisdictions sometimes lack parallel structures. This limitation matters, but it does not negate the principle; it reinforces its value. Users who recognise the principle can adapt by selecting tools with clear recourse where available.

Threaded through these principles is the motif of the *mirror rule*: whenever a system demands something of the user, it usually implies a reciprocal right. If a platform verifies identity, the user gains the right to have their identity protected. If a system sets thresholds, the user gains predictability about when scrutiny begins. If a rail provides recourse, the user gains clarity about responsibilities. These are not symmetrical relationships, but they are meaningful ones. The principle travels.

Counter-examples sharpen the picture. The 2022 freeze of certain decentralised stablecoin redemptions exposed a limitation in systems that claim to have no custodians. When redemptions halted for holders in specific regions, despite the asset's promise of neutrality, some users discovered the uncomfortable reality that "decentralised" governance still involves human decision-making. The event did not undermine the broader ecosystem, but it clarified a truth: when a tool crosses borders, any mismatch between its stated principles and its operational reality becomes visible. The lesson is not cynicism. It is discernment.

This discernment becomes practical when users examine tools not for their branding but for their structure. A wallet operated by a registered firm in Frankfurt with transparent recourse channels may align with protection principles more cleanly than a sleek, borderless app headquartered in an opaque jurisdiction. A rail that enforces clear identity checks may offer stronger continuity in emergencies than one that advertises total anonymity. When principles become the comparison metric, marketing loses its potency. Structure wins.

The chapter's arc deepens as these principles intersect. Identity obligations intersect with protection rights. Threshold logic intersects with cross-border portability. Accountability intersects with dignity. The connections are subtle but crucial. They reveal that financial freedom is not achieved by rejecting systems, nor by obeying them unthinkingly. It emerges from understanding what systems are trying to accomplish and deciding how to participate in them with intention.

This leads to the unresolved question that closes the section: *When you next adopt a financial tool that crosses borders—whether a wallet, a rail, or a token—what principle are you relying on, and what principle will you insist upon?*

Public goods and private choices

When the UK National Cyber Security Centre published its 2020 review of digital fraud patterns, a brief line in the executive summary startled even seasoned analysts: a single coordinated phishing campaign had generated more than 6,000 victim reports in under a week, with cases concentrated in Manchester and Birmingham. The attackers were not especially sophisticated. What made the surge possible was something simpler and more structural—a critical mass of users who ignored or deleted suspicious messages without reporting them. The cost of silence became collective. A few private choices had weakened a shared network.

A more constructive example appeared two years earlier. In September 2018, Transport for London quietly credited passengers who had been overcharged due to a malfunctioning Oyster reader at Holborn station. The refund was automatic. It rested on a system that recorded millions of taps, reconciled discrepancies, and pooled individual behaviour into a coherent whole. Every traveller who tapped correctly strengthened that system; every traveller who jumped the barrier degraded it. Here, too, personal actions shaped public goods, whether participants realised it or not. The rail works only when enough people choose to uphold the rules that keep it fair.

These vignettes expose a recurring motif: *every network is a commons*. Even when tools appear private—personal wallets, encrypted messages, individual accounts—their reliability depends on everyone else acting in ways that sustain them. The infrastructure beneath them is shared, and so are the consequences of neglect.

To see this clearly, start with fees. They are the most visible marker of a public good hiding in plain sight. Users often resent them, interpreting each charge as a penalty rather than a contribution. But fees measure something concrete: the cost of maintaining the rails, validating transactions, resolving errors, and filtering abuse. In October 2022, the Monetary Authority of Singapore published a study showing that digital payment providers spent significant fractions of operational budgets on fraud mitigation and system resilience—budget items that exist only to preserve the integrity of shared networks. When users choose the cheapest possible route without regard for these inputs, they participate in a subtle erosion. A network starved of maintenance eventually collapses into congestion, delay, or vulnerability.

The principle becomes tangible when we observe behaviour on high-traffic systems. Consider the 2021 payment outages reported by Brazil's PIX network. After a surge in micro-transactions designed to exploit fee structures, the system faced periodic slowdowns. Engineers adapted quickly, but the root cause was behavioural: thousands of users treating a public rail as if it were an unlimited private channel. The implication is not that individuals should overspend on fees, but that they must recognise the invisible labour they fund. Paying a fair price is a civic gesture, no less meaningful for being digital.

The second thread concerns vigilance. Avoiding scams is not just self-defence; it is safeguarding the network for others. A scam that succeeds at scale poisons the well. It forces platforms to raise friction, add verification steps, or throttle usage—burdens felt acutely by legitimate users. When a user takes the extra ten seconds to report a suspicious link, they create a measurable impact. Each complaint becomes a data point that platforms use to train filters, block senders, or refine heuristics. In the 2020 NCSC case, the lack of early reports allowed a crude phishing campaign to replicate faster than protective systems could learn. Silence is not neutral. It is a contribution to risk.

To anchor the point, examine email providers' spam-handling metrics. In 2019, Google stated publicly that user reports play a material role in tuning its defensive models, which block over 100 million phishing emails daily. The efficacy of those filters depends partly on unpaid, invisible labour spread across millions of inboxes. Reporting junk is as much an act of digital citizenship as returning a lost wallet to a station desk. It says, "This harms others; here is a signal."

There are limitations to this framing. Not every user has time or expertise to recognise scams. Some platforms mis-handle reports, responding slowly or imprecisely. And occasionally, overzealous filtering can silence legitimate communication.

But these imperfections do not negate the underlying principle. They invite refinement. Users who understand that vigilance strengthens public goods can push platforms to improve feedback loops, clarify reporting channels, or publish transparency dashboards. Private inconvenience becomes a lever for collective improvement.

A third principle emerges in the interplay between choice and constraint. Networks impose rules not merely to control behaviour but to protect the shared environment. Rate limits prevent overload. Identity checks deter serial abuse. Cooling-off periods slow impulsive transfers. These measures often feel restrictive to individuals eager to transact quickly. Yet each reflects a tension: how to preserve freedom without inviting chaos. A public good cannot function if participants treat its guardrails as negotiable.

Examples sharpen this tension. The rapid roll-out of Europe's PSD2 regulations in 2018 required stronger authentication on online payments. Many users disliked the extra steps. Yet fraud rates fell markedly across several markets, according to the European Banking Authority's 2020 review. The extra seconds saved the system millions. Meanwhile, Kenya's M-Pesa, celebrated for accessibility, has periodically tightened verification during high-risk periods such as election months. Some users found the rules intrusive, but the trade-off was stability: the rail stayed open, trusted, and orderly during political stress. These cases show that public goods are elastic—they adjust under pressure—but they depend on users who recognise that constraints serve a shared interest.

The motif of the commons returns here. A network is not a place where freedoms collide; it is a structure where freedoms coexist. Every tap, transfer, or report is a vote for the kind of network one wants to inhabit. Users who treat the rail as a commons behave differently. They pay fair fees, report abuse, avoid participating in schemes that degrade trust, and favour tools that strengthen rather than hollow out the infrastructure they rely on.

The most delicate part of this dynamic surfaces when considering responsibility. Unlike maintaining a park or safeguarding a water supply, digital stewardship lacks visible rituals. There is no weekly clean-up, no town meeting, no fence to repair. The work is distributed and ephemeral. A decision to avoid a suspicious link benefits strangers one will never meet. A careful identity check prevents collateral damage far downstream. A refusal to participate in grey-market shortcuts preserves the network's reputation. These are acts of citizenship that unfold silently, but their effects accumulate.

To appreciate their significance, return to the example of TfL's automated refunds. The system only functioned because the majority of travellers tapped consistently, enabling the detection of anomalies. Had widespread fare evasion become normal, the entire rule-set would have broken down. Digital networks operate under the same logic. They infer trustworthiness from patterns; they fail when patterns become unreliable.

A counter-example tests the argument. Some peer-to-peer networks pride themselves on operating without centralised oversight, suggesting that vigilance and fee structures can be left entirely to market behaviour. Certain cryptocurrency communities celebrate "self-regulation" as a defining virtue. But when exploit attempts escalate—as during the wave of decentralised finance vulnerabilities in 2021—these communities often revert to informal governance: emergency pauses, soft forks, unilateral decisions by core developers. The absence of explicit public-good structures did not eliminate the need for them. It only postponed recognition of interdependence. The commons reasserted itself, whether named or not.

This brings the narrative back to the individual. Every user faces a set of quiet tests: when you encounter a suspicious link, do you report it or simply delete it? When a service charges a fee that reflects genuine system costs, do you pay it or seek a workaround that shifts the burden onto others? When a tool introduces protections that slow you down, do you comply or attempt to circumvent them? These choices shape the network as surely as any regulation.

The unresolved question that closes the section is simple but uncomfortable: *What kind of digital citizen do you intend to be the next time a private choice touches a public rail?*

Dialogue, not dogma

In June 2016, the UK's Competition and Markets Authority released a report urging banks to improve data portability for customers who wanted to compare products or switch providers. The document did not make headlines. Yet within eighteen months—after sustained, politely relentless correspondence from consumer groups such as the Open Rights Group in London—major high-street banks began publishing clearer export formats for transaction histories. None of this happened through protest or posturing. It happened because citizens asked specific questions, framed in reasonable terms, and followed up. A few well-aimed letters shifted practice across an entire sector. Such change reveals a quiet truth: institutions tend to move when pressed with clarity rather than outrage.

The same year, a contrasting episode unfolded in San Francisco. A heated stand-off emerged between a coalition of cryptocurrency advocates and a local exchange over proposed withdrawal limits. Both sides dug in. Blogs circulated accusations. Anonymous forums filled with hostility. When the dust settled, nothing improved: limits remained, trust eroded, and engineers reported that the rancour delayed the technical fixes that might have softened the restrictions. Polarisation consumed energy that dialogue could have redirected into design. Anger produced heat, not movement.

Here lies the tension this section confronts. Digital finance invites strong views—privacy maximalists, compliance purists, open-source idealists, safety advocates. Yet systems do not function when factions retreat into dogma. They evolve when users articulate what they need, why they need it, and how an institution might reasonably provide it. Norms change through conversation.

A useful starting point is the behaviour one can observe in well-governed public institutions. Consider the Information Commissioner's Office in the UK. It publishes plain-English guidance, tracks complaints, and reports outcomes. Citizens ask questions; the office answers them. Each exchange shapes future expectations. The visible behaviour here is correspondence: a steady flow of letters, requests, follow-ups. Dialogue produces measurable shifts—revised forms, clearer notices, better defaults.

The motif running through this chapter is simple: *the letter matters*. Not because paper has mystical power, but because a written question demands a written reply. And replies shape practice.

Start with a major claim: polarisation wastes energy. Show it. The San Francisco case demonstrated lost time, increased hostility, and no resulting improvement. Name it. Explain that when users frame institutions as enemies, communication collapses into binary positions; engineers retreat; regulators become defensive; users disengage. Implication: a system built on coordination suffers when coordination fails.

A counter-example sharpens distinction. In 2019, Monzo Bank in the UK published extensive detail on how to export data from its platform after a wave of user letters requested clearer formats. The change was modest—a redesigned CSV file, improved labelling, more accessible metadata—but its significance was cultural. A bank listened because users asked concrete questions rather than demanding ideology. They measured the result in improvements they could verify, not in rhetorical victory. When dogma falls away, progress accelerates.

Dialogue begins with clarity. A user who writes, *"Please explain how I can export my full transaction history in a non-proprietary format, including timestamps and merchant fields,"* poses a solvable problem. A user who declares, *"You are violating my freedom,"* does not. Institutions—and the humans inside them—respond to specifics. They measure cost, feasibility, timelines. They cannot engage abstractions. A visible behaviour—precise questioning—reduces friction and increases the likelihood of change.

Another major claim follows: users can shape norms. Show it through a second example. In 2020, the Australian Digital Transformation Agency trialled expanded access to government data using machine-readable formats. The pilot emerged after civic-tech groups, notably Code for Australia, submitted structured feedback on the difficulty of parsing earlier exports. Not complaints; feedback. Named. Dated. Documented. The agency responded with revised schemas and public documentation. The implication is direct: norms shift when citizens describe needs in language institutions can absorb.

Reconciliation is necessary, because dialogue has limits. Some institutions respond slowly or defensively. Some platforms treat users as noise rather than signal. And some regulatory constraints cannot bend simply because users prefer flexibility. Yet these limits do not invalidate the model. They refine it. Even when institutions resist, a record of thoughtful correspondence creates pressure, reveals patterns, and provides leverage in future negotiations. Silence offers nothing.

To move from examples to principles, consider the structure of a constructive question. It pairs one abstraction with one visible request. Instead of "transparency", one asks for "a list of all data fields the platform stores about transactions". Instead of "interoperability", one asks for "export formats that can be read by widely used tools without loss of detail". Each visible behaviour—exporting, importing, reconciling—anchors the discussion in what users actually do. Institutions understand actions more readily than slogans.

Dialogue also reveals a form of citizenship. When users send clear, respectful letters to platforms, they not only seek services for themselves; they establish expectations for everyone else. A request for better export formats aids the next person who needs to switch apps or reconcile accounts. A question about retention periods pressures an institution to articulate limits that protect entire communities. Private requests become public signals. They move norms.

Thread the motif again: *the letter matters*. It is a rehearsal for democratic behaviour online. When financial life moves across borders, interfaces, and jurisdictions, the core skill is not outrage but articulation. A user who can express needs succinctly navigates systems more effectively than one who declares war on them.

A third major claim deepens the argument: constructive pressure outperforms antagonism. Show it with behaviour. Look at the European accessibility directives implemented across payment interfaces between 2019 and 2022. Disability-rights organisations submitted detailed submissions, specifying button sizes, contrast ratios, label structures, and navigation flows. Institutions complied because the requests were doable, measurable, and grounded in lived experience. Polarisation would have produced a stalemate. Dialogue produced regulation that improved usability for millions.

Limitations appear again. Not all dialogues succeed. Some letters vanish without reply. Some institutions hide behind boilerplate. Some platforms design opacity deliberately. Yet even unsuccessful attempts signal input; they create a paper trail. They allow journalists, auditors, and legislators to trace patterns of neglect. Dogma cannot do this. Dialogue can.

The motif recurs: *the letter matters*. Its power lies in iteration. A single message may be ignored; a hundred, written by different citizens with similar questions, become evidence. They reveal expectations. They force reconsideration. They make the shape of a norm visible.

As discussion advances, consider how digital polarisation mimics political polarisation. Both reduce complex issues to binary positions. Both reward anger more than accuracy. Both provide the illusion of participation without the substance. Dialogue breaks this pattern by insisting on mutual intelligibility. A question is an invitation. It creates a space in which institutions must think, not merely defend.

The most practical way to observe dialogue's value is to watch what happens after a platform changes a policy. If a fee structure shifts, a withdrawal rule tightens, or a privacy default alters, a user who sends a measured letter can trigger clarification. If enough users ask similar questions, institutions often publish updated FAQs, revised documentation, or clearer help articles. This pattern holds across banks, payment apps, co-operative platforms, and even decentralised networks. Collective curiosity becomes a form of governance.

The act of questioning also strengthens the questioner. Articulating needs forces one to examine assumptions, define boundaries, and identify what matters. It turns vague frustration into structured thinking. That clarity is itself a form of power. A user who knows what to ask knows how to navigate systems. A user who never asks remains subject to rules they do not understand.

The final thread returns to the motif with its fullest weight: *the letter matters because it is a mirror*. It reveals how a user perceives freedom, obligation, and dignity within digital finance. It reflects whether they treat platforms as partners in negotiation or monoliths to be assaulted. It shows whether they believe norms emerge from collective reasoning or from immutable ideology.

The unresolved tension at the close is deliberate. When you next disagree with a financial platform—over a data field, a limit, a fee, or a policy—will you choose the discipline of dialogue or the ease of dogma?

Designing for dignity

In March 2017, the Government Digital Service in London audited several welfare-related payment portals after a surge of complaints from citizens who could not access or correct their own records. One case, documented in internal review notes later summarised by the UK National Audit Office, described a woman in Manchester who spent nine days attempting to amend a mis-typed surname that blocked her benefit payment. The portal lacked a consent-aware override; it offered no clear explanation of who could adjust what, and under which conditions. A single missing feature turned a routine update into a protracted ordeal. Her difficulty was not a technical glitch but a design failure: the system treated her as a data point, not a person whose circumstances required dignity.

The episode triggered a redesign that restored a measure of agency. Fields became editable with logged consent flows. Customer-service staff gained a verification checklist. Users received time-stamped confirmations. The cost was modest; the relief was immediate. It showed that dignity is operational, not abstract—a set of decisions that either respect the contours of a person's life or crush them. When financial tools mediate identity, access, and autonomy, design choices become ethical choices.

A paradox shadows the entire domain. If a payment app can execute a transaction in under 300 milliseconds, why do so many interfaces still leave people confused about who sees what, when, and why? Speed has surged; clarity often has not. The gap between technical capability and human comprehension forms the terrain on which dignity is either built or eroded. A humane system matches capability with intelligibility.

The motif running quietly through this chapter is *the hinge*: small details—one permission toggle, one clear explanation, one respectful prompt—swing the entire experience towards or away from dignity. A hinge changes everything.

Begin with a major claim: finance should serve human dignity. Show it. The Manchester case makes the principle visible: a person blocked from essential funds by a design that failed to anticipate plausible human variation. Name it. Dignity here means the ability to understand, correct, and authorise one's financial data without friction or humiliation. Explain that this requires systems to treat users as full participants, not passive recipients. Implication: when dignity is absent, trust fractures and engagement declines. People avoid tools that make them feel small.

A second example clarifies the positive inverse. In 2021, the Norwegian Consumer Council published a review of digital banking interfaces across Oslo, Bergen, and Tromsø. One bank—SpareBank 1—earned specific praise for its context-rich consent model. Before granting access to a budgeting feature, users read a short paragraph describing precisely which data fields the feature needed and why. They could approve permanently, approve once, or decline. The behaviour was visible: users measured their exposure, not imagined it. Complaints dropped; adoption rose. A hinge moved.

Yet dignity is not merely about permissions. It is about context. One major claim follows: tools must reflect the situations in which people act. Show it by returning to Manchester. The original portal treated every update as if performed under ideal conditions, by a fluent user with spare time and perfect records. In reality, the woman juggling inconsistent documentation needed flexibility. Name this: contextual design. Explain that systems must adapt to varied literacy, device access, network constraints, and stress levels. Implication: a system that flexes for real lives prevents small errors becoming crises.

A counter-example sharpens the stakes. In 2022, a major US exchange—Coinbase, San Francisco—faced criticism after its identity-verification tool repeatedly rejected documents from users with older passports or non-standard lighting. The algorithm performed well under laboratory conditions but faltered in lived ones. Users reported hour-long loops of re-submission. The limitation does not imply malice; it reveals the danger of designing for the average rather than the actual. Reconciliation arrives through the response: the company later introduced a manual review path and clearer prompts. Hinges, once adjusted, realign the whole experience.

Another major claim: criteria for dignity can be operational. This means measurable, testable, repeatable. Show it through behaviour. A financial app that logs consent with timestamps, displays permissions in plain language, and supports easy revocation demonstrates operational dignity. These behaviours create a chain of evidence: what was approved, by whom, and for what purpose. Name this: dignity metrics. Explain that teams can score apps on categories such as clarity, consent, portability, and recovery. The implication is powerful: scoring trains taste. It turns intuition into practice.

The scoring exercise is not aesthetic. It is diagnostic. A user who takes two apps—say, Revolut's export flow and Monzo's card-freezing interface—and compares prompts, defaults, and explanations learns to recognise design that honours autonomy. Visible details shape discernment. A person cannot demand dignity from tools they cannot parse. Assessment builds fluency.

Return to the hinge. Small prompts can swing entire systems. When a payment interface asks, *"Do you want to share your location for this one transaction or for all future transactions?"* it acknowledges that context changes. It respects situational consent. Conversely, when an app buries its permissions under nested menus, it signals disregard. The hinge is not symbolic; it is structural.

A further major claim deepens the arc: dignity requires a path for error, illness, and absence. Show it with a real case. In 2019, a co-operative bank in Bristol updated its account-recovery process after a trustee temporarily incapacitated by injury found that no single document explained how deputies could access essential funds. The redesign produced a caretaker letter, a two-step verification path, and a documented contact list. Name this: continuity. Explain that systems acknowledging human vulnerability embed dignity into the recovery process. Implication: people trust tools that accommodate fragility.

A limitation should be clear. Not all design interventions land smoothly. Some users find prompts excessive; others resist granular consent flows. Too many hinges can overwhelm. The reconciliation lies in iteration: ask users, test assumptions, and refine. Dignity emerges from negotiated design, not rigid doctrine.

Next major claim: dignity is economical. Systems that reduce confusion lower support costs, shorten queues, and minimise disputes. Show it with behaviour. After the Manchester portal redesign, documented by the GDS case notes, call-centre volumes dropped. Staff spent less time resolving preventable errors. Name this: operational efficiency born from empathy. Explain that clear options reduce missteps. Implication: dignity is not a luxury but an efficiency strategy.

Across all these examples, the motif remains constant. Hinges matter. One permission. One path. One sentence. Small but decisive.

A final major claim: dignity avoids spectacle. Finance often rewards tools that appear clever but leave users disoriented. Show this through a visible behaviour: an app that auto-categorises expenses but hides its rules behind proprietary tags forces users to trust predictions they cannot inspect. Name it as opacity by design. Explain that such systems ask too much faith and too little verification. Implication: dignity requires legibility. Users should determine how their financial life is sorted, grouped, and analysed.

Thread the motif once more. Hinges restore legibility. A toggle that reveals categorisation rules. A button that exports raw data. A notification that explains why a transaction was flagged. Each hinge converts confusion into comprehension.

Collect the strands into forward momentum. When digital finance becomes global, fast, and automated, dignity becomes easy to forget. But dignity is simply thoughtful design, repeated until it becomes expectation. Its presence is measured in quiet actions: a user who edits their data without assistance; a parent who supervises a teen's allowance transparently; an elderly person who resets access after illness without shame.

The unresolved tension sits where design meets power. When you next evaluate a financial tool—whether for yourself, your team, or your community—will you score it by convenience alone, or by the dignity it protects when life becomes messy?

Chapter 12
A Personal Operating System for Borderless Money

On 6 January 1979, in a small flat in Hampstead, the psychoanalyst Wilfred Bion sat down to write a short note to himself before returning to clinical work after a long break. He did not compose a grand resolution or map out a heroic plan. Instead, he listed three simple daily checks: *What did I perceive? What did I assume? What did I ignore?* For Bion, discipline did not stem from willpower but from rituals that kept perception honest. The note survived among his papers. It reads like a private operating system—humble, repetitive, and quietly powerful.

A century earlier, in 1882, Friedrich Engels described the household routines he and Mary Burns had built in Manchester to keep both finances and political commitments sustainable. Their method was almost absurdly modest: review the books every Sunday, settle debts monthly, and each winter re-evaluate which obligations still aligned with their principles. The records show no drama, just continuity. Consistency allowed room for ambition. Engels called it *the economy of attention*: the belief that regularity protects freedom.

These vignettes frame a truth that threads through cross-border money management. The borderless world promises speed, reach, and optionality, yet it overwhelms quickly if not met with rhythm. Modern wallets stretch across currencies, jurisdictions, platforms, and counterparties; without a personal cadence, complexity wins. The tools multiply; the attention does not. A lightweight operating system becomes the hinge between fluidity and fatigue.

The premise is deceptively simple: rituals carry the weight that motivation cannot. Weekly, monthly, and annual reviews form a pulse. The individual steps matter less than the continuity they create. The motif in this chapter—the *metronome*—captures that idea. Regular beats, not grand movements, hold the structure together. What resembles routine is, on closer inspection, strategy.

The weekly review sits at the first tempo. It is the most modest but the most essential. Think of it as clearing the windshield: balances checked, pending invoices acknowledged, approvals granted or declined. The behaviour is visible and short. Twenty minutes is enough. A person who performs this consistently gains a subtle but growing form of agency—not through dramatic decisions but through drift avoided. The metronome clicks.

The monthly reset deepens the discipline. This is where rotation, reconciliation, and pruning occur. In a world where financial accounts proliferate like browser tabs, this monthly session brings order. It is neither administrative nor punitive; it is architectural. When a person reviews custody mixes, rotates hot-warm-cold storage, and verifies which services still deserve access, they are shaping their financial perimeter. A before-and-after snapshot does more than tidy a system; it clarifies identity. You see what has changed and what persists. The metronome slows, but it stays steady.

Annually comes reflection—the slow beat that articulates meaning. This is the moment to revisit assumptions: Why do I trust this issuer? Why does this rail still matter to my routines? Should any documentation be renewed, simplified, or revoked? A one-page "money map" reveals how a person's digital footprint has evolved. Reflection turns experience into judgement. It makes tacit knowledge explicit. What seemed accidental becomes comprehensible. The metronome sounds softer but deeper.

Across these layers—weekly, monthly, annual—a pattern emerges. A personal operating system is not a set of commands. It is a dialogue between tools and values. Without reflection, tools drift toward convenience and away from intention. Without tools, values become abstractions with no operational form. The shift toward borderless money intensifies this tension. Cross-border platforms promise frictionless movement but rarely teach comprehension. They provide functionality, not philosophy. The user must supply the meaning.

That meaning often arises at the hinge where responsibility meets freedom. A person who performs a weekly review discovers, eventually, that they no longer dread financial tasks. Anxiety subsides because surprises shrink. A monthly reset reveals where commitments have expanded beyond comfort. An annual reflection exposes whether your financial life still reflects your priorities—whether care, independence, and responsibility animate your choices, or whether momentum has taken over.

These rituals also counter the illusion of infinite optionality. Borderless money creates the impression that every rail is open, every tool interchangeable, every balance accessible everywhere. But optionality without structure is noise. A personal operating system converts noise into signal, excess into shape. It is the difference between a person led by transactions and a person who leads them.

Consider how this structure interacts with earlier themes in the book. Risk maps become more meaningful when rituals exist to update them. Shared wallets become safer when reviews prune access. Cross-border practices gain dignity when users maintain clarity about roles, permissions, and expectations. Nothing here stands alone. The metronome threads through everything.

We live in an age that celebrates optimisation but neglects rhythm. What elevates a personal operating system is not efficiency but coherence. Patterns create meaning. When a person repeats the same structure across weeks, months, and years, they accumulate a second kind of wealth: perspective. They begin to recognise the texture of their own behaviour. They notice the subtle drift of assumptions. They see where habits have hardened into norms and where those norms should now be refreshed.

The prize is not perfect control but a calmer life. Money becomes a servant again. That phrase may sound quaint in a world of real-time transfers and algorithmic suggestions, yet its relevance grows with each additional tool we adopt. Freedom increases only when routines support it. Responsibility becomes lighter when distributed across regular intervals. Care becomes actionable when woven into the system.

The question that lingers—and the question that carries us into the rest of this chapter—is simple but demanding: if your financial life already contains dozens of tools, contracts, and connections, what pattern will tie them together? What metronome will keep pace with your values rather than your inbox?

The weekly review

On 14 September 2008, in a cramped back office on Fleet Street, a junior accountant named Priya Mistry printed out a two-page reconciliation before leaving for the night. She had developed the habit after a near-miss earlier that year, when a misfiled invoice almost derailed a quarterly report. This evening, her check revealed a single anomalous entry: a small transfer logged twice. She raised it immediately. By the following morning, as Lehman Brothers collapsed in New York and markets shook from Hong Kong to Frankfurt, that minor discrepancy—spotted through a five-minute ritual—proved to be the first sign of a wider internal systems fault. Her diligence ring-fenced a problem that might otherwise have worsened under chaotic conditions. One quiet routine contained the noise.

That moment captures the core of the weekly review. When environments accelerate, rhythm protects. Borderless money magnifies this truth: transactions arrive at odd hours, approvals queue invisibly, invoices straddle jurisdictions, and balances move across rails with little ceremony. The ritual is not grandeur; it is calibration. It is the steady metronome that keeps pace while volatility demands attention elsewhere. The power lies in its ordinariness.

The weekly review begins with what can be seen—balances, pending invoices, outstanding approvals—but its significance lies in what is prevented. Drift is invisible until it is not. A missed subscription payment surfaces as a freeze; an unverified transfer hardens into a dispute; a forgotten small invoice becomes a strained relationship. These are not dramatic events but slow erosions. The ritual limits erosion.

Consider the structure of the routine. *Show*: a person opens their wallet interface and scans each balance. The visible behaviour is straightforward: confirm amounts, check timestamps, note variances. *Name*: this is the foundation of the ritual—regular balance verification. *Explain*: weekly verification creates a time series, an internal baseline that surfaces anomalies early. *Implication*: early detection shrinks both cost and stress. A 20-minute review saves hours later.

Two examples illustrate its value. In February 2022, the digital payments firm Wise reported a brief delay in outbound transfers from London after a partner bank's technical outage. Users who performed weekly checks noticed pending transfers queued for resolution; those who checked sporadically saw them only after several days, compounding uncertainty. The behaviour—reviewing timestamps—revealed the situation before support queues swelled.

A second example comes from Singapore in March 2021, when a major prepaid card issuer temporarily halted top-ups during a compliance review. Customers who kept a weekly ledger of expected inflows recognised the discrepancy immediately and rerouted payments. Those without a ritual discovered problems only when recurring obligations failed. The visible act—comparing last week's expected threshold with the present—created an escape path.

There is a credible limitation. A weekly review can produce a false sense of mastery: the ritual becomes mechanical, the eyes skim, the mind drifts. The weakness is real. Rituals decay into habit loops. Yet the reconciliation is straightforward: anchor the review in behaviour, not in autopilot. Speak the balances aloud. Note the oldest outstanding invoice. Commit one correction each week, however minor. The ritual stays alive because it produces action.

Three areas form the heart of the review: balances, invoices, approvals. Each maps to a specific risk. Balances protect against depletion, duplication, and unexpected holds. Invoices protect against reputational drift—missed payments, delayed responses, embarrassment when the sender has to nudge. Approvals protect against silent obligations accumulating unnoticed. These three checks cover exposure, reciprocity, and consent, the practical pillars of financial coordination.

The motif of the metronome returns here. The weekly review should feel like a click, not a burden. The short sentences inside the routine reinforce this: *Check. Confirm. Clear.* These diminutive verbs give the exercise momentum. A review longer than twenty minutes becomes something else. The constraint is the virtue. Short cycles strengthen attention; long ones drain it.

The borderless nature of modern money complicates matters. A person may hold value across bank accounts, mobile wallets, token systems, and stored-value cards. A weekly review is the only moment when these fragments are seen as one whole. It is the antidote to platform-induced myopia. The behaviour—opening every balance, not just the convenient ones—creates coherence. Without coherence, risks hide at the edges.

The review also tempers cognitive load. Many professionals underestimate the micro-tasks they accumulate: pending identity verifications, requests for transaction approvals, or platform notices that require acknowledgement. These linger like dust beneath furniture. A weekly routine lifts the furniture. The person moves from reactive mode to controlled response. The behaviour is visible: one inbox, one list, cleared each week.

A tension sits at the centre of the ritual. The review must be thorough enough to detect anomalies but light enough to repeat indefinitely. This is the paradox of maintenance. The temptation is always to extend the review—add more checks, incorporate forecasting, inspect contracts, optimise flows. Those belong to monthly or annual rhythms. The weekly review prevails because it stays small.

The weekly review draws strength from its consistency. Miss two cycles and entropy returns. Miss four and the ritual dissolves. That fragility is a feature. It signals how easily drift reclaims ground. When the review is restored, even after a lapse, its benefits reappear immediately. The metronome catches the beat again.

Historical habits echo this pattern. The writer George Orwell kept a weekly ledger during his years in Jura in the 1940s while drafting *Nineteen Eighty-Four*. His entries were sparse—expenses, receipts, occasional notes—but the discipline stabilised his chaotic environment. It was not the accuracy that mattered; it was the awareness. Early modern merchants in Amsterdam followed similar routines, not because regulations demanded them, but because rhythm protected judgement. The practice predates the tools but anticipates their logic.

The ritual also supports interpersonal coordination. When roles are shared—family accounts, joint projects, team budgets—a weekly review becomes the anchor that enables transparency. A person who completes their review arrives at conversations clearer, calmer, and with fewer surprises. The act of checking pending approvals signals attentiveness to others' needs. Drift in coordination often begins with drift in one person's review rhythm.

The metronome metaphor also speaks to emotional regulation. Money, left unchecked, accumulates ambiguity. Ambiguity breeds anxiety. A weekly glance converts ambiguity into facts and facts into decisions. Even unwelcome facts reduce stress because they replace vagueness. The behaviour—opening the tab, scanning, acknowledging—builds confidence over time.

Resilience grows through this rhythm. When a disruption occurs—a freeze, a delay, a platform maintenance window—the person with a weekly baseline knows what "normal" looks like. Restoration becomes easier because the drift is bounded. The weekly review constructs a personal reference frame.

The weekly ritual is not a forecast. It is not analysis. It is not aspiration. It is custodial: a way of keeping the system aligned with reality. Its value lies in repetition. The individual steps are humble, almost trivial. Yet from these trivialities, coherence emerges. A twenty-minute review each week gives shape to a borderless financial life.

One question remains, and it defines the unresolved tension that closes this subchapter: if twenty minutes each week can stabilise an entire financial system, what would prevent someone from doing it? And if they hesitate, what precisely fills the space where rhythm should be?

The monthly reset

On 31 August 2019, in a glass-walled office in Berlin, a small operations team at N26 gathered for their end-of-month close. Their dashboards showed near-perfect metrics: low failed-payment rates, reconciled customer balances, smooth card authorisations across borders. The snapshot looked harmless - almost. Then one analyst pulled a before-and-after export comparing June, July, and August custody balances. A pattern emerged: a tiny but persistent mismatch between funds held with one partner bank and aggregated customer balances in a specific currency corridor. The drift was measured in basis points, not headlines, but it was real. Because the team had a disciplined monthly reset—reconcile, rotate, prune—the discrepancy surfaced while it was still small enough to fix without crisis.

That scene captures what a monthly reset actually is: not a financial detox, not a heroic effort, but a recurring act of structural maintenance. Weekly reviews catch noise; monthly resets reveal shape. Where the weekly ritual asks, *"What is happening right now?"* the monthly one asks, *"What has this become?"* It is the moment when you compare snapshots, not just glance at the current frame. The rhythm is slower but the consequences are bigger.

The first major claim here is simple: maintenance is strategy. Show it. In the Berlin example, the visible behaviour was an export, a comparison, and a question. No algorithm demanded it. The team chose to take two snapshots—start of month, end of month—and place them side by side. Name it: this is the monthly reset. Explain it as a structured pause where you reconcile movements, rotate balances between "temperatures" of storage, and prune permissions and products that no longer serve you. Implication: strategy does not emerge from grand annual plans alone; it emerges from repeated, modest acts of alignment.

A personal version of this scene might unfold at a kitchen table in Lisbon or Lagos on the first Sunday of each month. A self-employed designer opens a laptop, pulls up their various wallets and accounts, and creates a simple before-and-after picture: total liquid balances at the start of the month, total at the end, and a short note on significant movements. That one page turns a stream of daily transactions into a pattern that the mind can hold. Borderless money without such snapshots becomes a blur. With them, it becomes legible.

The motif of the snapshot is central. Borderless systems bombard us with real-time views: constantly updating balances, instant notifications, moving charts. A monthly reset asks a different question: *What does the picture look like when you stop it?* Freezing the frame once a month enables judgement. You see what has accumulated, which rails you actually used, which tools justified their presence. The snapshot exposes drift.

Reconciliation is the first pillar. Show it through behaviour. A person sums balances across two bank accounts, three wallets, and a small allocation of stablecoins held for cross-border work. They write a single number for "liquid, accessible value". They then compare it with last month's number and with their own sense of what "right-sized" looks like. Name this: monthly reconciliation. Explain that it serves a different purpose from formal accounting; it is about alignment between your financial structure and your current life. Implication: if the structure diverges too far from your reality—too many tools, too much spread—the chances of failure in a shock increase.

The second pillar is rotation. After reconciliation, some movement usually makes sense. Hot balances for daily spend may have grown too fat. Cold storage may be too lean. A monthly reset is when you commit to moving a portion from one "temperature" to another. You do not need precision models to do this; you need a simple rule that matches your risk tolerance. The behaviour is again visible: deliberate transfers, recorded in your snapshot, from one rail or custody model to another. Name it: rotation. Explain that rotation counters inertia—those few extra hundred units a month that sit in a high-exposure wallet because nobody bothered to move them. Implication: regular rotation smooths risk exposure without requiring daily vigilance.

The third pillar is pruning access. Over a month, permissions proliferate. New apps connect to your main wallet. Merchants store card details. Trial subscriptions gain quiet continuity. The monthly reset is when you scroll through authorised connections, stored payment methods, and active subscriptions and ask, *"Which of these still deserves a key?"* The behaviour is tiny—revoking one permission, cancelling one card-on-file, closing one unused rail—but cumulative. Name it: pruning. Explain that pruning reduces your financial "attack surface", both technically and socially. Implication: the fewer unneeded doors remain open, the fewer ways your system can surprise you.

Two concrete examples show the power of pruning. In 2020, the UK's Financial Ombudsman Service highlighted several cases where unused recurring payments—small app subscriptions and forgotten services—contributed to overdraft spirals during income shocks. Customers who had regular habits of reviewing and cancelling dormant authorisations suffered fewer downstream issues. In a different domain, a 2021 internal audit at a European neo-broker found that stale API keys and third-party access tokens posed avoidable security risks; the firm instituted a monthly access-review protocol that cut active unneeded integrations sharply. In both cases, the act of pruning translated into fewer problems later.

There is a counterpoint. For some, the very idea of a monthly reset feels bureaucratic. Life already brims with admin. Why add another recurring chore? The limitation is real. If the reset becomes elaborate—pages of categories, colour-coded charts, perfectionist expectations—it will fail under its own weight. The reconciliation lies in minimalism. A functional monthly reset can rest on a single page: starting snapshot, ending snapshot, three or four deliberate changes. No more. The elegance comes from restraint.

In a borderless setting, the monthly reset also serves a subtler purpose: it reveals which rails really matter to you. Over 30 days, you might touch card networks, instant payment schemes, blockchain transfers, and platform-specific balances. Only at month's end, when you list which rails actually carried meaningful flows, can you see which deserve your attention and which merely clutter your options. The snapshot tells you whether your cross-border life depends overwhelmingly on one issuer or network. That awareness feeds directly into your risk maps.

The monthly reset, then, becomes the bridge between micro-habits and macro-structure. Weekly reviews track motion; annual reflection tracks direction. Monthly maintenance occupies the middle: it is where you can still make mid-course corrections without the drama of overhaul. Think of it as small-scale re-architecture. The motif returns: each month, you freeze the frame, mark it, and adjust.

Historical practice supports this idea. In the seventeenth century, merchants of the Dutch East India Company in Amsterdam performed regular *maandrekening*—monthly reckonings—to compare expected shipments, recorded credits, and outstanding obligations. The practice did more than keep books tidy. It allowed them to assess their exposure to particular routes and partners before a crisis forced recognition. Their environment was global, risky, and information-poor; monthly resets were how they imposed structure on uncertainty. Our tools are faster and shinier, but the underlying problem—too many moving parts, not enough attention—remains recognisable.

A modern analogue appears inside high-performing operations teams at fintech firms in London or Singapore. Even with real-time dashboards and automated alerts, they still hold monthly "hygiene" sessions: reconciling ledger snapshots, rotating balances between correspondent banks, and retiring outdated integrations. These meetings rarely make press releases. Yet when trouble arrives—a partner outage, a regulatory change, a sudden shift in volume—these are the teams that absorb the shock best. Maintenance is not separate from strategy; it is its spine.

The emotional dimension matters as much as the structural one. Borderless money can feel like an endless stream—notifications, rate changes, new rails, new stablecoins, new platforms. The monthly reset is the moment you step onto the riverbank and look at the flow rather than being carried along by it. The act of printing or saving a single-page snapshot—before and after, with a few handwritten notes—creates psychological distance. It says: *This is finite. This is knowable.* That feeling matters.

The motif of the snapshot also has a disciplinary edge. By preserving each month's frame, you create a quiet archive of your own behaviour. Patterns emerge: perhaps January always shows a spike in new tools adopted; perhaps June is when you habitually forget to rotate out of high-exposure wallets. You see not just what your money does, but what *you* do in relation to it. Experience, in this sense, is just snapshots revisited with curiosity.

The unresolved tension sits here: a monthly reset asks you to treat maintenance as a first-class citizen in your financial life, equal in importance to earning, saving, and spending. Yet the cultural script still glorifies intensity—big pushes, bold moves, aggressive optimisation—over gentle, repetitive care. The reset offers a different bet: that disciplined maintenance, quietly repeated twelve times a year, shapes your borderless money life more than any single "big decision" ever could.

So the forward test is blunt. If you were to capture one page at the end of this month—balances reconciled, rotations logged, permissions pruned—what story would it tell about how your financial system is actually built? And more sharply: are you willing to let that story accumulate, month after month, without editing it?

Annual reflection

In January 1995, the Bank of England published an internal review of its payment-system modernisation programme. Buried in the appendices was a quiet admission: the institution had underestimated how dramatically its own assumptions had shifted over twelve months—about custody partners, settlement rails, and the documentation required to prove resilience. The review did not lament failure. Instead, it treated the year's surprises as material for re-design. One line stood out: *"Only by studying our changed position side-by-side with last year's map do we understand what we have become."* That sentence captures the logic of annual reflection far better than any management mantra. A year is long enough for drift to accumulate and short enough for course corrections to matter. It is the interval at which experience becomes visible.

Picture a similar moment on a much smaller scale. A translator living between Copenhagen and Kuala Lumpur sits down each December with a single sheet of paper: a one-page money map showing where their funds begin, travel, pause, and rest. Twelve months of borderless activity appear as lines, boxes, and arrows. Some paths are thicker than others, marking habit rather than intention. Some tools have become central without conscious choice. Others linger unused yet still hold permissions. The map forces recognition: what looked like daily improvisation is, in fact, a pattern.

The motif of the map matters. Weekly reviews and monthly resets offer snapshots, but the annual map shows the terrain. It reveals the structures that formed while you were busy living—rails you relied on, custody choices you normalised, obligations you accumulated. Experience alone is not wisdom. Experience mapped, revisited, and questioned becomes something more stable.

Show first, then name. Imagine the translator examining their custody mix: funds spread across a Danish bank account, a Malaysian e-wallet, a euro-denominated stablecoin, and an international money-transfer platform that has quietly morphed into a de facto holding pen. Nothing dramatic happened over the year. Yet the total amount resting in the holding pen has doubled. That shift was never planned. It merely happened because the platform was convenient and always open. Name this phenomenon: behavioural drift. Explain it as the invisible accumulation of choices made under time pressure or habit. Implication: without an annual examination, drift becomes design by default.

Two grounded examples show why annual reflection matters across contexts. In July 2018, the Monetary Authority of Singapore released findings from a multi-bank operational review. It noted that organisations with explicit year-end audits of their custody arrangements—mapping which assets sat with which institutions and why—exhibited far lower exposure to single-point failures during correspondent disruptions. Their resilience stemmed less from technology and more from attention. Similarly, a 2022 audit of a mid-sized UK charity revealed that digital payment rails had proliferated over several years; a once-simple structure had become a maze of platform balances, card-on-file arrangements, and dormant access tokens. Only during the charity's annual governance review did trustees realise how many silent liabilities had accumulated. Both cases demonstrate that the visible behaviour—sitting down once a year to map the financial terrain—produces insights no dashboard can generate.

A credible counter-example sits nearby. Some individuals and teams argue that continuous monitoring removes the need for annual review. After all, real-time alerts and automated reconciliation make it easy to spot anomalies instantly. The limitation is that real-time systems excel at detecting events, not shifts in posture. They catch spikes, not drift. A year's worth of gradual reconfiguration—one new tool, one forgotten permission, one slowly thickening rail—evades daily attention. Reconciling this counterpoint clarifies the purpose of annual reflection: it is not about catching errors but about recognising how your system has changed shape.

Annual reflection also surfaces the difference between symbolic organisation and functional organisation. Many people maintain beautifully organised folder structures, colour-coded labels, or neat dashboards. Yet when asked which rails they actually used over the past year, they hesitate. The map tells the truth. If your largest flows ran through a platform you barely acknowledge, that dissonance is worth exploring. The act of drawing the year's map—literally sketching the path money travelled from origin to storage to usage—forces coherence between self-image and behaviour.

Documentation plays a central role. Consider an architect in Edinburgh who keeps meticulous transaction records but never updates her access instructions or emergency handover note. When she revisits her documents each December, she notices that a newly adopted savings app is absent from the instructions. Her partner would have no visibility of it if she were temporarily unable to act. The behaviour here—reviewing and updating documentation annually—may look pedestrian. Name it: continuity planning. Explain that continuity is not primarily about crisis scenarios but about reducing avoidable friction when life's disruptions occur. Implication: updating documentation once a year safeguards dignity for the people who may need to act on your behalf.

The motif of the map returns. A physical or digital one-page money map can track evolution over several years. It can show, for example, that the proportion of assets held in warm wallets has crept from 15 per cent to 32 per cent; that cross-border transfers now rely mostly on one provider rather than three; or that documentation for new tools lags adoption by two months on average. These are not abstractions. They are visible behaviours: the timing of your rotations, the density of your tools, the age of your instructions. With each yearly update, the map becomes a mirror.

Philosophically, annual reflection asks a deceptively hard question: *What assumptions have you been living under without noticing?* A man in Barcelona may realise, after a year of freelancing, that he has assumed uninterrupted access to his primary e-wallet. A woman in Nairobi may see that her reliance on a single mobile-money rail increased because clients defaulted to it, not because she chose it. A family in Vancouver may discover that their shared travel wallet, created for one summer, has become a semi-permanent fixture without anyone checking its permissions. These observations surface only when you step back far enough.

Historical precedent offers insight. In 1931, the economist John Maynard Keynes reviewed his personal accounts after the turbulence of the previous decade. He did not focus on gains or losses. Instead, he studied how his assumptions about liquidity and access had shifted during years of crisis. His diaries show an annual rhythm: in early January he reviewed custodial arrangements, exposure levels, and the interplay between his domestic and international obligations. His wisdom came not from perfect foresight but from repeated reflection on misjudgements and their causes. The discipline mattered more than the accuracy.

The counter-example to this pattern is equally instructive. There are years when reflection yields little. Perhaps there were no major shifts in custody mix or rail usage. Perhaps your documents remained accurate. The temptation then is to skip the exercise the following year. But reflection is not judged by its yield in any single cycle. It is judged by its cumulative effect. The reconciliation here is straightforward: the value of annual reflection lies in its regularity, not its novelty. Repetition creates the conditions for insight; insight arrives on its own schedule.

What, then, does annual reflection imply for a borderless money life? First, that the year is the right unit of re-assessment. A week is too short for deep shifts; a month detects drift but not transformation. A year captures the whole rhythm of a life: contracts won and lost, currencies touched, platforms adopted, habits formed. Second, that the act of mapping makes invisible structures visible. Third, that documentation is not bureaucratic clutter but a living record of how your financial system works when you are absent or vulnerable.

The emotional dimension surfaces again here. Annual reflection can be disconcerting. The map may reveal patterns you dislike: dependence on a single rail, sluggish rotation habits, permissions that linger without reason. Yet discomfort is a signal, not a failure. It is the point at which experience becomes wisdom. A map without friction teaches little; a map that challenges your assumptions has done its work.

The unresolved tension lies in how far to take this. Some will prefer a sparse, almost ascetic process: a single sheet, a few notes, a quiet hour. Others will produce multi-year charts, custody diagrams, and role-based access reviews. Both approaches have merit. The forward test is simpler: if you were to draw your one-page money map for the year just passed, would it clarify your financial life—or complicate it? And the sharper question: are you willing to let the map's truth guide your next year's design?

From tools to meaning

If you dedicate twenty minutes every Sunday to checking balances, scanning invoices, and approving transfers, why does your relationship with money so often feel unchanged by December? The paradox is familiar: the tools improve, the dashboards glow with ever sharper charts, yet the internal soundtrack—mild anxiety, low-grade vigilance, a sense of being chased—remains stubbornly the same. The rituals are in place. The calm is not.

In 2016, the Financial Conduct Authority in London raised a quiet concern: as financial products grow more sophisticated, it becomes easier for people to confuse *activity* with *alignment*. They may be endlessly signing up for apps, cards, and wallets without any corresponding shift in how money supports the life they actually want. That gap between the sleek surface of our tools and the deeper question of meaning is the terrain of this closing movement. The place where settings and spreadsheets meet care, freedom, and responsibility.

Consider one ordinary year in a single household. In January, a couple in Manchester agrees that both of them feel "crowded" by money. The accounts are not in crisis. Income is steady. Yet every unexpected bill feels like a personal failing, and every notification carries a small jolt. They decide—not dramatically, but deliberately—to treat the year as an experiment in rhythm rather than optimisation. A weekly review on Sunday evenings, a monthly reset on the first Monday, a brief annual reflection in December. No heroics. Just a quiet commitment to see whether a tiny operating system can change not only what money *does* but what it *means*.

By March, the visible behaviours are unremarkable. They tag receipts at the point of purchase. They keep a small stablecoin float for travel expenses. They shift a fixed amount each month into a cold wallet that neither of them touches without discussion. None of this would impress a technologist. Yet the couple notice something that cannot be plotted on a chart: arguments about money become rarer and more specific. They no longer quarrel about "being irresponsible"; they talk instead about a particular decision—a streaming bundle that no one uses, a freelance invoice that waited too long, a hotel booking that could have gone through a cheaper rail. The tools have not changed. But the conversation has.

Show first, then name. What is actually happening here? At the surface level, the couple's weekly, monthly, and annual practices form a simple scaffold around their wallets and accounts. At a deeper level, those practices are expressing a value: *care*. Care is not a feeling in this context. It is a pattern of attention. Checking that joint permissions still match reality is an act of care. Writing a two-line note in a wallet about the purpose of a transfer is an act of care. Each small action says, "Your future self matters; the people who rely on you matter." The implication is subtle but powerful: money is no longer just a set of balances to be maximised. It is an ongoing conversation about what and whom the household cares about.

A second value, *freedom*, emerges in a different story. In 2020, a software designer in Berlin leaves a salaried job to work across borders. Over twelve months, they receive payments in euros, dollars, and stablecoins. At first, every incoming transaction triggers a flurry of manual decisions: how much to keep in which rail, when to convert, which wallet to use for tax-related income. The designer feels, predictably, trapped by choices. More options, less freedom.

Halfway through the year, they create a personal rule set. Every invoice goes out in a single pricing currency. Each payment, no matter the rail, lands first in a "settlement" wallet. At the end of each week, they apply the same split: part to a euro account for near-term expenses, part to a longer-term reserve, part to a buffer in their preferred stablecoin. The behaviour is mechanical. The outcome is not. Within a few months, the designer reports a strange form of lightness: they are still dealing with the same volatility, but the decisions that once consumed attention have been turned into defaults. Freedom, in this case, is not the absence of structure but the presence of *chosen* structure.

The motif that runs through these scenes is a simple one: *who serves whom?* Does the person serve the tools, or do the tools serve the person's values? At the start of the year, both the Manchester couple and the Berlin freelancer are effectively serving their tools. Notifications dictate their attention. Platform quirks shape their behaviour. By year's end, the direction has shifted. The same rails and wallets remain, but they now sit inside a human-centred operating system. Money has become a servant again—not because balances have grown, but because meaning has been made explicit.

The third value, *responsibility*, often appears where care and freedom meet something less comfortable: obligation. Take a teacher in Nairobi who supports parents in Kisumu and pays school fees for a younger sibling. For years, her financial life is dominated by urgent transfers. She reacts to messages, scrapes funds together, and hopes that nothing overlaps. When she adopts digital wallets and cross-border rails, speed improves but stress does not. The obligations remain opaque; each month feels like an ambush.

Over the course of a year, she experiments with a different approach. She uses the weekly review not only to check balances but to list upcoming obligations: when term fees are due, which remittances have become de facto commitments, which contributions to community funds are genuinely optional. In her monthly reset, she compares these lists with her actual behaviour. Patterns emerge. Certain "emergency" requests repeat on a rhythm. Some contributions quietly replace others. She begins to treat these not as random shocks but as a portfolio of responsibilities. Responsibility here is no longer a vague moral weight; it is a set of specific, recognised flows. The implication is immediate: she feels more able to say yes with intention and no without guilt.

There is a counter-example worth acknowledging. Some people adopt elaborate systems—multiple buckets, colour-coded dashboards, strict rules—only to find that their anxiety worsens. They feel policed by their own tools. Money becomes a daily examination, not a servant. This is not a failure of discipline; it is a misalignment between values and design. A system built to express optimisation will not soothe a person whose primary value is security or generosity. Reconciling this limitation requires an uncomfortable shift of focus: away from the elegance of the system and towards the question, *What kind of person do I want to be in relation to money?* Tools are then chosen—and simplified—accordingly.

The language of values can easily drift into abstraction, so it is important to keep returning to visible behaviours. Care is visible in who gets access, and with what permissions. Freedom is visible in how often one needs to break one's own rules to cope with real life. Responsibility is visible in the promptness and transparency of meeting obligations, not in how loudly one talks about them.

A freelancer who claims freedom but cannot take a week off without checking a payments dashboard every few hours is living a different reality from their story. A parent who values care but keeps all recovery phrases in their head, with no documented plan for illness, is relying on luck rather than care. These discrepancies are not moral failings. They are signals for redesign.

One useful way to link tools to meaning is to observe the emotional residue left by recurring habits. A weekly review that consistently ends in tension or recrimination is saying something about how the system is framed. Perhaps it focuses solely on shortfalls, never on what went well. Perhaps it treats money as a permanent exam. By contrast, a weekly review that feels like a debrief—a mix of noticing, learning, and adjusting—indicates that the underlying values and tools are more closely aligned. The behaviour is the same: sit down, check, record. The meaning is not.

This is where the narrative of a single year matters. The story need not be dramatic. Imagine a calendar that begins with scattered, reactive behaviours: missed invoices, ad hoc transfers, permissions set and forgotten. By mid-year, small changes appear: a dedicated wallet for shared family expenses, a clearer distinction between hot and cold storage, a short note written when opening a new account about *why* it exists. By year's end, the external world may be more volatile than when the year began. Yet the person feels, quietly, calmer. Not because they have perfected anything, but because their daily, weekly, and monthly actions now tell a coherent story about what they value.

There is another named example that brings this into sharp relief. In 2019, a Dutch behavioural study at Tilburg University explored how people described "financial peace". Participants did not emphasise high returns or sophisticated products. They spoke instead about predictability, the sense that money-related surprises were rare and manageable, and the belief that their financial behaviour matched their personal standards. In other words, peace emerged less from objective metrics and more from alignment between tools and values. The study's details are less important than its core observation: meaning sits at the junction of design and self-respect.

A sceptic might argue that this focus on meaning is a luxury. For those under heavy pressure—unstable income, high obligations, political uncertainty—function must trump philosophy. The objection is understandable. Yet even in highly constrained circumstances, people already make value-laden choices: which obligation to honour first, which platform to trust, how much information to disclose. The tools are not neutral. They embody assumptions about whose needs matter. Naming those assumptions does not remove constraint, but it can prevent despair. It turns "I have no choice" into "Given these limits, this is the kind of person I choose to be."

The motif of service returns one last time. In a borderless world, money systems can quietly reverse the relationship. People start living in service of notification schedules, token incentives, or platform policies. They earn in a currency they do not understand because a client prefers it. They adopt a wallet whose permissions they do not control because it offers short-term rewards. They treat their attention and privacy as small, negotiable details. Over a year, these concessions add up. The person may remain technically solvent, even prosperous, while feeling continually diminished.

Reversing that pattern does not require grand gestures. It requires a shift in what counts as a "good" tool. Instead of asking only, "Is this efficient?" or "Is this cheap?", one can ask, "Does this help me care for the people and obligations I recognise?" "Does this expand or shrink my freedom to act without fear?" "Does this make it easier or harder to meet my responsibilities in a way I can stand by?" These questions do not produce instant scores. They produce conversations—with oneself, with family, with colleagues—that shape the operating system underneath the interface.

There is no final state where meaning is fixed and tools are perfect. Rails change. Laws evolve. Lives move through seasons of constraint and abundance. The unresolved tension is built-in: how do you keep reconfiguring a system that works with code and contracts so that it continues to honour values that are, by nature, human and evolving? A practical way to test this is simple, and quietly demanding. If someone who knew nothing about you examined your weekly routines, your monthly resets, and your annual map, what would they infer you cared about? Would they see a life where money is a frantic master, or a competent servant? And if their answer disturbed you, would you be willing to change the tools—or the story—until it did not?

About the Author

Darius Kelmori writes about the meeting point of money, technology, and everyday life. He has spent years working with independent workers, small teams, and migrant families on the practicalities of getting paid, sending support home, and staying safe online. His approach blends clear systems thinking with a humane focus on dignity and choice. Raised between ports and airports, he is drawn to histories of trade routes and the quiet rituals people invent to keep trust alive across distance. His work aims to replace hype with usable habits, and anxiety with a calm, border-aware way of managing cash in a world that moves at network speed.

www.ingramcontent.com/pod-product-compliance
Lightning Source LLC
Chambersburg PA
CBHW031337230926
51848CB00002B/275
9789374597019